The
NEW YORK
GRIMPENDIUM

Buffalo and Erie County Historical Society Building

The
NEW YORK
GRIMPENDIUM

A Guide to Macabre and Ghastly Sites

J. W. OCKER

THE COUNTRYMAN PRESS
WOODSTOCK, VERMONT

The New York Grimpendium

978-0-88150-990-8

Interior photographs by Lindsey Ocker or the author unless otherwise specified
Book design and composition by Eugenie S. Delaney
Cover concept, illustration, and design by Brian Weaver.

Published by The Countryman Press, P.O. Box 748, Woodstock, VT 05091
Distributed by W. W. Norton & Company, Inc., 500 Fifth Avenue, New York, NY 10110
Printed in the United States of America

10 9 8 7 6 5 4 3 2 1

For Lindsey and Esme.
Always for Lindsey and Esme.

contents

FIVE

CLASSIC MONSTERS 269

INTRODUCTION

NEW YORK MIGHT HAVE A SHINY NAME, but underneath it's as dark and wormy as any other state. Maybe more so. After all, it's the third most populous state in the United States, and it features the most populous city in the country by a long shot to the back of the head. It's also one of the oldest regions in the Union. Lots of lives plus lots of time equals lots of death.

And those macabre traces are everywhere in this Sphinx-shaped state. After all, this is the land that gave us the Headless Horseman, Son of Sam, Rosemary's baby, Rod Serling, the Addams Family, the electric chair, Albert Fish, Troma Studios, Typhoid Mary, Sing Sing, and the Amityville Horror. The state is full of the macabre, the grim, and the ghastly. And it's all there patiently waiting for us to drop by and say hello.

I've never lived in New York, but over the short course of the past year, I've probably single-handedly funded its Department of Transportation with my toll money. I've traveled from its northeast Canadian border to its southwest Pennsylvanian one. From the Great Lakes to the Finger Lakes to Lake Champlain. From the Adirondacks to the Catskills. From the Thousand Islands to Long Island. From Buffalo to the boroughs of NYC. From the tops of its skyscrapers to the bottoms of its crypts.

In fact, just in researching this book, I covered and re-covered some 9,000 miles of the state, crisscrossing its roads in the most inefficient itinerary anybody's ever put together. Granted, my travels have been of a particular cast, hue, and pall. Everything I've searched out is maggoty with death, whether it's a mass grave memorialized by a piece of stone, the home sweet home of a serial killer, the lock of hair of a horror author, the filming site of an obscure horror movie, or various public displays of the dead. Over the course of these GPScapades, I've seen some wonderful, ghastly, beautiful, morbid, fascinating, gruesome, exciting things.

Before I get to that part, though, I guess I should talk about the motivation. I mean, there are tourism brochures and websites overflowing with exceptional, life-changing sites and attractions in New York where you can go have a good time and forget about all the heavy stuff. Why obsess about its most ghastly bits? More generally, why be so engrossed with death at all?

I get asked this question pretty regularly. Mostly when I'm by myself. Sometimes I try to duck it by comparing the fascination with having a favorite color. I mean, I just happen to like green. I can't explain it. I also happen to like the way a jawless skull sits on a rounded gravestone or how nicely a human brain fills up a jar. It just appeals to me aesthetically.

Sometimes I try to take a more philosophical approach. I talk about death's being the ultimate commonality of humankind, one of our most defining features as a species, the most relevant part of our lives. When writing about that explanation, I often use lots of capital letters.

Other times, I answer more practically. That a better understanding of death yields a better way to live life. Knowing that it'll all end any second makes one better appreciate loved ones, beauty, and a good joke.

Then there are the times I go romantic with my rationalizations, calling it the great unknown, Shakespeare's undiscovered country, Yoda's forever sleep. That death seems a much more interesting thing to explore than my life of trying to get my phone to sync up to my printer and waiting for the gutters on my house to fall off.

In my rare honest moments, tapping away by myself at a keyboard, writing about a recent visit to a memorial dedicated to the horrible death of a child, I have to say, "I don't know." I hate that we all have to die. I hate that we all have to suffer, that some have to suffer more than others and all out of proportion to anything. I hate that there is so much uncertainty about life. That things have to end. And then I go to the refrigerator and get a Coke Zero because by that time I've imbibed everything alcoholic in the house.

So maybe I'm just getting to know my enemy better. Or maybe I'm forming a fast friendship. Regardless of my perspective on the matter, the fact stands on a herd of elephant legs that there's a lot of death in this world, and a lot of people who are into reading about it, discussing it, and going out to see its traces firsthand. It's a pretty common passion. Most of us are casket-shaped in one way or another.

In this book, this grimpendium, are more than 120 entries covering some 250 sites, attractions, and artifacts related to the macabre and the grim in some way that I hope will inspire the entire gamut of emotional reactions toward death, somberness, sadness, terror, hatred, grief, and uproarious laughter.

Like my previous book, *The New England Grimpendium* (Countryman Press, 2010), this one has three criteria that must be met for a site to be included within its pages. The first one I think I've covered to the point of smothering it, that it needs to be macabre in some way. Second, it needs to have a physical, visit-able component to it. So if it's a stray strain of folklore, legend, or historical anecdote, there needs to be something that can be inhaled into a camera, a foundation on which to almost literally jump up and down on. Finally, once those first two criteria are met, comes the third. I have to have visited it personally . . . with *visit* having a pretty wide definition that can include merely standing outside of the site in awkward uncertainty and embarrassment.

As a result, the book comes off as a hybrid guide book and travelogue. There is enough specific information for anybody to find everything I have included herein. And, where applicable, I interject my own experiences, descriptions, and opinions of it. Fair warning, though, I often mix up my left hand and my right, as well as three out of four cardinal directions.

As in the previous book, I've categorized the spookiness into five broad sections.

The first is "Legends and Personalities of the Macabre," which includes sites and artifacts connected to those famous and infamous artists, musicians, writers, directors, actors, entertainers, and historical personages whose biographies look best punched into tombstone.

The second section is dedicated to "Infamous Crimes, Killers, and Tragedies." It's full of tragedy and perversity and is generally a rough section to get through. I suggest skipping it.

For the "Horror Movie Filming Locales" section, I walked in the footprints of camera mounts and director chairs, searching out the canvases upon which some of our most indelibly terrifying moments of cinema were filmed.

The title "Notable Graves, Cemeteries, and Other Memento Mori" is about two-thirds self-explanatory. The rest of the section covers a broad swath of more uncategorizable items that range from a famous suicide note, to a shop that specializes in the morbid, to giant crow statues, to various ruins.

The last section, "Classic Monsters," explores all the sites connected to monsters of myth and story that have somehow managed to incarnate themselves into the real world in some way.

Admittedly, as you go through this book (which you can do either straight through or randomly), you'll see that I swing back and forth in tone, depending on the subject matter, my mood, and how close or far away I feel from death at the point that I wrote the entry, I guess. Certainly, overall, the book is meant to be a memento mori in itself . . . but it's also meant to be a good time.

Like I said, I just don't know what to do with death . . . except write a book about it.

Jason Ocker
Nashua, NH

Poe Park

ONE

Legends and Personalities of the Macabre

CHANCES ARE, if a person has achieved a high enough level of notability for his or her creative work, New York appears somewhere in that individual's biography. New York draws and expels the famous and the fame-minded like water through the gills and maw of some giant, sleeping ocean monster. Of course, in the pit of that brute's stomach is New York City itself, but often the famous spread out into the rest of the state, close enough to do business in the belly of the beast when they need to, but far enough away to avoid being digested within its suffocating innards.

Basically, whether their notoriety comes from blowing bubbles on the sunniest of children's shows or painting portraits of corpses with a palette of bodily fluids, the well-known find themselves in New York at some point.

And it's these latter types of the famous that this section is dedicated to, those legends and personalities of the macabre who plunge headfirst into the darkness of the universe, whether it's of the sort of darkness found in the crevices of the souls of man or in the multifarious terrors spewing from the crevasses of the planet, while the rest of us hang back. These creators in the dark take the grimmest truths of reality, interpret them, distill them, fit them into stories and onto canvases and into music measures. Some make it a lifestyle, some accomplish it against their will or unknowingly, some are masters at it. Others make valiant attempts to help us laugh at it.

Like gazing at a Gorgon, most of us can't always look straight into the eyes of the dismal and the ghastly, but these legends and personalities offer us the polished bronzed shield that reflects that real part of the real world and helps us when are forced to do battle with it ourselves. As we all will eventually have to do in our lives. Nobody is safe.

In this section are artists, actors, writers, directors, mediums, musicians, and even a magician who have either dedicated their lives and careers to the macabre or experimented with it in ways that have lasted long past what they themselves would have predicted. And of all the grim masters and characters who have tromped through the state of New York, these few have made lasting impressions on it in some tangible way that states unequivocally, "We were here."

Actually, some of these spooky sort are still in New York, quietly melding into its very loam beneath sinking headstones. Two are still living, the poor souls. Some have been commemorated with statues and monuments. Others are merely remembered as having a connection to a certain place, but the fact that it's still known and related from generation to generation is celebration enough. In one particularly special case in the following section, only a part of that person ever resided in New York, but that part has been sanctified as a relic ever since.

In every case, there is a physical trace of these legends and personalities that can be visited, where you can connect with them or their work . . . and then run screaming from it. But these are the type of people who are okay with that. They'd take it over a, "Nice work," any time.

Edgar Allan Poe
WEST POINT, BRONX, MANHATTAN

MOST PEOPLE have a bit of darkness in them. For some, it's way up in the rafter corners of their psyche, where they never have to deal with it. Others have it sliding down their walls, forcing them to take a more active approach to maintain their property values. Some of these latter tragic souls try to get rid of it by sweating it out through their pores. Others try to dilute it by dumping stuff into their body. Edgar Allan Poe, well, he seemed to dip his out one quill's worth at a time.

The darkness Poe faced made for a rotten life for himself at times, but a transcendent literary experience for the rest of us. Sometimes you have to break a few artists to make a legacy. And Poe's is one of the few indisputeds. He invented entire genres and used the English language in ways that an infinite number of monkeys on typewriters couldn't approach even if we spotted them all the transcendentalist writers and every best-selling novelist so far this century. Sure, his legacy is creatured with murderous orangutans, maniacs who steal the teeth from corpses, and personifications of plague, but like I said, most people have a bit of tar-pit darkness. It's just few have genius mired in it.

In his short life, Poe traveled to many places on the East Coast, looking for a spot to successfully bail his brain. What he didn't know is that he was spreading out his legacy for a wider swath of his future admirers to claim. Everywhere he placed a foot has sprung up memorials, plaques, and statues, and everywhere he so much as crooked an arm at a bar or nightmared his head on a pillow has been hallowed by posterity.

Poe spent about seven years of his measly 40 in New York. His first official foray into the state was at the U.S. Military Academy at West Point, about 50 miles north of New York City, where he enrolled in 1830 after a couple of unhappy years in the U.S. Army. The unhappiness continued, as a few months later he got himself court-martialed by just not caring about anything around him. That darkness again.

West Point has memorialized him with a marble doorway in the West Point Room of its former library building (its new library, Jefferson Hall Library and Learning Center, is across the street) that is inscribed with a few lines from his poem "To Helen" and a quote from Sir Francis Bacon that Poe himself used in his story "Ligeia": "There is no exquisite beauty without some strangeness in the proportion." The doorway was built in the early 1900s for an earlier library. As of the writing of this entry, the building that it currently resides in was under renovation, but even in less hard-hatted times is, like most of West Point, not open to the general public.

Of course, New York City, being the vortex of personalities that it has always been, sucked him in for a few years . . . and it has the memorials to prove it.

Poe lived at a number of residences throughout his sporadic New York life, in areas that back then were just outside the city and most of which don't exist anymore. One particular location he lived at before the city subsumed it now bears his name. A portion of West 84th Street between Broadway and Riverside Drive is now officially known as Edgar Allan Poe Street.

One of his last residences of both New York and his life was a three-story brick structure, 85 West 3rd Street, near Washington Square Park, in the Greenwich Village neighborhood of Manhattan. This one actually survived for about a century and a half after Poe's death, before being demolished in 2001 by New York University to make way for a law school expansion. After some public outcry and constant rappings on their window lattices, they compromised by, well, demolishing the house. However, they did rebuild its façade about a block away from the original location, incorporating it into the newly built Furman Hall. You can tell which section of the building it is due to the difference in the brick. A small rectangular plaque notes the significance of the wall, calling it an "interpretive reconstruction." Small signs in the first-floor window state that a "Poe Room" inside is open on Thursdays from nine to eleven AM and to ask for access at 245 Sullivan Street.

After living in Manhattan, Poe moved to a small cottage in the Bronx, which was his official residence at the time of his death in 1849. It was also the site where his wife, Virginia Clemm, had died less than three years before. Unlike so many characters in his stories, the cottage survived.

In 1913, the 200-year-old Poe Cottage was moved from Kingsbridge Road to just a little ways down that same street to what has since been called Poe Park, a glorified median between the extremely busy Grand Concourse and East Kingsbridge Road, where both intersect with East 192nd Street.

Other than its less-than peaceful location, which can be a bit scary at times for non-Poe reasons, the park in general is a nice tribute to the dark master, with gates that bear his signature and an a easily missed stone tile with an image of a raven on it. The park also features a large columned bandstand, as well as a playground.

The white, clapboard cottage at the north end of the park was always a humble, broken-looking little place, and on my recent visit it was even more so, as it was temporarily closed while in the throes of renovation. Interestingly, they were also putting the finishing touches on a second small building, a visitor's center for the cottage. With a design inspired by his poem "The Raven," the thin rectangular building is slightly cleft at one end to resemble a bird wing and features walls covered in dark shingles to resemble feathers. At the end facing the cottage is a large viewing window, making the thin building somewhat of a telescope.

About a mile away, at Bronx Community College at 2155 University Avenue, can be found another tribute to Poe, in the Hall of Fame of Great Americans. Founded in 1900 and situated at the back of the campus overlooking the Harlem River, the Hall of Fame is a covered walkway that arcs majestically behind the amazing Gould Memorial Library and connects the Hall of Languages on one side and the Hall of Philosophy on the other.

The terrace is lined by white columns interspersed with the contrasting dark bronze busts of approximately 100 prominent American scientists, teachers, soldiers, statesmen, artists, authors, and others. Poe finds himself in the impressive open-air colonnade adjacent to the bust of Mark Twain and not too far from Washington Irving (see page 23) on a pedestal decorated with a sigil bearing both a raven and a cat.

Poe's story officially ends in Baltimore, Maryland, where he died and is buried. Still, even without the relic of his remains, New York has managed to preserve quite a bit of Poe's tired, poor, huddled life.

Rod Serling

BINGHAMTON, INTERLAKEN

YOU KNOW HOW HARD IT IS to not open this entry with, "Imagine, if you will" or "Submitted for your approval"? Hard enough that I can't come up with any other introduction, other than to tell you that I can't come up with any other introduction. But because my brain is apparently forcing me to take the "needs no introduction" thing literally, it might as well be for Rod Serling. After all, he's a unique case in the history of storytelling. He was pretty much the first television writer to grab the immature medium by its bunny-ear antennas and tell it to grow up and start earning its keep or else.

Granted, it can take a while for new storytelling mediums to mature. But for some reason, it took television a long time. I mean, we still marvel at and study many of the first examples of film and literature. But early television? There's a reason that, even at this point in time when we've had plenty of excellent shows in this medium, television remains a punch line. And it could have been worse, if it hadn't been for a neat, well-dressed man with heavy eyebrows, an omnipresent cigarette, and a voice with a cadence so evenly measured, it was almost otherworldly.

Rod Serling was born in Syracuse on Christmas Day in 1924. Before he was two years old, his family moved 70 miles south to the town of Binghamton, where he spent the remainder of his youth. After high school, he joined the army, serving in World War II as a paratrooper and infantryman.

After completing his time in the military, he got a degree in literature and began writing for radio, before moving on to television. Eventually, he became frustrated at the compromises he had to make in his storytelling for that medium. He wanted to deal honestly with human issues without having to distort his stories due to network or sponsor censorship. He then made two realizations that would change television.

First, he realized that the only way he could fully tell the stories he wanted to tell was within the genres of science fiction and dark fantasy, where a writer could deal with contemporary social issues such as violence and racism and poverty when that society was depicted as 300 years in the future or on another planet. Sometimes extraterrestrials make the best human characters, and sometimes monsters reveal the most about humanity.

Second, he realized that the only way he could adequately fulfill his storytelling vision was to create his own show, under his own control.

Based on the strengths of some of his past storytelling successes, he was given a shot, one of the first shots, in fact, in the war against inane television. Now, 50 years after its debut, its music still disconcerts us, its title is still regularly used as a metaphor, and its stories have become legendary.

I'm speaking of, course, about *The Twilight Zone.*

The Twilight Zone first aired in October 1959. Over the course of the five seasons of the anthology series, Serling showed that brilliance could be consummated in half-hour, commercial-pocked increments if one tried hard enough, set higher goals for the medium, and was passionate about the message.

Whether they took place in the future, the past, on other planets or other dimensions, and no matter how creepy they got, *The Twilight Zone*'s tales were always human stories, with direct yet timeless applications. The black-and-white episodes were tightly told, often setting up endings that cleverly inverted the entire plot.

Serling wrote more than half of the 150-odd episodes of the series, and he personally narrated them all, often appearing on camera as the host. In fact, his image and voice remains as indelible in culture as the stories. The unique, monotone rhythm of his delivery and his dark features made him seem a disconnected observer of humanity and made the series seem even more surreal than the floating doors and eyeballs and eerie music of the opening sequence did.

Others would try to duplicate Serling's success with other anthology shows, and *The Twilight Zone* itself would be attempted again in the 1980s and the 2000s, as well as being released as a movie, but none of them achieved the cultural resonance of that original show.

Serling himself tried again in the early 1970s with *Night Gallery,* another anthology show that he introduced, narrated, and contributed stories for. *Night Gallery* was more horror-themed than *The Twilight Zone,* and though it lasted for more than 50 hour-long episodes and achieved landmarks of its own, it lacked the same vision because Serling didn't maintain creative control over the series.

He would go on to write a few movie scripts in his career, as well, the high point of which being a very high point indeed. He co-wrote the amazing *Planet of the Apes,* a movie that's as famous in that medium as *The Twilight Zone* is in its.

Serling lived much of his adult life in California, but his hometown of Binghamton continued to play a large role in his life throughout, and he returned frequently. And Binghamton loved Serling right back. The town has honored him in multiple ways. A sign outside of the high school he attended at 31 Main Street commemorates his life, and the fine arts program there is named after him. The town gave him a star on their walk of fame just outside the town's Metrocenter shopping mall at 41 Court Street and regularly host events celebrating his life and work. The Forum Theater, a performing arts theater at 236 Washington Street, has in its lobby a permanent exhibit of Serling memorabilia. You can even see his old house at 67 Bennett Avenue, although it's a private residence.

Most interestingly, just down the way from his house, on Beethoven Street, is Recreation Park, featuring a round, white, colonnaded bandstand and an adjacent indoor carousel. This park was Serling's inspiration for the much acclaimed first-season "Walking Distance" episode of *The Twilight Zone,* in which a man finds himself back in the town where he grew up . . . way back in the town where he grew up, in fact, trying to come to terms with the burden of growing up and away. A plaque in the middle of the floor of the bandstand attests to its significance to the episode.

When I first visited, the carousel was in the middle of being refurbished and was missing all its horses, leaving just the naked poles. A horseless carousel is now my default example for explaining *creepy.* However, I visited again after the job's completion. The canopy of the carousel had been repainted with about a dozen scenes inspired by iconic stories from *The Twilight Zone*. The artwork was created by Cortland Hull, great-nephew of actor Henry Hull (see page 62) and pretty much elevates the fairground attraction to the coolest herd of penetrated horses on the planet.

Serling died in 1975 of a heart attack at the age of 50. He's buried in nearby Interlaken, where his family owned a summer house throughout the years and where he was living while teaching at Ithaca College when he died. His grave is located in Lake View Cemetery at 3699 County Road 150 at the back of Lot G. His grave marker is a simple stone block set flush to the ground. It usually has a small flag staked beside it because of his military service. When I visited, the marker was covered with mementos from other visitors, including rocks, coins, a lighter, a miniature wrench, and a wristwatch. The stone acknowledges only his time in World War II and nothing about his writing career. I guess it doesn't have to.

Personally, I hope he wrung every last story out of himself before he died. Otherwise it just doubles the tragedy of his early death that we missed out on anything from his imagination.

But we can visit him and the stories he did tell anytime we want . . . in a place . . . called . . . *The Twilight Zone*.

Washington Irving
Sleepy Hollow, Tarrytown, Staten Island

SOMETIMES HALLOWEEN ENTERS ON WITCHES' BROOMS, sometimes on vampire wings, and sometimes on the epic swing of a Grim Reaper scythe. But more often than not, the holiday is borne on the broad, uninterrupted shoulders of a headless rider with a flaming jack-o'-lantern. And we can thank Washington Irving for that.

In 1820, he published his short story "The Legend of Sleepy Hollow," in which a trepidatious teacher named Ichabod Crane encounters a local New York ghostie, a headless Revolutionary War–era soldier that rides on a demonic black charger, searching for the head he lost to a cannonball . . . or, barring that, whoever's has the same hat size as he. With its harvest-time celebrations, seasonal Hudson Valley scenery descriptions, and spooky gallivantings, it has become one

of the foundational texts of autumn, in addition to a revered classic of literature by one of the original American voices.

Irving set his tale of a headless Hessian in a small Dutch-settled area on the eastern side of the Hudson River Valley region, about 30 miles north of Manhattan. And when I say set, I don't mean randomly picked a locale on a map or made one up in his head. Irving was in love with that area of New York. He eventually moved, lived, and was buried there, in fact.

As a result of his affinity for the region, he was able to incorporate the geography, history, and landmarks of the area directly into the story, making them traceable to this day, much to the delight of the local tourism board. Apparently, though, Sleepy Hollow wasn't a real town until about a decade or so ago, when North Tarrytown, which abuts Tarrytown and contains many of the landmarks of the story, officially incorporated itself under the mantle.

You're free to visit Sleepy Hollow in any season you want, of course, but I highly recommend autumn, the closer to Halloween the better. You see, the town knows what side of its pumpkin bread is pumpkin-buttered and plays up its unique ties to the season in appropriate fashion. The community is spooked out with decorations, throws a Halloween parade as far as it can, and conducts many Headless Horseman–themed events and tours.

No matter what time of year you visit, though, it won't take you long to figure out that this is the land of the Galloping Hessian of the Hollow. Images of the fiend abound, from the local school mascot to the sigils on the town police cars, and an impressive steel statue stands tall in the middle of the town, while various signs mark places of interest and local shops carry the requisite amount of Headless Horseman merchandise.

Route 9, also known as North Broadway, cuts through the town, and pretty much everything Headless Horseman—related that you want to see is situated on this road.

For instance, on that road stands an 18-foot-tall, oxidized steel testament to Irving's story. At the top of a hollow quadrilateral column are 20 fancifully sculpted rust-metal plates that overlap to depict Ichabod Crane being chased down by the jack-o' lantern-wielding Galloping Hessian. The unique effect of the stylized plates makes the image look as if it's made of smoke or gnarled tree branches or other eerie things.

Moving on down the road in the direction that Ichabod is riding for his life, you'll come across a little church, the Old Dutch Church by name, which was built in 1685 and was featured in Irving's story as demarcating the domain of the Headless Horseman. It was also around here that the climactic scene of the story takes place. In autumn, the church presents dramatic readings of Irving's story, complete with hot cider and seasonal snacks for the audience. Some moments in life should be crystallized into giant jawbreakers and sucked on forever.

The original bridge "famous in goblin story" that spanned the stream here beside the church is no longer standing, of course. However, a modern bridge has replaced it in the original location. These days, it's barely noticeable as a bridge, being one of those short paved stretches that "ices before road" in winter. It's now called the Sleepy Hollow Bridge and is dedicated to the author to whom the town owes its identity. A conspicuous blue and yellow sign identifies and commemorates the spot as "Headless Horseman Bridge."

You can actually trace the self-acclaimed legend's entire chase scene from terrifying start to pumpkin-shard-strewn end. It begins at Patriot's Park, a pleasant area along Route 9 south of the Old Dutch Church. Here you'll find a statue called the Captors' Monument that commemorates the spot where a British spy named Major John André, who was a conspirer with Benedict Arnold, found himself captured. In the Irving story, it was at this spot (pre-statue, of course) that Ichabod first sees the headless specter, "huge, misshapen and towering." From there, just follow North Broadway/Route 9 past the Sleepy Hollow statue and on to the supposed safety of the bridge and church.

Behind the Old Dutch Church is a cemetery known as the Old Dutch Burying Ground. Here it was in the story that the Headless Horseman was thought to be buried and where he "tethered his horse nightly among the graves," after sallying forth each night to go head shopping. The three-acre colonial burying ground has since been surrounded by the 85-acre Sleepy Hollow Cemetery. This latter cemetery dates back to 1849, and it is here that Irving, himself, is buried.

Sleepy Hollow is a real cemetery's cemetery, and probably my favorite in New York. The natural landscape is varied, with assorted hills and scenic irregularities; enough trees to drop showers of colors in autumn; and a pleasant, rock-strewn stream meandering through it. The unnatural landscape is also varied, with much-aged tombstones, statuary, and impressive mausoleums set into the hills.

Irving's grave is in the southern part of the cemetery (the north–south Route 9 borders the cemetery, and you can use it for a compass) right on Crane Way, which is just behind the church yard and not too from the gate behind the church. His plot is well demarcated, hemmed in as it is by a black cast-iron gate with the surname "Irving" emblazoned on it in white. The gravestone itself is white and round like a worn tooth and is crowded on all sides by other worn teeth that aren't as white or as round.

Another highlight of the cemetery can be found near the eastern border. Crossing the Pocantico River, which runs through and along the cemetery, is a wooden car bridge that locals unofficially call Headless Horseman Bridge. With its rustic crossed-stick railings, it fits the name more than the roadway bridge outside the cemetery, which spans the same river.

The cemetery also features graves from whose epitaphs Irving lifted the names for his characters in "The Legend of Sleepy Hollow," including Katrina Van Tassel and Brom Bones. No Ichabod Cranes, though.

To find the man whose name he used for his protagonist, you'll have to travel about 50 miles south to Asbury Methodist Cemetery on 2000 Richmond Avenue in Staten Island. Crane's grave is by the left side of the church, if you're facing it, in the rear, left corner of the small cemetery.

If the conditions are the same as when I visited, you'll pass through a few rows of relatively well-cared-for headstones until you hit a patch of overgrown scrubland that looks completely not worth venturing into. However, you'll just be able to make out the pointed tip of Crane's monument, which if I'm at all representative of my readership, will fortify you enough to vault the dead tree blocking the way and then fight off all the burrs, thorns, ticks, snakes, and other lesser-known minions of death and pain that have their own plans for you.

Back to the Hudson Valley, the preserved home of Washington Irving, which is in neighboring Tarrytown, is called Sunnyside, and is open for group tours. The house is a beautiful, large, red-roofed, cottagelike building overgrown with voluminous billows of creeper vine that can't help but beatifically overlook the Hudson River. It's an absolutely idyllic little place, the highlight of the tour of which is the author's own writing study.

Just down the road from Sunnyside, at the intersection of US 9 and West Sunnyside Lane, is the Washington Irving Memorial, a stone plaza that features a bronze bust of Irving flanked by bronze reliefs of two of Irving's non–*Sleepy Hollow* characters, Rip Van Winkle and King Boabdil, all carved by famed sculptor Daniel Chester French in the 1920s.

In the end, it's particularly gratifying to see that Sleepy Hollow has embraced not only Washington Irving, which you'd expect, but also the Headless Horseman himself. You might not be able to reason with a headless man, but you sure can celebrate him.

Oh, and I rarely point people to the websites that I steal information from, but you're going to want to check out sleepyhollowcemetery.org at some point in either your web or real-life travels, as it's pretty much the best resource for all things headless in Sleepy Hollow.

Fox Sisters
Lily Dale, Newark, Rochester, Brooklyn

IN 1692, A COUPLE OF GIRLS in Massachusetts turned a community upside down by pretending to be in cahoots with the devil. In 1848, a couple of girls in New York turned the country upside down by pretending to be in cahoots with the dead. Those are probably the only two historical anecdotes any alien race needs to work up a psychological profile of the human race.

It all started in a small cottage in a western New York hamlet that doesn't exist anymore, Hydesville. Today, that area is part of Newark, about 30 miles east of Rochester. On March 31, 1848, Kate and Margaret Fox, aged 11 and 15, respectively, told their parents about certain mysterious knocking sounds that they kept hearing. Soon after, the parents started hearing them as well. The girls insisted that it was a spirit, whom they nicknamed "Mr. Splitfoot." Eventually, Kate and Margaret were able to communicate with Mr. Splitfoot and discovered that the source of the sounds was actually a dead peddler named Charles B. Rosma who had been murdered on the property. Oh.

Word spread, neighbors dropped by to witness the supernatural shenanigans, and the entire community experienced an excitement that rivaled the Great Firefly Copulation of '39. The sisters were promoted to the bigger stage of nearby Rochester, where Kate and Margaret's older sister, Leah, lived. She immediately joined the party, making the mystical Fox sisters a proper female trinity along the mythic lines of the Fates, the Furies, and the Supremes.

They became celebrities. Both the living and the dead lined up to talk to them. They started touring the entire country, conducting public séances where the dead communicated with them through disembodied rappings. They even hit the proverbial big time in New York City.

From there, modern spiritualism became a Thing, and it took off faster than the soul leaves the body, with both supporters and skeptics. Some accounts claim that a couple million people were actively involved in talking to the dead. And there were probably ten times as many actively involved in denouncing or debunking it. Heck, when he wasn't bound by chains and hanging upside down in midair, Harry Houdini made exposing as counterfeit those who claimed to be communicating with the departed a part of his life's mission (see page 45).

Part of that rapid expansion was because the country was suddenly swollen with mediums. After all, if a couple of teenage girls could talk to the dead (and become famous by doing so), why couldn't anybody else? Just like today when anybody can grab a camera and run around an old house at night photographing orbs, back then anybody could put up a table for a séance and do more passive ghost hunting.

Far from any other claim, it's that spirit table that best supports spiritualism's entitlement to being considered a religion. Religions are often symbolized by furniture. Pulpits and altars and thrones. Crosses, depending how stretched your definition of furniture is. For spiritualism, it's the table. Just like the three-card monte dealer and the guy selling pirated movie DVDs on the street corner. In fact, the Rochester Historical Society has on display an example of a table used by

some charlatan lost to history, which has a spring-loaded rod and ball mecha-nism to simulate spectral rapping.

The fame of the three Fox sisters lasted for a remarkable four decades, but, as any medium worth his swami turban should know all too well, everything dies.

In the late 1880s, infighting arose among the sisters, especially between the two younger ones and Leah. The former were suffering from alcoholism and they all had different ideas about the practice of spiritualism. The situation got bad enough that in 1888, Margaret went onstage in front of a large audience, and, with the apparent support of Kate, publicly recanted the whole big fat spiritu-alism deal. Margaret explained that the noises she and her two sisters made were from their practiced ability to crack the joints in their toes. She demonstrated accordingly.

Still, the sins of the mothers didn't stop spiritualism, which is still practiced to this day, albeit in fewer numbers. The Fox sisters, on the other hand, con-tinued down their VH1 *Behind the Music* spiral to its conclusion. All three sisters were dead by 1893: Leah passed away in 1890, and Kate and Margaret ended up on the other side of the séance table in 1892 and 1893, respectively, and buried in adjoining graves.

In 1904, the Fox sisters found themselves posthumously spotlighted when a skeleton of the murdered peddler was claimed to have been found in a trunk in a false wall of their Hydesville cottage. Today, the discovery is touted as vindication by spiritualists and as not worth really even considering by skeptics.

Today, you can trace the lives of the Fox sisters almost entirely through memorials set up by those faithful spiritualists who were inspired by them. The Hydesville cottage where it all started was moved in 1916 from its original location to the spiritualist community of Lily Dale in western New York (see "Classic Monsters" . . . which sounds weird, but that's where I've categorized ghosts for the purposes of this book).

Unfortunately, in 1955, the cottage burned down as a result of unknown circumstances. A memorial garden and plaque-embedded rock now mark the site. Across the street, in the Lily Dale Museum, are whatever artifacts that were salvaged, including the aforementioned trunk claimed to hold the bones of the murdered peddler.

In Hydesville, on the spot where the cottage originally stood, the stone foundation has been excavated as carefully as a new species of dinosaur, and sheltered in a small, protective building. A sign on the front reads, "Hydesville Park, Birthplace of the Religion of Modern Spiritualism, March 31, 1848." The building sits at 1510 Hydesville Road, right where it intersects Parker Road, in Newark, nicely kept but lonely looking. It was locked when I visited, but ample windows all around give great views of the whole of the foundation.

In Rochester, near where the sisters lived, is an 18-foot-tall granite obelisk commemorating both them and the advent of spiritualism. Erected in 1927, the obelisk bears an image of the cottage, below which is a plaque with some dedicatory words that end with, "There is no death. There are no dead," which, if true, pretty much makes this entire grimpendium moot. The obelisk is located downtown on Troupe Street, right where it intersects Plymouth Avenue, across from which are a few grand old houses that date back to the Fox sisters' day.

And while there might be neither death nor dead, there are at least tombstones. Leah's grave can be found in the famous Green-Wood Cemetery at 500 25th Street in Brooklyn (see "Notable Graves, Cemeteries, and Other Memento Mori"). She's buried with her husband, Daniel Underhill, and their family in Section 172, beneath a squat, four-sided stone. Margaret and Kate are in a pauper's grave in Section 3 of Cyprus Hill Cemetery, also in Brooklyn. A headstone was erected later and reads, in barely legible script, MEDIUMS OF THE

ADVENT OF MODERN SPIRITUALISM. A small paper sign tacked into the ground designates the gravesite as one of Cyprus Hill Cemetery's notable ones.

To think that the whole thing got started because two teenage girls got bored one night in their bedroom.

Joe Coleman
BROOKLYN

"JOHN F. KENNEDY AND CHUCK BERRY DON'T NEED ME." That was one of my more legible notes from my night with Joe Coleman. And while it's a phrase that almost every person on the planet can utter with absolute accuracy, in Coleman's case it has a unique connotation.

Joe Coleman is an artist and collector of the sort that the phrase "of the macabre" fits like a hard-earned degree after each of those descriptors. He belongs in three or four sections of this book, but he's most famous for his paintings, which are often sold at prices that reach six figures and are collected by the type of people who can afford six-figure paintings.

I walked into his Brooklyn Heights apartment a bit gin-damp and somewhat February-cold and was immediately overwhelmed. The small space was wall-to-wall oddity. I didn't know where to start. I had a list of interview questions for him, but they were immediately defenestrated for: What's this—a wax figure of O. J. Simpson? What's that—a mummy? Is there something alive in here? No way that's a real creature, right? What's in those jars? Whose hair is that? Why is Fidel Castro holding a pair of panties?

It made me want to profusely express my gratitude at being invited into his sanctum and then to politely suggest that he leave his own home so that I could get to know every freakish inch of his collection at my leisure.

As it happened, I really didn't get a chance to scrutinize the vast array of what he likes to call his "children" because Coleman himself turned out to be just as interesting as the curiosities that surround him daily. We spent our time together conversing on an ornate hand-carved couch from the Philippines, cozily hemmed in by oddity and drinking mugs of red wine provided by his wife, Whitney, while wall-mounted death masks of celebrities and criminals peered blankly over our shoulders.

Coleman is short, in his 50s, with slicked-back black hair tinged with gray and a long goatee topped by a dangerously pointed handlebar mustache. His outfit was stylized but somehow not ostentatious, a dark jacket and vest, the latter of which was covered in chains and animal teeth and pins like war medals from some particularly gruesome campaign. He spoke almost tenderly and gave off the impression of a ringmaster from some dark and extremely fragile circus.

And it was that darkness that I wanted to know about, immediately asking him questions about his work that I probably had no business asking. But that was what the pre-interview gin was for. He answered my questions gently, thoughtfully, obviously struggling to communicate his ideas about depravity and the macabre in a way that would not come across as trite.

But he's definitely the guy to ask those types of questions. More often than not, the dark arts that he practices focus on the most depraved human beings to ever have their umbilical cords cut. Albert Fish, Timothy McVeigh, Charles Manson, Ed Gein. I mean, to call him a painter of serial killers is to limit his work unfairly, but these are the subjects that he seems to get the closest to wherever he's trying to go with his art. And even in his depictions of such people as P. T. Barnum or Harry Houdini or his own self-portraits (often especially his own self-portraits) can be found elements of dread and disgust.

"I'm not trying to get these guys out of prison and I'm not asking anybody to forgive them," he says of some of his more deviant subjects. "And I want them to be more than just cautionary tales . . . I'm trying to show the passion of these really dark characters as part of the human experience, which is so much a part of what human beings are, even though we try to deny it. It's like the suffering of the saints has its mirror aspect, or shadow self." Religion and religious art are pretty big influences on his work, actually. He was raised Roman Catholic in his home state of Connecticut, where as early as age five he would spend his time in church drawing the Stations of the Cross, with the blood accented in vibrant red crayon. He also characterized his paintings as fear responses. "I try to find the aspects of this person, who was a living person—what things in myself are like that person. And as scary as it is, I find these connections." He emphasized the humanity and the real lives of his subjects multiple times. "It's kind of like the 'losers don't get to tell their stories' thing. In my paintings, they at least get to have their say." Which is why he doesn't paint JFK or the Father of Rock 'n' Roll: "There're a lot of other people that could take care of them."

Stylistically, his brightly colored and crowded paintings are influenced by comic books, carnival posters, and (as he pointed out to me when I asked why an artist would incorporate as much text as he does into his works) illuminated manuscripts. He also described them as suggestive of the paintings seen on Egyptian sarcophagi in that they tell the life story of the dead person contained within.

His paintings are extremely biological, and most often pathological in the medical sense. Even his depictions of inanimate objects often appear diseased. The works are also achingly detailed, like a colorized electron microscope image of a virus. From afar, the works can seem cartoony, but the closer you get, further images and textures reveal themselves almost impossibly and often shockingly, an effect he achieves by painting with a single-hair brush while wearing a pair of jeweler's magnification lenses.

Coleman surrounds his subjects in a frame of smaller panels of images and text that encapsulate, contextualize, and narrate the main subject. He described the practice as, "Like the circle that the sorcerer might make to raise the dead." As a result, his paintings aren't just images that you can glance at in a gallery and check off as "seen." They're so brimming with details that they must be carefully and systematically explored. Of course, when they depict his usual subject matter of man's basic depravity, biology, and mortality, it makes for a daunting task.

At one point, he ushered me into an adjoining room where he had started work on a companion piece to one of his self-portraits. It's a scene I had seen in a million movies, where someone gets the privilege of walking in on an unfinished masterpiece, and it might have been my favorite part of the night.

This time, the painting was to be of his wife, Whitney. Incidentally, every article I've ever read on the artist mentions his wife of 11 years and she's often included in his paintings. Now that I've met her, I see why. Beautiful, tall, blond, with a voice like a full-body massage, she projects an undeniable presence both in general and in the life of her husband.

As to this particular work itself, the central figure was absent, and only a few of the surrounding cells had been created. The rest of the whitewashed wooden board (Coleman avoids painting on canvas because it has its own texture) was blank. He had already told me that he doesn't make preliminary sketches and has no plan in place for any particular work, as complex as they are. His method is to conduct a lot of research on his subject and then to concentrate on one square inch of the board at a time.

In fact, he described the overall effect of one of his paintings as a "collection" . . . which is interesting, because he also described his personal collection of oddity as a "work of art." Certainly, his collection and his painting are complementary, with the same themes of religion, science, pop culture, the sideshow, crime, and medicine. He's even put together art shows that combined the two.

Revealing again his fascination with fundamental human biology, he described culture, and his collection as a reflection of that culture, as a body, "These are from different elements of the culture. One is the lowest, like the sideshow. Maybe that's kind of like the guts. And then you have another aspect, which is science, so that's like the mind. And then you have maybe the other aspect being the heart, like religion."

Coleman's collection is full of taxidermy, holy relics, gaffs, life-size wax figures of the famous and infamous, indigenous artifacts, murderbilia (including the original Albert Fish letter that led to the capture of that cannibal of children . . . see "Infamous Crimes, Killers, and Tragedies"), and enough medical specimens to put together a body or two. On one shelf, the head of an Egyptian mummy sat under a glass dome. Resting on the floor was a large figural reliquary of a prostrate Saint Agnes that supposedly incorporated one of her actual bones.

Upon hearing that I grew up in Maryland, he pointed out the stage shirt of Baltimore native Johnny Eck, the sideshow performer who starred in Tod Browning's 1932 film *Freaks*. His body ended at his rib cage, and he used his arms and hands for locomotion and to do all sorts of cool things in his act. The shirt was gold colored, long sleeved, and sewn shut at the bottom.

As fantastic as the collection was, it was merely a fragment of the whole. The rest is in storage. I asked Coleman about the first piece in his collection, and he pointed to a set of Aurora monster models that he had put together as a child. His latest acquisition was a wax figure of Buffalo Bill. And, when I asked about his fire piece, that one artifact he'd grab to save if the place was burning down around him, he merely answered, "You're asking me to choose between my children."

Unfortunately, unlike almost everything in this book, Coleman's collection isn't usually accessible to the public. However, it is certainly something those of us who are into this type of stuff need to know exists. And, who knows, he told me he was more than open to creating his own public museum one day.

There are all shades of the macabre. In the too-few hours that we talked, I found Joe Coleman to be a right nice shade of it. Unforced, fascinating, with a body of work and a collection that matched. Granted, I may have caught him in a rare contemplative mood. Any other night he could be wearing the skeletons of conjoined infants around his neck and dancing with his wax figure of Charles Manson while his wife paints the walls of their bedroom in marsupial blood. Certainly he has a distant past in that, with performance art that includes blowing himself up with fireworks and biting the heads off live animals.

Still, if home is who you are, Coleman's personal odditorium and body of work testifies to a man who has honestly examined the grimmest aspects of life, regardless of discomfort and pain. A man who, in his own words is, "in awe of life and death."

Although it's probably more like "death and life."

Basil Rathbone
HARTSDALE

B ASIL RATHBONE WAS NOT TECHNICALLY a horror movie actor, but when, in the course of your career, you get to trade lines with the likes of Vincent Price, Boris Karloff, Bela Lugosi, and Lon Chaney Jr., the horror cachet kind of rubs off on you.

Rathbone was born in 1892, in Johannesburg, South Africa, but his family left just a few years later for England. Actually, they were chased out on the pretense that his father was a British spy sometime during the Boer War. "Rathbone" was just too cool a name for anybody to think otherwise.

Other than his stint in World War I, during which time he was awarded the British Military Cross for living up to his name with some bad-assery inside enemy lines, his entire life was devoted to acting, on the stage and on both sizes of screen. That devotion yielded him quite the respected career in which he appeared in more than 80 films, in addition to a resume-load of plays and television series. Over the course of that career, he won a Tony Award in 1948 for his work in the play *The Heiress* and two Academy Award nominations, one in 1937 and one in 1939, for his supporting roles in *If I Were King* and *Romeo and Juliet*, respectively.

Although he was never typecast as a horror movie actor, he was stereotyped in other ways. For instance, he often played villains of the sort that ranged from Mr. Murdstone in *David Copperfield* (1935) to Sir Guy of Gisbourne in *The Adventures of Robin Hood* (1938). However, he is most famous for playing Sherlock Holmes in some 14 major films.

Nevertheless, in between bouts of being condescending to Dr. Watson or fencing with Errol Flynn, he found himself shoulder to shoulder with some of the scariest fiends of the screen.

By my count, he was in four horror movies, five horror comedies, and one film—*Tower of London* (1939)—that wasn't horror but which also starred Vincent Price and Boris Karloff, so it should be mentioned. And that's in addition to turns in the main roles on various anthology television shows, in stories based on *A Christmas Carol* and *Strange Case of Dr Jekyll and Mr Hyde*. Those four straight horror movies are *Planet of Blood* (1966), *Tales of Terror* (1962), *The Black Sleep* (1956), and, most iconically, the Universal Studios picture *Son of Frankenstein* (1939), in which he played the titular role with Boris Karloff as the monster and Bela Lugosi as Ygor.

His horror comedies were *The Black Cat* (1941); *The Comedy of Terrors* (1963); *The Ghost in the Invisible Bikini* (1966); *Hillbillys in a Haunted House* (1967); and, to top off his career, a strange little Mexican production called, in translation, *Autopsy of a Ghost* (1968), which was posthumously released.

All in all, it's more than enough for an induction into the Fiend Club and actually makes me want to revise my introduction here to state unequivocally that Rathbone *was* a horror actor.

He died of a heart attack at the age of 75 in New York, and, despite his British citizenship, is still here. His earthly remains can be found at Ferncliff Cemetery and Mausoleum at 280-284 Secor Road in Hartsdale, just about 15 miles above New York City.

Now, Ferncliff is a place that would have gotten its own entry in this book were it not for the fact that it will get two other mentions in this section (for the grave markers of Joan Crawford and Conrad Veidt, which follow this entry). It's where famous people go when they die on the East Coast. Besides those above-mentioned three, this 80-year-old cemetery is also the last location of Judy Garland, Thelonious Monk, Edward, Sullivan, and Malcolm X. It was also where the remains of such as Jim Henson, Christopher Reeve, and John Lennon were cremated. The place is populated with more famous names than any given Los Angeles movie set.

To find Rathbone's or any other famous grave, I would certainly suggest asking the Ferncliff staff for help, as we found them to be super-super-helpful. They pretty much did everything except disinter the bodies for us (which we had to do ourselves). We were given a map in the offices within the main mausoleum (also called Ferncliff), with directions and burial spots highlighted for the many graves we were there to see. Then, several times while we were wandering the cold, marble halls of the mausoleums, we were further helped by various random staff members, and at one point I think a corpse even swung open the face of his crypt to help us find our way. Definitely some of the best service of any service industry of which I've been a patron. It's as if all the celebrities buried there specifically

inserted "Make sure my public finds me" clauses in their burial contract.

Rathbone is interred next to his wife, Ouida, in the Shrine of Memories mausoleum (Unit 1, Tier K, Crypt 117—although I don't remember seeing any labels for the units, tiers, and crypts in this particular mausoleum). The Shrine of Memories, like most modern mausoleums, is an austere place. Lots of marble, the dead floor-to-ceiling in drawers, no epitaphs, only names and dates of existence. A central corridor goes down the middle of the building, with hallways branching off on both sides that end in wall-size stained-glass windows of varying design.

To get to Rathbone, enter the front door of the building and head down the central corridor until you get to the last left. Take that, and he'll be in the very top row about halfway down that hall . . . so unless you're superhuman with camera angles, you'll probably not be getting in a good picture with him.

Which is fine. It's not as if any of us are of the caliber of Boris Karloff or Bela Lugosi.

Joan Crawford

HARTSDALE

WHAT THE HECK'S JOAN CRAWFORD doing in this book, right? She's an Oscar-winning silver screen—era movie star, not a bleeding-throat horror film legend like, say, actresses Karen Black or Barbara Steele. It's a fair question, and I'm glad you called me out on it.

Here's the thing. In the corresponding section to this one in the precursor to this book, *The New England Grimpendium,* I included Bette Davis and her plaque-adorned childhood home in Lowell, Massachusetts. I did this on the foundation that Davis topped off her impressive career with a trilogy of classic horror movies, interspersed with a few less memorable made-for-TV genre efforts. In addition, in those latter movies she exhibited an ability to terrify that transcended any rubber-masked fiend.

Well, when you talk about Bette, you've got to bring up Joan. It's kind of like an equal-time rule. They had somewhat of an acrimonious rivalry, for reasons both personal and professional. More relevant, both of their star trajectories ended in the exact same place . . . at a twilight horror career. But let's start at Crawford's dawn.

Crawford was born in 1905 in San Antonio, Texas, as Lucille Fay LeSueur. Her career began as a chorus dancer in a traveling show, and she was able to parlay that into an MGM contract and a movie career that started in 1925 with *Pretty Ladies*. Despite not having any schooling in acting, she went on to work with everybody from Lon Chaney to Spencer Tracy to Clark Gable, and embodied the Hollywood glamour girl ideal.

You know what? Let's fast-forward to the horror movies. Basically, her life box score was four adopted children, five husbands, 80 or so movies, one Oscar for her lead role in *Mildred Pierce*, and one seat on Pepsi's board of directors.

Her horror career took up the 1960s. In 1962, she starred alongside Bette Davis, herself, in the film *Whatever Happened to Baby Jane?*, about two sisters growing old and crazy together in a miasmic old house. The film was a hit, garnering multiple Oscar nominations (none for Crawford, however), and resuscitating the careers of the "two old broads."

Actually, *resurrecting* might be a better term, as the two women, who were both in their fifties, shuffled zombielike straight into the horror genre from there. After a few television dalliances and dropping out of a reunion with Bette Davis for *Hush . . . Hush, Sweet Charlotte* in 1964 (due to the aforementioned rivalry or illness, depending on which story you believe), Crawford found herself in the camp of famous B-movie purveyor William Castle for a pair of movies. These were *Strait-Jacket* (1964), written by genre author Robert Bloch, in which she played an ex-mental patient axe-murderer, and *I Saw What You Did* (1965) about a couple of girls who accidentally prank call a murderer. In the latter, Crawford portrayed a neighbor who is in love with the murderer.

Her next horror role was in the 1967 film *Berserk*, about a circus with a serial killer for a main attraction. Crawford played the owner and ringmaster of the circus who tries to capitalize on the piling bodies that are making her circus famous.

After a few more television appearance that included a stint on Rod Serling's *Night Gallery* (see page 22), she had one of the lead roles in the 1970 film *Trog*. This crazy, notorious little jaunt of a film is about an anthropologist (Crawford), who tries to communicate with a living Ice Age troglodyte that has been discovered in a cave in England. Hilariously, the caveman is costumed in what is generally understood to be a monkey suit from Stanley Kubrick's 1968 film *2001: A Space Oddity* that looked like it had been found in the trash and run over for good measure before it was recycled to be Crawford's leading man in the pic.

Actually, stop reading this book and go stream the movie online or something.

Unfortunately, *Trog* was to be her final movie appearance, although she had a couple more television ones, including a role in 1972 in the supernatural mystery series *The Sixth Sense* (in an episode titled "Dear Joan: We're Going to Scare You to Death"). She lived until 1977, her final years a period (in the punctuation sense as well) of seclusion and illness.

After a service at the Frank E. Campbell Funeral Home (see "Notable Graves, Cemeteries, and Other Memento Mori"), she was buried in Ferncliff Cemetery, the final resting place for many movies stars from Judy Garland to Basil Rathbone. You can read more about the cemetery itself in Rathbone's entry.

For Crawford, the grave that Blue Oyster Cult sings that she's risen from is actually a mausoleum wall. She's interred alongside her last husband, Alfred Steele, in Unit 8, Alcove E, Crypt 42 of the main Ferncliff Mausoleum. It's about chest height on the wall, depending on the latitude of your chest.

Looking over it all, Crawford's 50-year career started in glamour and ended in horror. And while that might've bummed her out, I'd personally call it an upward trajectory.

Conrad Veidt

HARTSDALE

IT'S EASY TO WRITE OFF the horrors of the silent film era of early cinema as quaint, tame, not too scary—that the movies have great atmosphere, but without the sounds of soul-stopping shrieks, chainsaw engines, and gloppy intestines falling to the floor, and without the vivid colors of various bodily fluids, horror fans just aren't ravaged by the nightmares and psychological scars that we yearn for from our horror flicks.

But then we run into one of the many terrifying horror movie visages of actor Conrad Veidt.

Veidt was born in 1893 in Berlin, Germany, and, after serving briefly in World War I, went on to a major acting career that spanned his homeland, the United States, and England, where he eventually became a citizen after leaving Germany due to the rise of a certain dictator who birthed a horror subgenre all his own.

In addition to live theater, Veidt acted in more than 100 movies in an auspicious and nearly three-decade cinema career that spanned silent films, talkies, and—just once near the end—full-color films.

Due to genetics, God, the deeds of a past life . . . somehow Veidt found himself with the face of a villain, and he played some of the best. His roles included Rasputin, Ivan the Terrible, Mr. Hyde, Cesare Borgia, Jaffar (in the aforementioned 1940 color film *The Thief of Bagdad*), Satan himself, and Nazi character Major Strasser in *Casablanca* (1942), a film in which he was the highest-paid actor in an all-star cast.

However, not only did he have a face for villainy, he had features that were the perfect canvas for creepy makeup, which is evidenced to the point of unanimous conviction by his roles in the two silent horror films for which he has achieved genre and cinema immortality: Cesare the sleepwalker in the 1920 German expressionist film *The Cabinet of Dr. Caligari* and Gwynplaine in the titular role of the 1928 movie *The Man Who Laughs*.

In *The Cabinet of Dr. Caligari*, Veidt played a somnambulist serial killer under the control of a hypnotist named Dr. Caligari. With its painted shadows and angular, crooked sets, the movie establishes an unreal and unsettling backdrop, through which wafts the strange, haunting sleepwalker with his death-pale face, dark-rimmed eyes, and limp black hair. He's dressed head to toe in silhouette black and carries a wicked dagger, but it's his face, that God-damned face, which makes a date with our nightmares. It's one of the most indelible images of cinema in a movie full of influential images.

In *The Man Who Laughs*, based on the Victor Hugo novel of the same name, Veidt portrayed the son of a 17th-century English nobleman who offends the king. As punishment, the king sentences the father to death by the Iron Maiden and his young son to a lifetime of facial disfigurement. His mouth is permanently carved into a large, toothy rictus. Google the image at your own risk. As proof of its ineffaceable ability to shock, the image of Veidt's mutilated face was chosen by the creator of Batman as the basis for the look of the superhero's maniacal archnemesis the Joker.

Veidt was in other horror films—*Eerie Tales* (1919), *The Hands of Orlac* (1924), *Waxworks* (1924), and *The Student of Prague* (1926)—but almost as interesting is the horror film that he wasn't in. Apparently, Veidt had but didn't take the chance to perform Dracula in the 1931 Tod Browning picture, a role that eventually made Bela Lugosi the horror legend that he is.

Veidt died in 1943 in Los Angeles while playing golf, and was cremated. However, his ashes weren't interred immediately. Not until the 1960s, in fact, when he was entombed in Ferncliff Cemetery at 280–284 Secor Road, in Hartsdale, a Westchester cemetery full of the corpses of famous actors and actresses. As mentioned in the previous two entries, it's the same cemetery where reposes the remains of Basil Rathbone and Joan Crawford, the latter of whom starred with Veidt in *A Woman's Face* (1941) and his last film, *Above Suspicion* (1943).

However, New York wouldn't be his final, final resting place. In the 1980s, his remains were moved to California to the possession of a family member and then, in the 1990s, a group of his admirers calling themselves the Conrad Veidt Society raised the money to have his ashes interred in the country of his chosen citizenship, England, where they sit today in Golders Green Crematorium in London.

However, the small, plain-faced urn repository in Hartsdale still bears his name as a memorial, although, strangely, no birth or death dates. When we visited, the person at the help desk couldn't find any record of this actor in their system, but based on the information we'd gathered from the Internet, we found the tiny monument to Veidt in Ferncliff Mausoleum at Unit 6, Tier AC, Column A. This is one of the end cap walls interspersed throughout the mausoleum (between Tiers A and C, in this case) where they keep cremated remains. His name is found on the bottom left corner of the column.

Were we all a little more comfortable with the aesthetic spookiness of cemeteries and mausoleums, the mini-crypt would also bear the images of the face of Cesare on one end and that of Gwynplaine on the other.

Man, that's the tattoo I've been waiting for.

H. P. Lovecraft
Brooklyn

H. P. LOVECRAFT WAS A WRITER of some of the most horrific stories in the genre, yet for himself, it was the borough of Brooklyn that he found utterly horrific.

Literarily, Lovecraft's bio would read, "Invoked the blind terrors of the universe; dwarfed humanity in an indifferent cosmos; and incarnated giant, elder

monsters incapable of considering the hurt feelings of an entire human race."
Geographically, the Rhode Island native's bio would read, "Providence, Providence, Providence, Providence . . . Brooklyn . . . Providence, Providence."

Lovecraft lived in Brooklyn for a mere two years, from March 1924 to April
1926, when he was in his mid-30s. The reason that this extremely New England
horror author moved was, well, he met a girl.

Her name was Sonia Greene, and they met in 1921 in Boston. They eventually married in early 1924, and Lovecraft uprooted his slimy tentacles and moved
to New York City, where his wife owned a hat shop. For a few months, they lived
in the central Brooklyn neighborhood of Flatbush, where he penned "The
Shunned House," his, well, Lovecraftian take on the old haunted house trope.
And then he entered one of the worst phases of his life, in a life that involved
both parents going insane, poverty, and the frustrations of an author whose vision
wasn't widely appreciated.

Lovecraft, as was his habit, wasn't doing too well financially at the time, and
Sonia's business started failing as well, followed by her mental health due to the
financial stress. As a result, she moved to Ohio to pursue a job opportunity there.
Lovecraft didn't go with her, and it was the beginning of the end for that strange,
brief marriage.

Instead, he ended up in a small apartment in the northwest corner of a
building in Brooklyn Heights at 169 Clinton Street, bordering the neighborhood
of Red Hook, which was named for the color of its soil and the hooklike strip of
land that curves into the East River at its southern end.

Back then, Red Hook was a bit more slumlike. Lovecraft felt the decrepitude
of the area and his apartment keenly, once writing in a letter, "Something
unwholesome—something furtive—something vast lying subterrenely in obnox-
ious slumber—that was the soul of 169 Clinton St."

He was also . . . let's be kind and say, extremely uncomfortable with the mul-
tiethnicity of the area. Another letter written to fellow author Frank Belknap
Long (see page 65) describes some of his fellow Brooklynites as

> Monstrous and nubulous adumbrations of the pithecanthropoids
> and moebal; vaguely molded from some stinking viscous slime of
> earth's corruption, and slithering and oozing in and on the filthy
> streets or in and out of windows and doorways in a fashion suggestive
> of nothing but infesting worms or deep-sea unnamabilites.

Granted, from an author like Love-craft, those types of epithets could be considered high praise, but the truth is he was miserable. Of course, sometimes an unhappy writer is an inspired one. Sucks for the author, rocks for the readers. The stories that came out of his New York period were "He," about a stranger with a strange New York lair; "In the Vault," about an undertaker trapped in his own receiving tomb; "Cool Air," about a weird scientist neighbor; and most notably, "The Horror at Red Hook," about a disturbing cult. All but "In the Vault" featured New York settings. It was also where he began penning "Supernatural Horror in Literature," a long-form essay about the horror genre in general.

But it wasn't all blood sacrifices and animated dead people for Lovecraft in Brooklyn. He did have some friends in the city. It was here that his Kalem Club flourished (named so because its founding members all had surnames that started with the letters *K, L,* or *M*), which was a literary circle of half a dozen or so like-minded authors that included Frank Belknap Long. It was also in New York that he cultivated a friendship with famous escape artist Harry Houdini (see page 45), for whom he ghostwrote an article debunking astrology and a short story entitled "Under the Pyramids."

Still, all that fellowship wasn't enough to alleviate the daily gloom of his New York life. He finally went back to Providence in the spring of 1926 where, a few months later, he would write the story "The Call of Cthulhu," inventing the winged, tentacled, ocean-slumbering creature that would secure his future and, sadly, posthumous fame.

Today, the brown-painted four-story townhouse on Clinton Street still stands. It's at the end of the row, right where Clinton intersects with State Street. The ivy-covered edifice offers no clue about its previous tenant, apparently focusing on projecting its nightmarish influence onto its current residents instead.

New York City is the type of place that can leave scars, no doubt, but for a horror author—heck, any author—that's sometimes exactly what he needs.

Harry Houdini
QUEENS

ONE COULD SAY THAT, as a man who dedicated his life to defying death, Harry Houdini was the opposite of macabre . . . except that to defy it, you kind of have to be obsessed with it. And Harry Houdini was.

Houdini was born more or less Erich Weiss in 1874 in Hungary and died definitely Harry Houdini in 1926 in Detroit on Halloween. In between he made a name for himself by becoming more magician than magician, seeping deep into the bones of human culture by mystifying audiences with feats astounding enough to make their ears pop as if they were adjusting to a new reality. The best magic does that to a person.

Of course, Houdini was actually more of an escape artist than a magician. The phrase "greatest escape artist the world has ever known" is Houdini in a nutshell . . . or a casket . . . or a prison cell . . . or a straitjacket . . . or whatever else he's ever escaped from.

However, most relevant to this book and as part of his obsession with death, a big part of his life was spent crusading against charlatan psychics and mediums, Scooby Doo-ing their masks off with aplomb. You see, Houdini more than anybody was qualified for such a cause, because those fraudulent spiritualists were using the tricks of magicians to fool the bereaved.

Typical of a showman, Houdini's exposures were accomplished in quite the dramatic fashion. I'm talking spy networks, headline-grabbing reward offers, disguises whipped off at climactic moments, booby trapped apparatuses, the whole deal. This enraged the spiritualist community to such a degree that they started making threats on his life . . . through the ghosts that they channeled. Death is a weird threat, coming from a ghost.

But all that's only relevant to Houdini's life. Without his aforementioned Halloween death, we wouldn't have his grave to visit.

The story of his death starts backstage at the Princess Theater in Montreal where Houdini, after a brief speaking engagement to the kids at McGill

University, entertained three of those same students. One of the students wanted to test Houdini's much-proclaimed ability to take a punch in the gut, insistently launching an oafish volley of punches at the abdomen of a prone and unprepared Houdini. While not killing him directly as the story sometimes goes, they at least contributed indirectly to his death. Houdini mistook the pains in his stomach for minor injuries from that altercation, instead of going to the hospital to learn that they were being caused by acute appendicitis. His appendix ruptured, and he died in a Detroit hospital, pus-filled and weak, nine days later at the age of 52.

Houdini's grave can be found in Machpelah Cemetery, a Jewish corpse repository in the borough of Queens in New York City, at Cyprus Hills Street in Glendale. Machpelah is one of a cluster of cemeteries whose borders overlap and which are filled to the point that the sides of the tombstones, and assumedly the shoulders below them, almost touch. At some points, the place seems more like storage for a headstone factory than an actual cemetery.

The bit of real estate that Houdini chose for his sole inescapable situation sticks out from all that, though, and is located just inside Machpelah's front gates, like the best show car at a dealership. Part bench, part sculpture, part monument, it's a nice little place to entertain visitors.

A life-size statue of a grieving women throws herself on the long, semicircular bench and dais of the grave. The large, colorful seal of the Society of American Magicians, of which Houdini was a president for a while, adorns it prominently. Just above the seal is a place for a bust of Houdini, but that's been stolen enough times that people just gave up on that embellishment, so his grave remains headless.

Directly in front of the bench, in what pretty much looks like a front yard, are a few cement decorations and a series of long grave markers that denote the exact resting places of Houdini and his immediate family. Houdini's wife, Bess, is actually not buried in Machpelah because of her lack of Jewish genetics. Gentile bodies just don't seem to decay right in Jewish hallowed ground. However, because Houdini had planned for her to be buried there, her name nevertheless adorns his marker. That makes Houdini's grave officially mislabeled. You can tell because its artisans left Bess's death year incomplete and patiently waiting . . . although they assumed the "19" part of it.

In practical terms, Harry Houdini's obsession with death was basically just an intense desire to not be forgotten. We all have that. Unlike most of us, though, Houdini was more successful at eluding it.

Peter Steele
FARMINGDALE

A T SIX FOOT EIGHT, with long dark hair, an intimidating build, and a voice that went six foot eight in the other direction, Peter Steele was put together in Frankenstein's laboratory to be a Goth metal singer. And that dark destiny was fulfilled as the front man, bassist, and songwriter for the band Type O Negative. And then his other dark destiny was fulfilled, the one that he shares with the rest of us, when he died of a heart attack at the age of 48 on April 14, 2010.

Born in Brooklyn on January 4, 1962, as Petrus Ratajczyk, Steele's first attempt at a rock -and- roll phantasmagoria began in the 1980s with metal bands Fallout and Carnivore. These lasted only a few years before going to the place where broken rock groups go . . . other rock groups.

This time, one of those other rock groups was Type O Negative. It would be this band that would validate Steele's decision to have fangs implanted in his mouth and shove so many *E*'s in his name. Formed in 1989 with keyboardist Josh Silver, guitarist Kenny Hickey, and drummer Sal Abruscato (later replaced by

Johnny Kelly after the *Bloody Kisses* album), these Brooklynites gelled into a fiendish musical force of soaring and sinking melodies led by Steele's bone-vibrating bass-baritone and poetically macabre lyrics. It took only two studio albums for them to find a mainstream audience.

Type O Negative's first album came out in 1991 and was called *Slow, Deep and Hard.* The second was a "live" album called *The Origin of the Feces* that they faked to half-ass a contract clause. Their aforementioned official second studio album, *Bloody Kisses,* was released in 1993, and it went platinum, roughly equivalent in its day to "heavily downloaded."

It's easy to write off Goth bands as a cliché, because most of them are. And at a superficial glance of song titles and album covers, it's easy to lump Type O Negative in with the rest of them. However, whether it was due to the group's lengthy, keyboard-reliant orchestrations; the intensely personal lyrics that still managed to exceed the genre quota of death references; or the probability that I'm being completely subjective, somehow Type O Negative seemed a different type of Goth band. Mostly, I think, it can be attributed to Steele's haunting voice.

The band did have room in its doom and gloom for some buffoonery. You can almost hear the performers cracking up behind such songs as "Black No. 1" (named after a shade of hair dye) and "My Girlfriend's Girlfriend." They also sabotaged the atmosphere of many of their albums by inserting practical joke tracks that included the sounds of an unplugged speaker, CD skip noises, long periods of silence, and tracks where they addressed the listener, at one point apologizing for one of the albums.

Of course, they had their earnest songs about death and despair, as well, such as "Red Water (Christmas Mourning)," about the death of Steele's father, and the simple but sweeping "Everything Dies."

According to many that knew him, Steele himself swung wildly between being hilariously self-deprecating and worryingly morose. He had his personal demons, which in the show biz world is almost always a euphemism for illegal substances. Being a big guy, he was able to take a lot of bodily abuse from hard-hitting drugs. He even once found himself in jail at Rikers Island, at the age of 43, for charges related to drug use, as well as in a mental institution for rehabilitation.

However, the oddest places that Steele ended up at was in the pages of *Playgirl* magazine, where he posed nude, and on talk shows such as *Ricki Lake* and *Jerry Springer,* the former for a fan fantasy fulfillment segment and the latter for a show about groupies. Ha. Why not?

Back to the less awkward topic of his morbid music, the follow-up album to *Bloody Kisses* was *October Rust,* which came out in 1996 and was similarly popular, achieving gold status (lots of downloads). The band also released three more albums together before Steele's death: *World Coming Down* in 1999, *Life Is Killing Me* in 2003, and *Dead Again* in 2007. And then the premature death of Steele, due to a heart failure that's never really been elaborated on, took Type O Negative with him.

He's buried in Saint Charles Cemetery at 2015 Wellwood Avenue in the village of Farmingdale on Long Island, in what I assume is a very big coffin. Neither of his names, real nor stage, adorns the simple stone, which he shares with his parents, but the overflowing grave offerings of stones and shells and candles and marbles attest to his presence. The grave is at the back of the cemetery in Section 47, within view of the local airport. It is at the end of the row designated Range N, close to the road itself.

It'd be easy and trite to end this jaunt with any of Type O Negative's relevant song titles—"Die with Me," "The Dream Is Dead," "Halloween in Heaven"—but they only sound good when heard out of Steele's subterranean pipes.

Lloyd Kaufman
QUEENS

THE BUILDING'S METAL GARAGE SHUTTER bore a brightly painted mural of a horribly mutated man holding a mop and wearing a pink tutu, with a word bubble above his head that said, "No parking, please."

"Think this is the place?" I asked, as my wife and I approached the adjacent door. We were in Long Island City in Queens, near the East River, on a block that was mostly residential. We tested the door, which opened onto a "Lady and the Tiger" scenario that involved a short, dingy hallway to the right and a short, dingy staircase to the left. No signs indicated the right path. A pair of foam buttocks with an accurately placed orifice leaned against the wall in a corner.

"Yup, this is the place," answered my wife.

We were standing at 36-40 11th Street, in the entryway of Tromaville, the headquarters of the famous-to-those-who-know-them Troma Studios, and we were there to meet one of its founders and the company face, Lloyd Kaufman.

Troma Studios was established in the 1970s by Kaufman and his partner Michael Herz. They got their start making sex comedies, and then switched over to horror comedies because, according to Kaufman, "It was what not to do."

In 1985, they debuted *The Toxic Avenger,* a movie about a mutated monster superhero, which got them as close to the mainstream as they've ever been. The movie has had three sequels, a Saturday morning cartoon, an off-Broadway play,

and tons of merchandising. No Macy's Thanksgiving Day parade float yet, though. Toxie, as he's affectionately come to be known, has become the company symbol, mascot, and official "no parking" sign.

A proudly independent movie studio by necessity, Troma somehow managed to not only survive for almost four decades in an industry where multibillion-dollar corporate studios fade monthly, but has assembled a strong fan base that acts as the team's life support. A lot of that is due to the popularity of Toxie. A lot of is also due to the popularity and showmanship of Kaufman. Most, though, is due to the questionable tastes of their fans.

You can almost learn everything you need to know about the studio by perusing the titles of the movies that Troma makes or distributes: *Surf Nazis Must Die, Rabid Grannies, Class of Nuke 'Em High, Chopper Chicks in Zombietown.* The thing is, Troma movies are almost without exception extremely low-budget, over-the-top affairs that exist in a strange spatial geometry devoid of any lines of decency. The movies are profane, obscene, disgusting, sex-and-gore obsessed . . . they're Troma. However, they're made in such obvious defiance of the movie system and with such a strong will and self-awareness that it's hard to disparage them. Also they take descriptors such as the above as compliments. So it's literally hard to disparage them.

My introduction to Troma was on VHS from my local movie rental shop. And that's also how we were all introduced to Kaufman and Tromaville. Every VHS copy of a Troma movie came with an introduction by Kaufman, where he would wander through the halls of Tromaville with a microphone, talking in his trademark animated, self-deprecating way, to the various residents of the studio. These were invariably recurring actors from their movies, costumed characters such as Toxie and Sgt. Kabukiman (from *Sgt. Kabukiman, N.Y.P.D.*), and plenty of random scantily clad females, all just there to put in a day's work at Tromaville. Basically, Kaufman almost singlehandedly invented the DVD extra before those things ever existed, and in so doing, he made Tromaville a real space. In reality, of course, he was just trying to take advantage of one of the few advertising outlets that the small studio could afford.

However, that was at Tromaville's previous location, in Manhattan's Hell's Kitchen, back when that moniker made sense. Over the past few decades, Hell's Kitchen gentrified quite a bit to the point where Troma studio couldn't turn down the price it could get for its property. According to Kaufman, "We were the nicest building on the block, and by the time we left, every other building was really nice and we were the slum."

Eventually, my wife and I made our way up the stairs and saw the real Tromaville. It was a large, cluttered room lined with Troma posters and full of desks and college-age kids working busily around a bunch of half-packed boxes as they prepared for an imminent convention. It felt more like some kind of volunteer effort than a movie studio.

After meeting Kaufman's secretary Chelsea, a young girl with a Troma bumper sticker stuck to her shirt, we learned that the first thing on our docket was a tour of the facilities, which we were taken on by Troma's PR guy, Mike. Both Mike and Chelsea were enthusiastic and probably years from being born when *The Toxic Avenger* came out.

By *facilities*, they meant the storage room. At the end of that first-floor hallway is the small room where the props, stocks of DVDs, film reels, marketing materials, and fan art are stored. Any other studio would probably call these archives, the contents of which would be carefully logged, arranged, and safe-guarded, but not Troma.

Stuff was everywhere—DVDs, actual film reels from the earlier movies, paintings that fans had created and sent in, props. However, the entirety of the contents was pretty scant for a movie studio that had been around for almost 40 years, especially when it came to props.

The few they had were piled on top of a bank of filing cabinets and were mostly from the last movie that they had made (three years earlier), *Poultrygeist: Night of the Chicken Dead*—zombie chicken masks, giant veined eggs, buckets of guts, less identifiable things. I'd find out later from Kaufman that because most of the people who work on Troma movies are fans, they always swipe the props afterward. "It's publicity. It's advertising. I don't mind."

Finally, after wading through all the Tromabilia and getting loaded up with DVDs by Mike, it was time to meet Lloyd Kaufman.

Kaufman's office was just a large, empty room that he shared with Michael Herz, whom he met at Yale. Herz is the silent partner, meaning he doesn't go in front of the camera. In the Tromaville introductory scenes, Herz was played by a morbidly obese actor named Joe Fleishaker who has a recurring role in most Troma movies whenever there's a spot for a particularly disgusting bathroom joke. In reality, Herz is a slim, dark-haired man who doesn't seem to have a reason to be camera shy. According to Kaufman, Herz just hates the publicity aspects of the job. He was actually there for much of our interview with Kaufman, but mostly ignored us, only reluctantly throwing in acerbic jokes when addressed directly by Kaufman.

Their desks told the story better than I just did. Herz's desk was basic: a com-puter, business and personal paraphernalia. Kaufman's, on the other hand was spilling over with Troma merchandise, almost to the point that it couldn't be used as a desk. Behind him was a continuous backdrop of Troma posters bearing the tagline "40 Years of Reel Independence." A green screen was taped to a nearby wall. It wasn't so much a desk as it was a set.

Kaufman is short, in his late 60s, and in real life seemed just a muted ver-sion of the one I'd seen in Tromaville segments in the 1980s and '90s, although he was missing his bowtie. He was friendly and had no problem discussing any-thing I wanted to bring up. However, most impressively, he was probably the best

at self-deprecatory humor that I've ever seen. I guess he has an advantage being the head of a company known for its penis monsters, cannibal musicals, feces play, and hermaphrodite serial killers.

When I told him he'd be one of only two living people to be in the "Legends and Personalities" section of the book, his partner chimed in with, "That could change really fast." To which Kaufman said, "Yeah, just waiting to die. A sad clown just waiting to die. I'll soon be throwing off these mortal clown coils. A life wasted. A good chapter head for you: A life wasted." Actually, I could just fill this entry up with his quotes.

Kaufman is not only one of the founders of Troma Entertainment, he regularly directs and produces the movies, in addition to often acting in them. He also writes books about the independent film business, including *Make Your Own Damn Movie!* and *Produce Your Own Damn Movie!*, books that are a fun read even if you aren't trying to make a movie.

It didn't take us long to get to the company's certain but limited success in the business. Kaufman blamed the industry and used the phrase "economically blacklisted" regularly. Second, in fact, only to "conglomerate," which he used as a swear word.

"Troma is more famous than ever, but yet we're economically blacklisted. In the '80s, before the conglomerates got rid of the rules and laws that protected the public against monopoly, the playing field was never level, but at least we had a chance to compete. The playing field now is impossible for an independent movie studio. It's like a perpendicular stripper's pole that's greased. You cannot climb up. It's impossible."

I obviously don't know the ends and outs of Hollywood politics (or much about stripper poles), but there could be some truth in what he says, even if he doesn't seem to be taking into account the utter amoral chaos of a Troma movie. The studio has been around for decades, has multiple titles that sold half a million units without advertising, and has helped launched the careers of Matt Stone and Trey Parker, Kevin Costner, Samuel Jackson, Billy Bob Thornton, Marisa Tomei, and Vincent D'Onofrio, who have all been in Troma movies. Troma is also frequently cited as inspirations by some of the biggest directors out there, including Quentin Tarantino and Peter Jackson, and just about every horror movie director. Honestly, Disney should have absorbed these guys years ago.

Nevertheless, according to Kaufman, Troma films can get only extremely limited theatrical releases, if that; they have no content deal with any of the cable companies; and they were never carried by Blockbuster, which they've almost outlived, as well. Kaufman likes to attribute their continued success despite all that to the fan base . . . which bootlegs Troma stuff.

"It's really thanks to the fans . . . the fans distribute our movie, the bootleggers distribute our movie. We make money because our stuff is bootlegged. All that stuff keeps us out there. I'm totally pro-piracy. Yeah, a hundred percent. Absolutely. I'm not pro-China stealing our movies and then selling them. I don't think that's such a good idea. But no question, the file-sharing, we make money."

I asked him whether Tromaville is open to the public, and he answered that people come by just about every day. "We had tourists today from Australia and from Germany and then . . . from Michigan." So there's your invitation.

We talked for about 45 minutes, covering a wide range of topics that I can't at all fit into this space, from his family (he's married to the New York State film commissioner and has three adult daughters) to Buffalo, where they filmed *Poultrygeist* in an abandoned McDonald's (see "Horror Movie Filming Locales") to his beliefs about copyright law ("an obscenity") and his expertise with whores.

All in all, I left ready to steel myself for another Troma movie, although I'll never forgive myself for not swiping a prop on the way out.

Charles Addams
SAGAPONACK

I T'S ONE OF THE MORE TERRIFYING PROPOSITIONS a person can be offered: "I want you to meet my family." And when cartoonist Charles Addams offered it, it should have been doubly so. Instead, meeting the Addams Family turned out to be delightful . . . or, rather, darkly delightful.

Charles Addams was born in 1912 in Whitefield, New Jersey. His career as a guy who drew pictures in little boxes started not long after that when, at age 21, he got a comic published in *The New Yorker* magazine. That publishing relationship would continue throughout his life. In fact, those characters known collectively as the Addams Family first appeared in that publication.

However, the Addamses as we know them now are far from the Addamses as they were conceived. None of the characters had names, and they weren't even a family. They were just part of a larger cast of characters that populated the offbeat and often macabre cartoon world of Charles Addams.

Over the years, the more creepy, kooky characters gravitated toward one another in Addams's comics and became familial. According to H. Kevin Miserocchi in his book, *The Addams Family: An Evilution,* they were given Addams's own surname by the media, which sometimes referred to the characters as "Addams's family of ghouls."

The popularity of the Addamses grew from the first appearance of an Addams in 1938 until it blossomed blackly into a television show, where it entrenched itself into our culture to the point where Uncle Fester's deep-set eyeballs peer into our nightmares to this day . . . our more hilarious ones, at least.

The Addams Family television show aired from 1964 to 1966 and really codified the Addamses as we know them, as the eccentric, macabre family with a zeal for life. The show contrasted the group against conventional society, which found them strange, terrifying, and dangerous . . . in a lighthearted, set-up-and-punch-line sort of way.

Charles Addams himself was heavily involved in the series, helping design costumes and sets, casting actors, and writing more than half the scripts. He even came up with the names. Gomez, Morticia, Wednesday, Pugsley, Lurch, Grandma Frump, Uncle Fester . . . names so apt it was as if these characters had always been called that.

Looking back on the show after half a century of television-watching savvy, the pacing is a bit stilted, like all shows of that era, and sometimes the episodes lean too hard on their gags, but the charm of the series survives much more intact than does many of its contemporaries'. After all, you can't fault it for being dated. With *The Addams Family*, "The world's not like that anymore" is a completely irrelevant criticism. The world was never like what it was inside the Addams house . . . and that's too bad.

Just about everything we find wicked and worth avoiding about life, the Addamses find good and embrace it, but that's not because they're contrarian or evil. The pleasure they find is of the exquisite variety, not the decadent. They find good in almost everything . . . with the exception of blandness, that is. They hate that. They're like children in both those respects.

Prominent among those exquisite pleasures are, strangely enough, kindness and compassion. Sure, they might try to skewer you with a sword, feed you to a carnivorous plant, or lock you in a medieval torture device, but it's because they think you'll derive as much pleasure from it as they do. And at the very least it will fight off the blandness for you.

As to the characters, while they all bring something to the Addams family dinner table, and as much as I like the dish best served cold who is Morticia and the perennial agony and befuddlement of Lurch, Gomez Addams carries the show on his pin-striped back.

You know that enlightened third-eye concept present in Hinduism and Buddhism? Well, Gomez (as played by John Astin) has two of them, each outlined in black eyeliner and never blinking, voraciously eating up everything he sees. Sure, it's the gaze of a maniac, but it's also the look of one who is imbibing wonders, like one's first glimpse of the ocean or a skyscraper. Gomez looks at everything that way.

It might seem surprising at first that something so entrenched in popular culture as *The Addams Family* only ran for two seasons (64 half-hour episodes), but the Addamses never really left us, having been reincarnated as three movies, two cartoon series, a second television series, and, most recently, a Broadway play. Oh, and Scooby-Doo met them once in the 1970s. And that's only as of the time of this writing. Plans always seem underway to further exhume the characters.

Meanwhile, Charles Addams, though his life bore no real similarity to the Addams family aesthetic, relished his role as a patriarch, never tiring of his famous creations. In addition to his Addams Family endeavors, he undertook a range of different drawing projects, from illustrating book jackets to exhibiting in galleries to publishing about a dozen books of his own artwork. In 1980, Addams married his third wife, Marilyn Matthew Miller, or Tee, as she was called.

He died eight years later at the age of 76 of a heart attack while waiting in his car in New York City. The Grim Reaper always fills in the last panel.

Addams kept a few homes, including an apartment in Manhattan at 25 West 54th Street, behind the Museum of Modern Art. However, he settled into the end of his life at what he called The Swamp.

Its address is 510 Sagaponack Road in Sagaponack, almost at the tip of Long Island, and situated within a nature sanctuary. Today, it's the headquarters of the Tee and Charles Addams Foundation, which Mrs. Addams set up before she passed away in 2002 to further and protect her husband's legacy and works. Charles and Tee Addams's ashes are buried on the grounds there at its pet cemetery (fitting, given he married Tee in another pet cemetery).

It's also the site of Addams's last studio, and while the site isn't really a museum, it is open to the public by appointment from April 15 to June 15 and again from September 15 to November 15, if you can nab one. I wasn't able to take advantage of those time slots, unfortunately (something I hope to remedy at some point in my life), but I was able to drive up to the house during one particularly snowless winter month. Besides being secluded at the far end of the island, the low-built but sprawling house isn't visible from the main road. A narrow quarter-mile unpaved driveway wends its way through the property to the front of the house. No signs that I could see announce its current role or previous claim to fame.

Hopefully, one day the house will become a full-fledged, year-round museum, where people can come to see him. Until then, there's always 0001 Cemetery Ridge.

Mary Shelley

MANHATTAN

IF A MAD SCIENTIST TODAY stitched together corpse parts with the purpose of reanimating them into a monster, I hope he'd have the sense of style to actually incorporate a lock of Mary Shelley's hair into his creation. I mean, all he'd have to do is borrow it from the library.

Mary Shelley, of course, was the teenage girl who put every single horror author to shame before there even really were horror authors, by writing her 1818 novel *Frankenstein: The Modern Prometheus*. In it, a genius but myopic scientist creates a monster that secures the acting career of Boris Karloff, inspires a strawberry-flavored cereal, and gifts the world a metaphor on a silver platter for anything assembled from disparate parts.

Legend has it that the book came out of a friendly horror story competition one night among a group of 20-something literary lights staying at a Lake Geneva summer house. Besides the 19-year-old Mary, the participants included Shelley's future husband Percy Bysshe Shelley, Lord Byron, Mary's stepsister Claire Clairmont, and physician John Polidori. The other completed work that came out of the game was Polidori's "The Vampyre," the first vampire story in English. So that single night birthed two enduring legends. Last night I vacuumed beneath my couch.

Now, 200 years after it was shorn from Shelley's nightmare-filled head, a lock of her hair resides in the grand collection of the New York Public Library. In 2011, the library temporarily displayed it for all to marvel at, among other, probably-more-august-but-not-to-me literary treasures.

The occasion for the special exhibit was the centennial of the Stephen A. Schwarzman Building, the main branch of the New York Public Library in midtown Manhattan. The New York landmark at Fifth Avenue and 42nd Street is famous for its massive stone lion—guarded marble architecture and, um, for being the locale of the first scene of *Ghostbusters* (see "Horror Movie Filming Locales").

Some of the items in this large, yearlong exhibit were the original plush animals that inspired A. A. Milne to create Winnie-the-Pooh and his friends, a Gutenberg Bible, the writing desk of Charlotte Brontë, the cane that Virginia Woolf used to walk into the river where she committed suicide, George Washington's handwritten farewell address, sketches made by Beethoven, the typewriter of E. E. Cummings, and a letter from Houdini.

But even with all that crazy, crazy, fascinating stuff, I could only feign interest on my visit, about a month before the exhibit closed, as I looked frantically for just one glass case in particular.

The tresses were on display beside a first edition of Mary Shelley's famous work, as well as a comic book version, for some perspective on how long this work has captivated us. Interestingly enough, it also shared a case with the letter opener of Charles Dickens, which he had made from the paw of his pet cat. The blade was inscribed with "C.D. In Memory of Bob 1862."

As to the hair itself, I was expecting (and would still have been enthralled by) a locket-size few strands, but instead it was a long, thick rope of hair, its brunette color hardly dimmed by age and still wig-worthy.

The story behind the hair specimen is as strange as the artifact itself. Percy was a big proponent of free love and wanted to encourage it between his wife and friend. Shelley sent a length of hair to Thomas J. Hogg, a friend of her husband's, in 1815, a year or so prior to that fateful and frightful June night, along with a civil-sounding letter. They had a much different attitude toward awkwardness back then. Apparently nothing came of it, though, other than an artifact for posterity.

If you're reading this grimpendium from the beginning, I'm not sure whether you're going to find a better entry than a length of hair from a dead woman famous for a story that includes grave robbing as a major plot point. I also realize this entry borders almost on fetishism. It's just that, of all the deceased legends and personalities in this section, the closest I've been able to get to them is about 6 feet of thick earth away. But to see an actual biological part of an actual legendary author gives a different kind of shiver than the one Mary Shelley officially bequeathed us.

Charles Fort
MENANDS

YOU'VE DONE ALL RIGHT IN LIFE if your name gets turned into an adjective. Or at least, you've done something unique—for instance, pioneering a distinct style or perspective, or giving form to an idea that hadn't been incarnated before. In the case of Charles Hoy Fort, whose name inspired the term "Fortean" (and, in its noun form, "Forteana"), he delineated a space that was previously amorphous . . . a wild space filled with monsters and aliens and ghosts and strange artifacts and unexplained occurrences.

Over the years, we've accumulated a baggage-weighted raft of terms that covers all the more fringe aspects of life: the supernatural, the paranormal, the preternatural, the unknown, the occult, the weird, none of which really catches the gist of the whole thing. After all, Bigfoot's not paranormal (I assume), aliens aren't supernatural (still assuming), and fish falling from the sky and humans spontaneously combusting aren't either of those descriptors (assuming again). Charles Fort, as a writer and researcher of the strange and bizarre in all its iterations, gave us a way to succinctly group all of that oddity together.

Far from being a Carl Kolchak or a Fox Mulder, though, Fort hung out for hours on end at libraries, tirelessly sorting through scientific journals and newspaper accounts and writing an Iron Mountain truckload of notes about anything that deviated from scientifically accepted ideas about the world. Such as rains of blood. And demonic footprints. And extraterrestrial visitors.

Born in 1874 in Albany, Fort was an unsuccessful writer by trade. An inheritance from his uncle freed him up, though, to write without caring that he was an unsuccessful writer. In fact, most of his work went unpublished, including a large stack of novels and an autobiography. However, the few books that did make it into print largely influenced certain circles in a way that continues to this day.

Even though Fort is connected with a field that many believe is reserved for the gullible or deluded, he was actually a skeptic. Of everything. Specifically, he called himself an intermediatist, meaning that he believed that the foundational truth of reality was too interconnected and melded to ever tease out, that theories and natural laws and facts and philosophies could only be established or arrived at by excluding data that didn't fit in with those ideas, meaning that one was wrong the second that one said one was right. He was antiauthoritarian and antiabsolutism about all dogma, especially that of science. Hilariously, he

referred to science as a "mutilated octopus." He basically disagreed with and poked fun at anybody—theologians, philosophers, scientists—who said that they had any kind of answer.

And that was the main point of his obsessive "data-collecting," to show how much had to be ignored to come up with sensible models of the world. Besides developing a sore butt from his days in the library and his lifetime of fence sitting, he produced a massive collection of clippings and notes, the latter numbering in the tens of thousands. He ended up burning most of them, an act that has been attributed to depression, but which I think is also a common impulse among a certain type of collector. Some of the surviving notes are kept at the New York Public Library's Rare Book Room.

The four books that he's most famous for are *The Book of the Damned*, published in 1919 (Fort used *damned* as a kind of antonym to *dogma*), *New Lands* in 1923, *Lo!* in 1931 (in which he coined the term *teleportation*), and *Wild Talents* in 1932.

Most of his life was spent in New York, and most of his researching was done at the New York Public Library, but he also spent about a decade in London, where the British Museum Library was his home base.

The Fortean Society was established during his lifetime, a society to which he declined leadership due to that aforementioned antiauthoritarian streak, and to this day there are many other organizations and periodicals that have taken on both his name and his purpose.

He died at the age of 57 in 1932 in New York and was buried in Albany Rural Cemetery in Menands, the same cemetery where President Chester A. Arthur is buried (see "Notable Graves, Cemeteries, and Other Memento Mori").

The cemetery is located at the end of Cemetery Avenue, and the Fort family plot can be found in Lot 8. The lots are well marked and easy to find, and the Fort plot within the lot is equally so, due to the tall obelisk mounted by a figural statue that marks the plot. As I mentioned, it's a family grave, and there are two Charles Forts buried there. You're looking for Charles H., not Charles N. Unless you're looking for Charles N.

Now, I realize that Fort wasn't a practitioner of the macabre, per se, but he did entertain and popularize ideas that were monstrous and that, for the purposes of this book, we've included in our definition of *macabre.* Mostly, though, I think the thing about Charles Fort is that, and I'm sure he'd disagree, he just wanted explanations to be bigger than what science gave. Less mundane. He wanted there to be giant creatures swimming in space, gelatinous pockets in the sky full of water and animals and artifacts, mysterious, undiscovered planets that come so close they pulled things off our own, and extraterrestrials and giants and fairies and ghosts, so he advanced wild theories that incorporated them based on mounds of anecdotal evidence he accumulated. And then the punch line was, he didn't believe a word of his theories, even when his adherents tried to convince him of the truth of his own conjectures. Because that's just the way he was.

In the end, I think the moral of the story of Charles Fort is this: Being indefinable only works until your own name is used to define you.

Henry Hull
SPARKILL

IN 1941, LON CHANEY JR., made the Wolf Man famous. However, by that time, the Universal Studios stable of monsters had already chained a werewolf within its cobwebbed depths for years.

In 1935, they released the less atmospheric *Werewolf of London,* starring Henry Hull as both star and monstar of the film. *Werewolf of London* wasn't the world's first werewolf movie, as there had been three or four other independent and obscure films and shorts that featured the creature, but *Werewolf of London* was the movie that really made the lycanthrope mainstream, and a viable enough creature with which to seed the nightmares of children.

In the story, Henry Hull plays Dr. Wilfred Glendon, a rather unsympathetic botanist with a conservatory full of exotic and carnivorous plants, including one with six-foot tentacles that eats frogs and probably should have had its own movie. *Werewolf of London* opens with Glendon in Tibet, where he's tracking down an ultrarare species of plant known as *Marifasa lupina lumina*, the phosphorescent Wolf Flower, and gets attacked by a hairy humanoid creature.

Turns out, it's a werewolf, one played by Warner Oland, the Swedish actor who made a career out of playing Asian characters, including famous, multimovie stints as both Fu Manchu and Charlie Chan. In this movie he portrayed another Asian character, a Dr. Yogami, who, upon meeting Glendon back in London under less lupine terms, insists that "werewolfery" is real, present in London, and that the Wolf Flower plant that Glendon has brought back from Tibet is the only way to keep the monster at bay, a monster that is "neither man, nor wolf but a satanic creature with the worst qualities of both," a monster that always attacks those it loves.

From that point in the story, it's werewolf movie 101, albeit before there was a 101, with Glendon turning into a werewolf from the bite sustained during his tussle in Tibet and then trying to find a way to stop himself from killing during the full moon, especially before it's too late for his wife.

Other than the fact that he's killing women on a nightly basis, Hull's werewolf is a pretty civilized one, not leaving the house without a coat, hat, and scarf, and eloquently thanking his shooter through his fangs for the bullet that puts him out of his misery at the end. He also looks more man than wolf, as he's often well dressed, especially during his first "transvection" when he's wearing a tie and lounging jacket. In addition, the hirsuteness of his beast form is basically confined to the peripheral areas of his face.

Jack Pierce did the werewolf makeup for the *Werewolf of London*. Apparently, he wanted the werewolf to be more bestial, but Hull didn't want to sit through the hours-long process of makeup application, so Pierce invented a less hairy, less obscuring, easier-to-apply look. It works pretty well and is pretty distinctive with its pointed ears and fluffy widow's peak and sideburns. However, the O. Henry ending to that story is that six years later Pierce would get a second chance to try his original makeup idea, this time on a much more amenable Lon Chaney Jr., creating the iconic Universal Studios werewolf look that horror fans revere to this day.

Henry Hull didn't do any horror movies after *Werewolf of London,* or even really before that, unless you want to count a turn as Rasputin in a 1917 film about the mad monk. A large portion of his career focused on Broadway, although he did act in the Western genre quite a bit, for both movies and television, and had roles in other movies that included the 1948 *Portrait of Jennie* and in Alfred Hitchcock's 1944 *Lifeboat.* His last movie role was in the 1966 *The Chase,* starring Marlon Brando and Robert Redford. But his place in the Universal horror canon, and in the annals of cinema itself, is secured through just his single werewolf role.

Hull was born in Kentucky in 1890 but lived in all the places that actors do, California, Connecticut, New York. He died in England in 1977, where he had moved to live with his daughter after his wife died in 1971. He's buried beside her in Rockland Cemetery in Sparkill, on the west bank of the Hudson River just about where it starts to widen into the Tappan Zee.

The cemetery address is 201 Kings Highway. His grave, where I'm sure he rolls every time somebody compares his werewolf to Chaney's, is located in the upper part of that cemetery with a great view of the river. To get to there, head to the back of the cemetery, and then take the road that winds steeply up the hill into the woods. If after a few moments you're wondering whether you're on the right road, that means you're on the right road. It'll finally open onto a smaller, higher-up section of the cemetery. Once you enter that part, take the road past the tall obelisk on the right. This is the final resting place of Henry Honychurch Gorringe, the man who was in charge of transporting the massive Cleopatra's Needle from Egypt to the United States. It now stands in Central Park just behind the Metropolitan Museum of Art. Like that anecdote, the road veers to the left at this point, which you'll follow just a few car lengths until you see a large, squat monument on your left. Hull's simple headstone is just behind this monument.

Incidentally, that monument is dedicated to General John Charles Frémont, who was a famous Civil War–era military officer, explorer, and politician. Hull married Frémont's daughter, which is why he shares a burial plot with him.

It's a shame that Hull didn't stick around at the Universal Studios horror department, though. *Werewolf of London vs. The Wolf Man* would have been a great little flick to see.

Frank Belknap Long
BRONX

AUTHOR FRANK BELKNAP LONG is less known in horror literature for his actual stories than for the seminal horror community of which he had a large part. He was a frequent contributor to the influential *Weird Tales* fiction magazine during its original run and a personal friend of H. P. Lovecraft (see page 42). Rare is the piece on Long that doesn't include multiple Lovecraft references, and it might not even exist. The Elder Gods know I can't do it.

Long was born, lived, and died in New York City, but that easily stated life arc encompassed a span of more than 90 years from 1901 to 1994. Basically, Long helped lay the foundation for modern horror, witnessed its many phases over the course of the 20th century, and lived to see it acknowledged as a genuine cultural force.

Any discussion of Long's work starts with a discussion of Lovecraft, both biographically and stylistically. In 1921, Long published the short story "The Eye Above the Mantel" in an amateur publication that Lovecraft happened to read. Lovecraft was impressed enough with the story that he started a correspondence with Long that developed into a friendship that would last about 15 years, until Lovecraft's death in 1937.

Lovecraft, a native of Providence, Rhode Island, visited Long in New York, and when Lovecraft moved to that city for a couple of years in the mid-1920s, saw him often. In fact, Long was a founding member of Lovecraft's Kalem Club literary group. Long even wrote a biography of Lovecraft, entitled *Howard Phillips Lovecraft: Dreamer on the Nightside,* and used him as a character in his story "The Space-Eaters."

Lovecraft couldn't help but be an influential force on anybody who has ever read his stories, and Long's work was often Lovecraftian; some might say at its best, even. Sometimes his work was literally so, as Long published stories set within Lovecraft's Cthulhu Mythos. His most famous in that vein, and perhaps his most famous story overall, is "The Hounds of Tindalos," in which a man attracts the attention of malevolent otherworldly beings who exist in "angular time" and so attempts to round out every example of that geometry from his apartment to keep them from attacking him.

Like Lovecraft, Long's horror was often cosmic, but unlike Lovecraft, he would often cross the genre line to write full-fledged science fiction (even though his science fiction always kept some horrific element in it).

Horror aside, Long holds a similarly august place in the annals of science fiction. He was an earlier contributor to *Astounding Science Fiction* (now known by the sadly less pulpy name *Analog Science Fiction and Fact*), the magazine that influenced and launched such giants of the genre as Isaac Asimov, Ray Bradbury, and Robert Heinlein, an extremely daunting peer group.

Long also wrote freelance articles and poetry, as well as more than two dozen novels, but it is his short stories, some 150 all told, where his legacy lies. Unfortunately, it wasn't enough of a legacy to guarantee financial stability. He died poor, without even the wherewithal for his own grave. However, his peers, friends, and fans got together and

gave him a proper burial in his family plot in Woodlawn Cemetery in the Bronx.

The address of the 150-year-old, 400-acre cemetery is 501 East 233rd Street. Next to Sleepy Hollow Cemetery, Woodlawn is probably my favorite graveyard in New York. The cemetery contains the graves of everybody from Herman Melville and Bat Masterson to Irving Berlin and Duke Ellington and features a varied topography with large trees, hills, ponds, and winding paths that portend the discovery of something new and interesting around every bend. I'd also suggest checking out the grave of Lieutenant Commander George Washington DeLong, the arctic explorer, who is buried with members of his last expedition, which ended in tragedy somewhere in Siberia. His grave has a life-size statue of him in a winter parka, standing in and back-dropped by a snowdrift, his hand to his eyes peering across what is obviously some icy, uncharted landscape. The locations of all the aforementioned graves can be found on the maps in the cemetery office.

However, Long's grave is not listed among those notables, and that, combined with the size of the cemetery and the wonderfully confusing landscape, means that his grave can be hard to find without prior intelligence. And while I might not be able to offer that, I can at least give you directions. Long's plot is in Prospect section, near the intersection of Prospect Avenue and Lawn Avenue. It's easily found from there as it's near the road and marked by a tall stone obelisk with a carved shroud adorning its apex. His name is engraved in relatively fresh letters on the base of the monument.

Today, even with the resources available to us through the Internet, much of his work is difficult to find. Meanwhile, his legacy struggles between obscurity and a Lovecraft footnote. Fortunately, with Lovecraft's ever-expanding stature in the genre, the link might be enough to maintain Long's works in the sphere until he can be appreciated in his own right.

John Lennon Memorial

TWO

Infamous Crimes, Killers, and Tragedies

OTENTIAL IS A TWO-WAY STREET, and New York is a great example
of the dichotomy. For every momentous event that has taken place
here, a great tragedy has befallen. For every success story, there's a tale of
victimhood. For every noble act, there is an equal and opposite depraved one.

Honestly, this is the uncomfortable section of the book. Elsewhere, when
we talk about storytellers who focus on the macabre or the filming locales of
horror movies or historic cemeteries or the classic monsters of our mytholo-
gies, there's still a certain distance from the topic of death that enables amiable
and even pleasurable discussion of it. At some point the blade has to hit the flesh,
though. These kinds of stories and sites exist because people die. And too often,
they die horribly.

Worse, this section of the book doesn't merely comprise true stories of
crimes, killers, and tragedies. After all, treating them as stories, true or not, still
gives us a bit of distance. The story of a lynch mob's graphically earning its name
and the story of an inquisitive monkey and a man in a yellow hat have that much
in common.

Instead, within the following pages are the actual sites, artifacts, memorials,
and even body parts connected to those events of New York history about which
you have to check to see if there's any children around before you talk about them.
I admit, it's somewhat strange how seeing the house of a serial killer or the mass
grave of theater fire victims or the skull and noose of an executed criminal better

imbues such events with reality than do simply the facts of the incident. But that's just the way it is.

Despite all that, though, this section is the one that needs to be included in this book the most. These things happened. They're moments of New York history, of U.S. history, of human history, just as much as George Washington's taking the first presidential oath of the country or the delivery of the Statue of Liberty or the invention of the martini. They need to be written about. Why? Well, I'm not totally sure. I'm willing to be flexible on that point.

Heck, just as I started on this book in early 2011, reports were rampant that the discovered remains of multiple victims on a Long Island beach meant a new and terrifyingly successful serial killer was in town. As the months progressed, more victims were found in the same area for a total of ten victims, including a toddler, and the investigators reevaluated their theories, considering it to be the work of three or four different serial killers. By the end of this book project here in early 2012, the investigators had reverted back to the single serial killer hypothesis. Oh, and most relevant, they still haven't found him. I shudder to think what the next twist in the case will be by the time this book is published. But the point is that this chain of events should be the plot of an over-the-top horror novel, not solemnly transcribed items on a police report. Geez, New York.

Unfortunately, a small community's worth of murderers appear in this section of the book. And in addition to those dregs of the dregs of humankind are included fires and plagues, bombings and crashes, torture and execution, accidents and assassinations . . . even toxic sludge—all told, enough to make you want to leave New York. Maybe even the planet.

Of course, listing them all like that may make it look as if New York is a cursed land or the entry point for the apocalypse. But the answer has nothing to do with New York itself. It's just people. Lots and lots of people. New York is the third-largest state by population and only the 27th largest by area. So not only does it have a lot of people, it has a lot of people in a relatively small area, and mostly concentrated around New York City (which is, admittedly, the elephant in the state, so to speak, when it comes to this topic of tragedy and atrocity).

And where there are people, there are accidents, crimes, evil, death. The more people, the more brutality. It's obvious, but it still needs to be said. After all, our instinct is to push it away from us, turn it into a story, distance ourselves from it, survive the telling by holding our fingers to our ears and hoping it'll never be relevant to our individual lives.

But you know what? It will be. Your odds just increase if you're here in New York.

So please read on . . . just make sure you're sitting in a seat with plenty of squirm room.

Son of Sam Locations
YONKERS

H*E CALLED HIMSELF THE SON OF SAM*, but after his yearlong murder spree in New York City in the late 1970s, it's hard to imagine that any parent would claim him.

The Son of Sam's real name was David Berkowitz, and he's almost always mentioned in the same listings as the most infamous, depraved serial killers in America. He killed six people and injured seven others over thirteen months from the summer of 1976 to the summer of 1977 throughout the Bronx, Queens, and Brooklyn before he was finally caught.

However, Berkowitz's murders were different from those of most serial killers. Quite simply, he shot his victims. No kidnapping, no torture, no violations, no dismembering and disposing of bodies. He simply walked up, pulled the trigger, and walked away. Quickly, I assume. And it's one of the reasons his victims had a 50-50 chance of living. It was almost thuggery. In fact, the name the media originally gave him, when authorities realized that it wasn't just a bunch of ordinary, unrelated shootings, was the gangsta rap name of ".44 Caliber Killer," for the bullets left behind.

But just because he wasn't a fetishist doesn't mean he wasn't messed up in the 'mygdala. They just had to catch him to learn the extent of it.

Berkowitz was born in 1953. He was adopted right after his birth and raised in the Bronx, where he lived as normal a life as anybody else, with maybe a few more downswings of fortune than average. His adopted mother died of breast cancer when he was a young teenager, and his father married a few years later and moved to Florida without his 18-year-old son. Berkowitz spent about three bad years in the army before exiting the service. In 1976, he moved to Yonkers, got a job at the post office, and became a serial killer.

He attacked mostly young women, but also couples sitting in cars. All told,

there were eight separate attacks over the course of those 13 months, often enough and over a long enough period to really add to the miasma of the city. New Yorkers reacted accordingly and added yet another reason not to go out at night. Hundreds of cops were put on the case.

Berkowitz sent notes to both police and the media. The hand-scrawled missives were incoherent, self-obsessed, perverse . . . all in all, sterling examples of the genre. But they did give him his name. Actually they gave him a few, most of them alliterative: "Mr. Monster," "Duke of Death," but it was "Son of Sam" that stuck.

And then, in perhaps the most mundane way possible, he was captured.

In a twist that is probably still used at police academies everywhere as an example of the importance of even the most trivial-seeming assignments, Berkowitz was busted as a result of a parking ticket. He parked his yellow Ford Galaxie too close to a hydrant on Bay 17th Street in Brooklyn during his last attack that killed a young woman and permanently blinded her boyfriend. Somebody had witnessed a man throwing a parking ticket away nearby on the night of the shootings. The police traced it to Berkowitz, who lived in an apartment in Yonkers, and presto, "I'm the Son of Sam."

Then the story gets weird. Berkowitz claimed he killed people because his neighbor's possessed black Labrador told him to during its nightly howlings. The neighbor's name was Sam Carr, from whom Berkowitz derived his alias. The dog's name was Harvey. Berkowitz actually ended up shooting the animal at some point, and though the dog apparently survived, the telepathic demon angle was never verified.

At the time of the crimes, Berkowitz lived in a building called Pine Hill Towers, at 35 Pine Street. His apartment was 7E. He was arrested right outside of the building. Today, the red-brick residence is called Horizon Hill, and they've changed the address to 42 Pine Street to distance the place from being the location of the so-called Satan's Lair. The house where Sam Carr lived still stands nearby at 316 Warburton Avenue.

Later, Berkowitz would recant the demon dog explanation, but he maintained full weirdo status by claiming that he was only responsible for about a third of the attacks and that he was part of a Satanist enclave that was responsible for the rest of the killings. Basically, the Son of Sam had siblings.

Regardless, he was sent to prison in 1978 to serve the life span of a tortoise or two at the Sullivan Correctional Facility in Fallsburg. He's found God. God's only response so far has been, "No comment."

However, the Satanism angle gives us a much more interesting place to visit than some old apartment building. The story goes that Berkowitz and his fellow Satanists met in Untermyer Park, a property on the Hudson River about a mile and a half from his Yonkers apartment. Here they would supposedly sacrifice animals, traffic in pedophilia, and do just about anything to serve the forces of chaos . . . like planning a city-wide murder spree.

Located at 945 North Broadway, the park was originally the estate of a multimillionaire lawyer after whom the park is named and whose first name just happens to be Sam. The park's various gardens, pools, statuary, Grecian pillars, and gazebo still reflect that this is a different class of park.

Just off to the side of the garden area, a long set of stone stairs leads out to a colonnaded viewing platform above the river. Just below this platform, and accessible by the path that parallels the river, are the ruins of a large stone building, set back slightly into the overgrown forest area. Its walls are thickly covered in graffiti, its roof is gone, and it is guarded by a large stone lion and a matching, albeit headless, stone horse. It apparently was once the entrance house to the Untermyer estate.

Other than the fact that it's pretty easily accessed and that it's obviously regularly done so by teenagers, it seems a pretty good spot to jumpstart a lethal occult conspiracy. When David Berkowitz finally bites it himself, this is certainly where his doomed soul should haunt.

Grave of a Jack the Ripper Suspect
ROCHESTER

I DON'T CARE WHO REALLY SHOT JFK, what Coca-Cola's secret formula is, or how the universe came into being. Of all the mysteries that we banter about on dark, Madeira-fueled nights while watching hastily put-together cable TV specials, I really just want to know who Jack the Ripper was. And I have no good reason for that.

I certainly don't think the answer would be at all interesting. I mean, in our stories, serial killers are often portrayed as evil geniuses with some type of deranged cultural message, inherently intriguing just for that fact, while the truth of the matter is that in real life they're almost always just dumpy animal trash. Uninteresting as people, barely interesting as aberrations. We study them to stop them.

But Jack the Ripper . . . in the midst of all the advancement, reform, and invention going on in the late 1800s, he dug in his bloody knives, and in the space of just a few months, singlehandedly dragged mankind backward as a species. Suddenly serial killers were a reality and had to be added to the burgeoning list of despicable things that humanity was capable of producing.

Since that time, he has somehow passed from mere infamy to mythology. We use him regularly in our fictions, and he's still as much a part of contemporary popular culture as are Superman, Elvis, and Darth Vader, despite the fact that he prowled some 120 years ago and that in the intervening years we've had more than our share of monsters out-monster him. Heck, we've pretty much thrown the entire weight of our anorexic popular culture at the fiend, siccing H. G. Wells, Maxwell Smart, Sherlock Holmes, Johnny Depp, Kolchak the Night Stalker, Dr. Who, David Hasselhoff, Captain James T. Kirk, and others on him at one time or another. I think even the Fantasy Island guy got involved once. The tall one.

Sadly, the real story of Jack the Ripper doesn't involve Starfleet captains and *Baywatch* stars. The real story has few components, although those fragments have spiderwebbed into so many theories, ideas, and exaggerations that there's no longer any discernible single thread of story and wading into it all just makes you feel sticky and sucked bloodless.

There are basically two facts in the Jack the Ripper murders. One, a bunch of prostitutes were killed in the Whitechapel area of London in the fall of 1888. Two, we don't know who did it. From there, history and its too many experts guess that

it was a single killer, that there was no one killer, that the killer sent letters and part of one of the victim's kidneys to the media, that the letters were fake and the organ was from a medical cadaver, that he was a media invention anyway, that the nature of the wounds pointed to the subtle skill of a doctor, that the nature of the wounds pointed to the unsubtle skill of a butcher, that he killed five women, that he killed more than five women. On top of that, hundreds of suspects have been pushed forward over the years. Even Lewis Carroll, author of *Alice in Wonderland,* has been dubitably suggested.

If you ever visit London, you can take an after-dark tour of the streets of Whitechapel and see the spots where the Ripper's victims were found. You can also visit some of their graves. On this side of the Atlantic, however, there's little around that allows us to physically access the story. Here's one, though.

Of the many Whitechapel suspects, a few had American roots. And in this case, when I say suspects, I don't merely mean random name thrown out by a researcher to sell a book a hundred years after the fact. I mean suspects, as in pulled by the scruff of their neck into Scotland Yard and questioned brusquely by someone with a British accent.

One such suspect was Francis Tumblety, and he's buried in the city of Rochester, making his grave one bit of Ripper lore that we Yanks can see firsthand.

Tumblety was born sometime in the early 1830s, after which time his family settled in the Rochester area. He was a crazy kind of cat, traveling all over America and Europe, impersonating doctors and military men. Apparently he would truck around in an unearned military uniform on a white horse led by a pair of greyhounds, while collecting human uteri and making a nice little fortune selling snake oil. The one picture of him that shows up the most on the Internet depicts a guy in a Sergeant Pepper outfit, with a mustache the size of a ferret.

For the reasons outlined above (impersonations, snake oil, ferret mustache) and more, Tumblety regularly got into trouble with the law on both sides of the ocean. On our side, the biggest mark on his rap sheet was being arrested for conspiring in Lincoln's assassination. In England, it was the Whitechapel murders. Obviously, he was either the original Mr. Wrong Place at the Wrong Time or the actual subject of the Rolling Stones' "Sympathy for the Devil."

He was cleared of the Lincoln accusation within a few weeks, but he just plumb ran away from the Ripper one, eventually coming back to the United States and somehow avoiding extradition. Some say that's because he wasn't really a serious suspect, in addition to the fact that his arrest in London was actually for homosexuality, a crime punishable by imprisonment back then and there, but not one worth pulling someone back across the ocean for.

After dying in St. Louis, Missouri, in 1903, he was buried in the family plot in Holy Sepulchre Cemetery in Rochester. The large cemetery can be found at 2461 Lake Avenue and extends to both sides of the street. Tumblety's grave is on the east side, which is the one with the gothic-looking chapel right through the front gates. His grave is easy to find from there. It's in Section 13, to the left of the chapel.

The family grave is marked by a single, pinkish, urn-topped pillar that, for some reason, is jammed up against the slab of the adjoining plot. On the pillar, Tumblety's name is spelled "Fransis Tumuelty," but that's the guy. It also marks him as "Dr.," although it seems that more evidence supports his being a serial killer than a genuine man of medicine.

I admit that visiting the grave of a Ripper suspect who probably was only a weak one at that is a rather mundane experience, given the mythology surrounding the Whitechapel murderer. However, I can also tell you that I did that aforementioned after-dark Jack the Ripper tour while in London years and years ago. The grisly locations where the bodies of the eviscerated prostitutes were found are now modern office buildings, parking lots, and random bits of sidewalk, which, according to my math, is 1.3 million times more mundane than a 100-year-old grave. That said, both are probably more interesting than the real identity of the Ripper himself.

I still want to know, though.

Skull and Noose of a Murderer
ELIZABETHTOWN

MOST OF US MEMBERS of the law-abiding set will probably get a plain piece of granite shoved into the ground where our body ends up. It will be visited only by relatives and then only rarely, until it's eventually a forgotten rock above the remains of a corpse indistinguishable from the surrounding loam. The earthly remains of wife murderer Henry Delectnack Debosnys, on the other hand, have received a special kind of perpetual care. His skull and the artifacts associated with his execution have been preserved and placed on display like holy relics for all posterity . . . an extremely grateful posterity, I hope.

I had to cram in some of the sites and artifacts sideways to make them fit this grimpendium just because I wanted to write about them, but this type of exhibit is exactly what the book is about. Honestly, this might be one of my favorite entries, to the point that I tried to get my publisher to insert a permanent bookmark here so that it always opens to this page when people flip through it.

The story of Debosnys's life runs a lot like a novel, and that might be because most of what we know of it is drawn from his prison autobiography and is probably fictitious. If it is to be believed, though, he was born in Portugal in 1836 and then traveled the world for a bit, becoming fluent in about half a dozen languages. He was present on a couple of arctic expeditions and fought in a few wars, including the Battle of Gettysburg. In the United States, he lived in various states, including New York, where he eventually settled down, murdered a few wives, and then spent his retirement at the end of a noose in 1883. Actually, the epilogue of his biography is the stone dead truth, although officially, his first two wives died under mysterious, unprosecutable circumstances.

Debosnys met and married his third wife, Elizabeth Wells, in the Lake Champlain town of Essex in 1882. A few months later, he made a big show of telling everybody that she would be staying with relatives in the nearby town of

Port Henry for a while. Apparently the story was suspicious (it probably always should be), because neighbors did some poking around and found Elizabeth's dead body bejeweled with stab wounds to the throat and a pair of bullet holes in the head.

Authorities tracked down Debosnys, who was apparently heavily laden with physical evidence, and then executed him by rope about a year later, on April 27, 1883. He was the last man of two ever hanged in Essex County.

His skeleton, by a previous arrangement that involved trading his postexecution body to a doctor for a $15 dollar suit, I assume, to die in, ended up at a school as an anatomic specimen. Somehow, over the years, only the jawless skull of that skeleton survived.

You can see it and the noose that fit over it at the Adirondack History Center Museum, the headquarters for the Essex County Historical Society, in Elizabethtown.

The Adirondack History Center Museum is a large museum as far as local historical society museums go. It's housed in a hundred-year-old high school building that is a better accommodation than most of these types of societies get. The layout might've changed a bit since my visit as the building was undergoing renovations, but the basement floor is filled with carriages and various other antique vehicles, while the first floor has various displays on Essex County life, as well as a small gift shop in the entryway. It's on the second floor, just past an antique doll collection and in a room full of other random antiques, that a simple glass case holds the astonishing array of morbid treasures related to Debosnys.

If the exhibit only contained Debosnys's skull and the short, slip-knotted length of dingy rope that made it famous, my statement about how much I dig this display would still stand. But it has so much more, namely facsimiles of fascinating documents and artwork related to Debosnys (the originals are kept safely in the museum archives). For instance, one of the tickets to the event is present, signed by the county sheriff and made out to an "A. K. Dudley." "Not Transferrable," the ticket says.

Also included are reproductions of a few pages from the autograph book of the 17-year-old turnkey who was working at the prison during Debosnys's stint there. The murderer signed the teenager's book with entreaties to remember him and random aphorisms, accompanied by somewhat skilled drawings that included a self-portrait, an African camp, and a dog with its leg caught in a steel-jaw trap.

Finally, the exhibit features a range of macabre drawings and poems composed by Debosnys while in prison. These morbid little artworks showcase a neat, even hand and more of his drawing skills. The poems include such titles as "The City of Death" and "My Own Grave." One is even dedicated to his "poor" wife, in which he describes her death as "like golden insect in the dew, calm and pure." The images that accompany the poems include a skeleton in a cemetery with a broken chain around its ankle and a giant, pumpkin-covered gravestone . . . his own, and something he would never get . . . unlike us law-abiding folk.

The Adirondack History Center Museum is at 7590 Court Street, where it intersects with Hand Avenue and just down the road from a New York history sign touting the location of an overnight stop for the body of abolitionist John Brown on his funeral journey home to North Elba, New York, after being hanged for his raid on Harper's Ferry, West Virginia. The museum is only open from late May to mid-October, but if you happen to show up in winter, it's worth camping out on the doorstep for a few months to see this fascinating little display on the death of Henry Debosnys.

Wall Street Bomb Damage
Manhattan

As humans, we bear the scars of the worst of our wounds throughout our entire lives. Sure, they fade, but they never totally heal. Buildings, on the other hand, get their worst scars plastered over, repainted, the boards and stones replaced with newer, unmarred ones. However, one Wall Street building has retained on its exterior walls the last evidence of a horse-drawn time bomb that went off more than 90 years ago.

It was noon on September 16, 1920. World War I was a short but comfortable enough distance in the past, and the busy workers of the financial district

had lunch on their mind. A simple, horse-drawn carriage drew slowly up the street . . . and then exploded in what one surviving eyewitness described as a mushroom cloud of yellow-green smoke and fire 100 feet high.

In the twisted aftermath of severed body parts, shards of glass, and over-turned cars, it was discovered that 38 people (and one horse) were dead. Hundreds were injured. Property damaged numbered in the millions, a lot of it located in what was then the headquarters for the influential J. P. Morgan & Company bank.

Later investigations ruled out accidental causes when it was revealed that the source of the explosion in the carriage was a timer strapped to about 100 pounds of dynamite and 500 pounds of cast-iron sash weights, the latter acting as missiles from the force of the explosion. Foreign anarchists seemed the mostly likely cause, due to similar past incidents. Fingers were pointed at Italian and Russian sects.

Later, the anarchist angle was pretty much confirmed when it was revealed that fliers had been discovered nearby just before the explosion that read, "Remember, we will not tolerate any longer. Free the political prisoners, or it will be sure death for all of you." It was signed "American Anarchist Fighters." Unfortunately, the true identities of the bombers were never determined, even after years of investigation.

The next day, the Stock Exchange opened as usual. A previously planned rally celebrating Constitution Day was also held, with thousands showing up to an event that had changed its focus to one of solidarity and defiance. Whatever vague message the anarchists thought they were clearly sending disappeared like the smoke from their attack. It's a lesson that still hasn't been learned a century later. Bombs are the worst medium of communication.

Today, the only public indications of that bombing on Wall Street is a series of small, irregular craters in the exterior limestone walls of 23 Wall Street, the aforementioned Morgan Building, which was caused by the metal shrapnel in the carriage. These days, the headquarters of that financial institution is down the road a few blocks, while the 100-year-old, four-story, bomb-scarred edifice is now a residential property connected to the 42-story building behind it.

The building is right at the intersection of Wall Street and Broad Street, and scores of pockmarks can clearly be seen on the northeast, Wall Street side of the limestone building. Some of the shallow craters are as big as a hand and others as small as a marble. Many are right at eye level. Still, even with that, the damage is subtle, though, and can easily be missed or just chalked up to age.

Incidentally, the bomb went off right under the stone gaze of George Washington's statue, which . . . somehow undamaged from the blast . . . still stands in front of the Federal Hill building across the street from the Morgan Building, marking the place where the country's first president took his oath of office. I guess that's as good an answer as any for the long-dead terrorists.

Sing Sing Prison Exhibit
Ossining

COMMUNITY CENTERS ARE GREAT PLACES for a wide range of local functions such as children's activities, public meetings, and educational sessions. For the Joseph G. Caputo Community Center in the Hudson River Valley town of Ossining, it's also a great place to show off wicked-looking shanks, ominous electric chairs, and depressing prison cells, all in the name of community . . . a community that used to be named Sing Sing.

"Sing Sing" was derived from a Native American name meaning "stone upon stone," but the village changed the delightful name to Ossining in 1901 to distance itself from the infamy of its local prison. But that hasn't changed the fact that

Ossining's most prominent landmark is still the notorious Sing Sing Correctional Facility.

Completed in 1828, the large prison sits right on the banks of the Hudson River and has a history like many of the old prisons in the United States . . . over-crowding, stretches of brutality and inhuman conditions, in-house crimes, and dramatic escape attempts.

In the early 1900s, it became the go-to place for state executions, so many of the most notorious were housed on Death Row there. More than 600 convicts were executed on the premises by electric chair before the state stopped the practice in the 1960s.

During that time of electric justice, many of the most infamous criminals in history had their seats warmed there: William Kemmler, Ruth Snyder, Albert Fish, Edward Haight, Lonely Hearts Killers Raymond Fernandez and Martha Beck.

Today, you can tease their ghosts almost right from the walls of this still-active prison, although it has since expanded from its original cell block that now stands abandoned on the property. Public residential roads State, Hudson, Hunter, and South Streets take you right up to the chain-link fence that sur-rounds the prison, only a few score feet from the tall concrete walls and promi-nent guard towers.

In fact, you can get close enough that it's terrifyingly easy to imagine Sing Sing's 2,000 inmates pouring over those walls straight at you, their fingers bran-dishing homemade weapons and the body parts of unfortunate guards, their eyes blazing crazily with freedom and bloodlust against the law-abiding. Like a video game, except you don't have a chainsaw-equipped shotgun, just a small digital point-and-shoot that you brought because all you wanted was a photo that may or may not make it into the book you were writing . . .

Where was I?

Ah, the Joseph G. Caputo Community Center. Less than a mile from the prison itself at 95 Broadway is the community center that houses an exhibit dedicated to Sing Sing Prison. The humble brick building with its scuffed floors and walls furry with fliers was filled with activity when we visited.

After making our way through a crowd of sweaty middle-school-age children in karate uniforms, we hesitatingly asked the attendant at the front desk about the exhibit. He quickly led us to a nearby glass door, unlocked it, flipped a light switch, and let us wander around on our own.

The exhibit is mostly made of up informational placards and pictures, but the few artifacts that it does display are pretty impressive and well worth the free cost of admission. The first thing you come across is a glass case in which are mounted about 20 or so homemade, er, prison-made weapons confiscated from the inmates over the years. Shanks, all my years of watching prison movies tell me that they're called. Each roughly made stabbing implement was completely unique and rigged together from materials that included plastic forks with broken tines, screwdrivers, random prongs of metal, and less identifiable supplies. The handles were taped or wrapped with cloth, the ends were all pointy, and they all looked more monstrous than an actual Bowie knife dripping with fresh blood.

Next were full-size replica cells using actual doors from the prisons and filled with the meager holdings of the incarcerated . . . a cot and some pictures tacked to the wall. Or taped, actually, since I'm sure some crafty criminal could turn a pushpin into a deadly shank without straining a neuron. There were only three cells, each one with an open door allowing for photo ops, but the walls on either side was cleverly mirrored to give the illusion of an eternally long row of cells.

Next was a replica of the infamous electric chair of Sing Sing, which makes up for its being a mere replica by having been made by genuine prisoners, according to the placard, which also states that the original seat of dishonor is being kept at the Green Haven Correctional Facility in Dutchess County. The chair is all wood and leather straps, with a head cap like an innocent reading lamp affixed to the back.

The final object was a heavy, iron door set into the wall that was used for one of the original cells before we got better at treating our prisoners. It was made of thick, crosshatched, studded iron straps that let in very little light, and the darkness behind it must have been tiny. This seemed more like a solitary confinement pen than the more open, barred prison cells in which we'd just lightheartedly taken our pictures.

From there the museum leaves the bleakness of prison history and turns more to local history. All told, it can take just a few minutes to get the full effect of the exhibit, although the more meditative could certainly find reason to stick around longer.

For the past few years, there have been efforts in creating an official Sing Sing museum in the original prison building itself, but so far that hasn't come to pass. Until then, this exhibit will do nicely, I think.

Grave and Quarantine Island of Typhoid Mary
BRONX, NORTH BROTHER ISLAND

MUSTANG SALLY. RUNAROUND SUE. Sweet Caroline. Typhoid Mary. One of these things is not like the others. Unless you're a death metal fan, you're probably not going to hear a song about that last one. However, you can't avoid hearing about her legend.

It's a legend that makes it easy to imagine Typhoid Mary as some personification of disease, like Poe's Red Death, although instead of ominous aloofness, she laughs maniacally as she decimates cities, casting plagues on anybody she so much as trails her fingertips across.

Of course, as always, the truth is much more prosaic.

It's been estimated that thousands of people died from typhoid fever in New York in the early 1900s. Mary was the direct cause of only three of them, although she caused nonfatal illnesses in somewhere around 50 people.

Her real name was Mary Mallon. She was born in 1869 in Ireland and immigrated to New York in her teens. She became a private cook for various wealthy families, a dangerous position for an asymptomatic carrier of a pathogen that gets passed by ingestion.

The state health authorities thought so, too. In 1907, they locked up Mallon for three years in New York's Riverside Hospital, a quarantine facility on North Brother Island in the East River. Mary went kicking and screaming into infamy.

It's understandable, though. You're feeling fine, cooking some stew, and then somebody in a dark suit and shades knocks on your door, tells you that you've actually got a deadly disease even though you haven't had a symptom in your life,

asks for your bodily fluids and excretions, and then imprisons you in an island hospital.

Still, even back when it wasn't commonly understood that healthy people could spread fatal diseases, the proof was pretty damning.

Over the previous decade, Mallon had worked as a cook for some seven families all along the Long Island Sound in such places as Mamaroneck, Manhattan, and Oyster Bay. Every family suffered an outbreak of typhoid fever shortly after her employ. One person even died.

She simmered on North Brother Island for three years, developing the beginnings of an extremely impressive persecution complex that she would perfect later and which can be admired to this day in her letters and interviews. Authorities eventually decided to let her go, under the stipulation that she no longer find employment as a cook and that she keep as sanitary as possible.

In 1915, a typhoid cluster broke out at Sloane's Hospital for Women in Manhattan. It didn't take long to discover that Mallon had returned to her evil/naive cookery under the pseudonym Mary Brown. More than a score of people grew ill. Two died.

This time, her quarantine on North Brother Island was permanent. She spent the last 23 years of her life on the island, dying in 1938 at the age of 69 of pneumonia.

In death, she finally escaped from North Brother Island, but not from the

nickname that she hated and which was given to her by the media. Various editorial cartoons from the time depict her dropping skulls into a frying pan like so many cracked eggs or cleaning house with the Grim Reaper.

You can find her grave in Old Saint Raymond Cemetery at 1201 Balcom Avenue in the Bronx. She's in Section 15, which is the back part of the graveyard parallel to Balcom Avenue, grave number 55 in Row 19. Be careful not to confuse this cemetery with the nearby New Saint Raymond Cemetery at 2600 Lafayette Avenue. It's a mistake I've already made for you. An easy way to tell the difference between the two is that the new cemetery, in addition to being new, uses saints as naming conventions for its lot divisions, instead of numbers.

These days, the tiny North Brother Island, which was also the site of the General Slocum wreck three years before Mallon's tenure there (see page 138), is abandoned real estate, and Riverside Hospital just a decaying hulk. You can easily see the island and some of its ruins, the ones not covered in thick forest, from multiple points along the south shore of the Hunts Point neighborhood, along with the island's smaller compatriot South Brother Island.

Today, even though we've pretty much eradicated typhoid fever in the developed world due to the creation of vaccines and the implementation of modern sanitation practices, "Typhoid Mary" is still a name of dread. And I guess, in the end, that's the moral of Mary Mallon's story. Sometimes life just hates you.

Cory Lidle Crash Site
MANHATTAN

IN LIFE, CORY LIDLE GOT PAID to throw a 3-inch-diameter sphere at a 30-inch-tall rectangle. For his death, he flew a 38-foot-wingspan plane into a 50-story one.

Lidle's Major League Baseball career as a pitcher spanned stints with seven teams, including a debut with the Mets and a short roster appearance with the Yankees at the end. He had a career ERA of 4.57 and a lifetime record of 82 wins and 72 losses. Baseball is a game of numbers.

So is airplane piloting . . . minus the game, of course.

It was October 2006. The Yankees, who had the best record in the American League that year, lost their Eastern Conference Division Series to the wildcard Detroit Tigers. Detroit would go on to beat the Oakland Athletics for the American League Championship and then lose to the St. Louis Cardinals in the World Series. Lidle would never find out the final outcome of that 2006 season, though. On the afternoon of October 11, just four days after the Yankee's season ended, the 34-year-old died making use of both his newly found free time and the newly earned pilot's license he had picked up in the previous offseason.

Lidle took off from a New Jersey airport in his four-seater Cirrus SR20 with his flight instructor, Tyler Stanger. After flying around the Statue of Liberty and heading north up the eastern coast of Manhattan, the plane performed a tight turn at the tip of Roosevelt Island. No one is sure exactly what happened at that point. It has been conjectured that the men miscompensated for a crosswind in a notoriously tricky bit of urban airspace, but whatever the reason, the outcome was that the small plane crashed directly into the top floors of the north side of

Belair Apartments, a high-rise building on the shore of the East River.

Cirrus SR20s have two sets of controls, so it's unknown whether it was Lidle or Stanger who should be assigned the error. What is certain is that they both died, the crash injuring 21 people, including building residents as well as responding firefighters.

Complicating the immediate media and witness responses was the fact that it was only five years after 9/11 (see page 100) and the image of hurtling aircraft missiles and smoldering skyscrapers like upright cigarettes was a terrifying one. Eventually, the truth—non-terrorist-related but no less sad for the loved ones and colleagues of the two men on the plane—came out.

For a while after the accident, the 500-foot-tall Belair building bore the highly visible black eye of a fire-stained smudge that extended multiple stories around the 40th floor of its frontward-facing side. It would be a year before it was completely fixed. These days, the reddish building with the staggered crown at 524 East 72nd Street bears no scar from the accident, gazing serenely with its many window-eyes over the East River and Roosevelt Island into an airspace that has since been better configured for pilots.

Both men were buried in the state of California where they grew up. The next season, the Yankees wore black mourning bands on their uniforms in memory of their fallen teammate

Cory Lidle achieved one of the seven dreams of modern man: to play professional sports. Which makes it just that much more tragic that he also suffered one of the seven nightmares of modern man: dying in a plane crash.

The Butcher of Tompkins Square Park
MANHATTAN

THE BUTCHER OF AMRITSAR ordered the shooting deaths of more than 1,000 men, women, and children. The Butcher of Lyon tortured and killed some 14,000. The Butcher of Baghdad headed a brutal dictatorship responsible for near genocides. The Butcher of Tompkins Square Park, well, he killed his roommate, boiled her remains into a soup, and then served it to homeless people in the park whose name he usurped. He also got high a lot.

Had Daniel Rakowitz not been so dubbed by the newspapers, the only place his name would ever have been inked would have been on his birth certificate. But, to all accounts, we'd have thought of him as merely a screwball instead of dangerously screw-loose. The long-haired, bearded young man from Texas would often walk around the 10.5-acre park and the surrounding East Village with his pet rooster, smoking, selling, and extolling marijuana, as well as spouting nonsensicalities as if they were divinely inspired.

And he fit right in because, back then, the East Village was that kind of place.

In 1989, at the age of 28, he began a literally short-lived cohabitation with a 26-year-old Swiss dancer (possibly "exotic," possibly legit, possibly both) named Monika Beerle, who didn't know him too well but moved in with him at

his apartment at 700 East Ninth Street because she needed a place to stay. From here the details get sketchy, tabloid enough that I almost skipped putting the story in here. But being the avowed monster of such a definite, confined physical space fits this book too well.

The story goes in a few different directions at this point, before converging back at Rakowitz's arrest. Some say that Beerle was killed as part of a Satanic or otherwise strange ceremony with multiple accomplices, of whom Rakowitz was only a participant. Or that she was accidentally killed during an altercation at the apartment with a bunch of high, drunk derelicts, of whom Rakowitz was only one. Also that Rakowitz killed her on his own, of course, for whatever passes for a motive for that kind of person.

After her death from one of these three scenarios, the story continues that Rakowitz made a soup of her brains and flesh, which he then ate and served to homeless people in Tompkins Square Park. He was just that kind of guy.

What is certain is that Beerle did die, that Rakowitz did strip and sterilize her bones, that he packed them in kitty litter, and that he hid them in the baggage room of the Port Authority Bus Terminal. We know that because he led the police right there.

For about a month previous, rumors of murder and purposeful and accidental cannibalism circulated around the East Village, with everybody racking their brain trying to remember whether they'd ever been given anything to eat at Tompkins Square. The cops eventually investigated and were led right to Rakowitz, who some say had been bragging about the crime.

During the trial, Rakowitz continued to be nutty, with random outbursts, strange answers to questioning, and his usual litany of marijuana references. The closest the prosecutors got to proving the cannibalism part of the story were producing a witness who claimed he had seen a finger floating in a soup that Rakowitz had served to the homeless . . . a situation not that harrowing to those of us who are more acclimatized to a suburban world of fast-food joints.

Not surprisingly, the jury found him not guilty by reason of insanity, and he was put away at the Kirby Forensic Psychiatric Center on Ward's Island in the East River. Since that time, he has proved docile in captivity, although deemed on multiple occasions not to be competent enough to be released. He probably wouldn't like the East Village that much these days anyway.

That's because Tompkins Square Park and its surrounding neighborhoods have changed a lot. The entrance to Tompkins is at East Seventh Street and Avenue A. It's most famous for a few historical riots, and it's also the location of a 9-foot-tall monument to the General Slocum Tragedy (see page 138).

Of course, some things have stayed the same. When I visited, old men were playing chess and homeless men were washing up in the bathroom. It's still a Manhattan park, after all.

Except I didn't see any food vendors.

American Merchant Mariners' Memorial
MANHATTAN

THERE ARE UNCOUNTED WAYS to honor the wartime sacrifices of the merchant mariners that would not have made it into this book, extremely civic-looking memorials of the sort that proliferate in our cities and towns to the point of anonymity. But when you create a statue based on the last image of a group of doomed mariners on the point of drowning, and then actively drown them every day, you've done something truly affecting. And pretty macabre.

The merchant mariners don't get a whole lot of press or any snazzy recruitment commercials with market-tested slogans. These sailors crew civilian-owned supply and support vessels that, during wartime, change from their peaceable alter egos into a duly appointed part of the U.S. Navy, with their mission being to deliver supplies and troops and support various initiatives across battle lines.

For some perspective on their roles it has been said that during World War

II, the merchant mariners had the highest casualty rate of any service. Makes sense. Being a supply ship makes you a prime target in any engagement. And navigating the seas means that you're facing death even in times of peace.

Sometime during the 1970s and '80s, a group banded together with the express purpose of creating a lasting and prominent monument to the sacrifices of these mariners. The task was awarded to Marisol Escobar, a Venezuelan artist born in Paris, who has been a resident of New York for much of her life. She was given the commission based on the design she submitted, the merits of which are immediately apparent in both fore- and hindsight.

In 1991, her multipart bronze figural sculpture was officially dedicated off the shores of Battery Park at the southern tip of Manhattan. What she created was haunting, for two main reasons.

First, she based her tableau on an actual photograph. It was taken by a crewmember of a Nazi U-boat that had just torpedoed a merchant marine vessel into casualty. A small group temporarily survived, which the wartime photographer captured in their last moments before leaving them to die at sea. Basically, these victims are saying "cheese" to their killers.

Second, it's the way Escobar depicted the men. She captured well their hollow, hopeless look, certainly, but it's how she took advantage of her subjects' grouping that really pushes this piece to something special.

The statue is placed on a stone breakwater out in New York Harbor, about a dozen or so feet from the western edge of Battery Park. It shows four mariners

and a plain, tilted geometric shape designed to express the sinking ship that three of them are on. The men are obviously all at the point of despondency and grim realization; one calls out without much vigor for help or to other victims, while another just perches on his knees and stares hopelessly into oblivion. A third takes some comfort in activity, reaching down into the waters of the harbor, where just beyond his fingertips, their fourth companion strains and reaches desperately out of the water. Depending on the tide, that latter sailor can be up to his waist or up to his wrist in water.

And it is this latter element that really seals the complete picture. Of course, the sculpture is at its most affecting during high tide when all that futilely breaks the water is that last sailor's hand.

The aged green figures are often seagull spattered, giving them an even more forlorn appearance. When I visited, it was low tide, the water coming up to the thighs of the overboard victim. The dark water stain on the small quay behind him extended all the way up to his wrist.

Honestly, if you find yourself in the vicinity of this statue, it probably wasn't on purpose. Most people that see it are the ones in line to board the nearby ferry to see the most famous statue in the harbor, the other one with the upraised hand, that one in hope instead of desperation. The American Merchant Mariners' Memorial is worth a look and more than a few thoughts, though, on your way.

Rulloff's Brain
ITHACA

THERE'S A REASON why the phrase goes "a gentleman and a scholar" and not "a criminal and a scholar." The latter are too rare to get their own cliché. But they do exist. Cornell College in Ithaca has the evidence on display in a large jar of formaldehyde.

Edward H. Rulloff was born in New Brunswick, Canada, in 1819. He was a self-taught man, both in the academic field and the criminal, and it didn't take him long to go full Jekyll and Hyde. At the age of 20, while working as a clerk and studying law, he was arrested for a series of thefts that earned him a two-year scholarship in the local penitentiary.

After graduating from that prison, he moved across the border to western

Used with permission of the Wilder Brain
Collection at Cornell University

New York and started teaching, as well as practicing pharmacy, a skill he also picked up in his younger days. There, in 1843, he married one of his students, much to the horror of her family, who apparently saw through the thin veneer that was his civilized face. The pair had a baby not long after. At some point during this time, it has been surmised that he poisoned one or two of his wife's more distrustful relatives, as they died under his apothecary care.

Lending further credence to the theory, his own wife and infant daughter disappeared in 1845. Their bodies were never found, leading some to believe that he dropped them to the bottom of Lake Cayuga in the Finger Lakes region.

Although he was never convicted for their murders because of the lack of physical evidence, he was found guilty of their abduction. That earned him a decade's worth of tenure in the Auburn Correctional Facility (see page 133). The second he got out, they tried to put him right back in for the same crimes. During the new trial, he escaped from the county jail where they were holding him.

While on the run in Pennsylvania and Ohio, he continued his life of academia and felony, but was eventually captured and brought to Ithaca, where he was greeted by a lynch mob of 2,000 who assumedly were all holding up polite limousine driver signs that read RULLOFF. Not only did he survive the mob, he also survived the subsequent trial, being let go due to lack of bodily evidence.

Next, he went to New York City, where his strange pattern continued. On the academic side, he starting to write about linguistics, going so far as submitting a paper to the American Philologist Convention on the formation of languages, a paper that he was working on expanding into a book. Meanwhile, he padded the criminal side of his curriculum vitae with more thievery and more prison stints in such august institutions as Sing Sing (see page 81) and Wethersfield State Prison in Connecticut.

Finally, in 1870, a store break-in in Binghamton became his final bad break. During the robbery, which he undertook with two of his regular cohorts of ill-repute, one of the clerks was shot and killed, ostensibly by Rulloff himself. In the chaos that followed, both his accomplices drowned in their attempted escape by water. Rulloff was caught (for while some, including himself, claim that he was a genius, he was certainly not a criminal one) and finally hanged in

Binghamton in what is often touted as the last public hanging in the entire state.

Rulloff's brain was welcomed with open jars into the Wilder Brain Collection at Cornell University, where you can see it on display to this very day (see "Notable Graves, Cemeteries, and Other Memento Mori").

Rulloff had a notoriously large ego, and in his death, his big head was at least physically proven: His brain is believed to be the second-largest human specimen ever measured, at 3.9 pounds, give or take a few decimal places. The Russian novelist Ivan Turgenev's brain weighed almost 4.5 pounds. There are also Internet rumors of an anonymous 5-pound brain that might knock Rulloff down to bronze, although I'm not sure that anybody's kept an official biggest brain list.

Now, Ithaca's fascination with Rulloff goes beyond a thousands-strong lynch mob and the display of his brain. About half a mile from the building that currently plays skull to Rulloff's brain is a tavern that is named after Rulloff. In his honor, I guess. I'm not sure.

Rulloff's Pub, at 411 College Avenue, has been around since 1977, just over a century after the hanging of its namesake. Its symbol is a drawing of his face, and the backstory its website gives about Rulloff is a bit more extraordinary than the bio within Cornell's exhibit. Certainly, he at least lived a life that was easy to embellish.

For instance, the pub's website describes him as an objectively certifiable genius in that he spoke 28 languages and had expertise in philology, history, philosophy, mineralogy, biology, and anatomy. Most interesting, though, are the Rulloff quotations highlighted there. According to that website and various others, Rulloff said in his final newspaper interview:

> You cannot kill an unquiet spirit, and I know that my impending death will not mean the end of Rulloff. In the dead of night, walking along Cayuga Street, you will sense my presence. When you wake to a sudden chill, I will be in the room. And when you find yourself alone at the lake shore, gazing at gray Cayuga, know that I was cut short and your ancestors killed me.

Then Rulloff further cemented both his legend and future ghost tales with what are supposed to be his last words, spoken on the gallows: "Hurry it up! I want to be in hell in time for dinner."

To me, that makes it much more appropriate to name a restaurant after him.

World's Fair Bomb Plaque
QUEENS

IN THE MIDDLE of all the future-facing wonders left over from the 1939 and 1964 world's fairs at what is now known as Flushing Meadows Corona Park in Queens—the undulating Hall of Science, the 12-story Unisphere, the large and decaying New York Pavilion, the science fiction–looking sculpture *Forms in Transit*—is a 30 by 35.5-inch dark square that argues against all the vaunted progress touted by those fairs.

The 1939 New York World's Fair was built on the ashes of a trash dump, and it seems as if certain societal unsavories wanted to reduce it back to that . . . with a homemade time bomb.

Although we think of time bombs as a modern phenomenon sometimes, the truth is they were pretty common in the early part of the century (see page 79). One of the more obvious evidences of that is when a ticking satchel was found in the British Pavilion in the afternoon of July 4, 1940 (the 1939 World's Fair extended into the next year), New York already had in place an official bomb squad to dispatch.

Technically, it was the Bomb and Forgery Squad, but only half of that purview comes with the danger of being blown into the type of confetti you don't want to be covered in at a party. I mean, I've never met anyone assigned to a bomb squad,

but I know exactly what I would say to them: "You're awesome, but I'm sorry to hear that."

When this particular time bomb was discovered, the squad heroically moved the threat out of the fairgrounds and away from the hundreds of thousands of attendees. After transferring the ticking package, it was investigated, confirmed to be a bomb, and then procedures were started to extinguish the threat. Unfortunately, it went off, instantly killing 33-year-old Detective Joseph J. Lynch and 35-year-old Detective Ferdinand A. Socha, the two men who were actively attempting to defuse the bomb, while wounding other officers.

You'd think that such a dramatic act on such an international stage in such a time as the beginnings of the Nazi threat and the Second World War would evolve into a story full of plot and intrigue. Unfortunately, this story ends with both a bang and a whimper.

The bang, we've covered. The whimper? The culprits were never caught. No group, Nazi, anarchist, or otherwise, ever claimed responsibility, and the investigation ended up as empty as the large crater left behind by the explosion. Not even a $26,000 reward shook loose any information.

Today, the only evidence of the two-man tragedy is the aforementioned dark square, a plaque memorializing the event and the two men who lost their lives while saving so many others. It's located just in front of the Queens Museum of Art (which faces the massive Unisphere), on the left-hand side if you're facing the front of the building.

Flushing Meadows is a park worth seeing for many, many reasons. However, after tilting your head up to take in the wonders of the Unisphere and the Pavilion, make sure you also tilt it down toward the ground to both see the plaque and to pay your respects, 70 years into the "World of Tomorrow" that the fair was celebrating.

Yankee Leaper Sites
ROCHESTER

SAM PATCH SOUNDS like the safest name in existence. Like an affable character from some innocent fairy tale or the setup to a particularly funny limerick. Which is why it's surprising that this is actually the name of a real-life . . . and real-dead . . . daredevil, also known as the Yankee Leaper.

Patch was born in 1807 in Massachusetts, but grew up in Pawtucket, Rhode Island, where, they say, he would jump off the 50-foot falls that powered the local mill. He doesn't have a very full biography, though, and the skeleton that does exist is fossilized with conflicting facts. However, it can be stated with certainty that there was a two-year section of his life where Sam Patch jumped off waterfalls a lot. The final two-year section of it, in fact.

Sam Patch probably started jumping off waterfalls for fame. And money. And because what else was a 20-something in the early 1800s supposed to do. Video games wouldn't be invented for another century and a half or so.

Before he was the Yankee Leaper, he was the New Jersey Jumper, having moved to that state before officially starting his career as a daredevil. His first jump into the public imagination was in September 1827, when he dodged the police and jumped 80 feet from a ledge over the Passaic Falls in Paterson. The feat was accomplished in front of a large crowd that had gathered to watch a new bridge being hoisted into place at the spot. It was the first of multiple jumps from this particular bit of wet gravity.

His next big jump was in August of the following year, when he split close to 100 feet of air over a waterfall in the town of Hoboken.

By this time, Patch's celebrity had started to spread. The newspapers were printing stories about him, advertisements were circulated in advance of his jumpmanship, and people showed up in the thousands to see him. Again, video games kind of solved this problem for most of us, but at that point watching a man hurtle himself toward a percentage of death that ranged crazily for every single jump was something not to be missed.

In between stationary jumps, Patch would often jump from ship mastheads, as well, sometimes while en route to other jumps. He was also known for his motto, "Some things can be done as well as others," which while not exactly "Geronimo!" I reckon has its own poetry.

In October 1829, he was hired for the largest diving board of his career . . . Niagara Falls. Local business owners had put together a public relations event that included everything from sending derelict boats over the falls to blasting the surrounding cliff rocks with gunpowder. Among all that delightful violence and destruction, Patch was the main attraction. And that's *attraction* as in the natural force that pulls small objects toward hard, unforgiving large ones.

His jump took place on a platform erected on Goat Island, that bit of rock that separates the U.S. side of the falls from the Canadian side. All told, that means about 85 feet was between him and the horizontal cement that the Niagara River could be at that height. Then, with his back to the record machine, he became the first man to survive the jump over Niagara Falls (and was duly inducted into the Hall of Dubitable Honors as a result).

Although the jump was successful, the crowd turnout was less so, due to inclement weather and the fact that Patch had arrived late to the event. As a result (and, according to some reports, to take advantage of the masses that would be present in the area for a public hanging that was happening at the time), he decided that if at first you succeed, try again. This time, the platform that was built ascended him to a height of more than 100 feet. Those crowds were more to his satisfaction, and the successful jump was a smash in the nonlethal definition of the term.

His next stop was in early November to the 100-foot-tall High Falls of the Genesee River in Rochester, New York. There, an audience of thousands showed up to watch him Yankee-leap from a rock ledge at the top of the falls. Along the way from Buffalo to Rochester, he had picked up a small, tame bear, which he threw into the water first. The bruin struggled to the shore wet, confused, and totally vowing violent things when it grew up. Patch then followed with another successful mockery of self-preservation.

Apparently, despite the large crowds, Patch was unsatisfied with the amount of money he raised for that gig, so just as at Niagara, he decided to dare the devil again. The next week he increased the height to 125 feet with a platform, got up there, and boasted about doing what great men like Napoleon and Wellington could not. Then he was airborne, in the opposite way that word is normally used.

However, it was quickly realized that something was wrong with this jump. Instead of his usual feet-down, arrow-straight posture, his body tilted and his limbs flailed. He hit the water with a loud eulogy and then disappeared.

At first, folks thought it was part of the show. A week later, some still held on to that hope. Eventually, everybody realized that Patch had jumped not just into the water but, to use a word from one of the local news commentators, into "eternity." He was 22 years old.

Everybody is sure why Patch died, but none knows why it was on that jump versus any other one. A bad wind and too much drink to keep warm on that mid-November afternoon in northern New York have both been offered, albeit weakly. Sometimes people just die when they jump over waterfalls.

Patch's body was finally found the following spring in some lingering ice at the mouth of the Genesee River. The news yielded a lot of mourning, a lot of "I told you so" and a lot of "I guess the moral of this story is . . ." The best commentary seems to have come from none other than Nathaniel Hawthorne himself, who visited the spot shortly after Patch's disappearance. He wrote about Patch in a piece on the city of Rochester: "Why do we call him a madman or a fool, when he has left his memory around the falls of the Genesee, more permanently than if the letters of his name had been hewn into the forehead of the precipice."

Patch was buried in Charlotte Cemetery, not too far from the area where his body was discovered. Charlotte Cemetery is located at 28 River Street, and Patch's grave is easily found in the northern corner right beside an adjoining residential parking lot. The front of the rectangular stone bears his name and the years of his existence. On the back, a plaque gives a short synopsis of his short life

The High Falls are still an attraction in Rochester, and something you should see if you're ever in town regardless of your perverse interest in tragedy. A large pedestrian bridge called the Pont De Rennes Bridge spans the Genesee and connects Platt and Cataract Streets, offering a great view of the powerful falling water and the city behind it.

I'm not sure whether they keep track of the life spans of daredevils as they do with lumberjacks and Alaskan king crab fishermen, but Patch's couple of decades on the planet seem about par. After all, it's all fun and games until someone gets dead . . . and secures his fame.

9/11 Memorial at Ground Zero
MANHATTAN

AS A GENERAL RULE, tragedies aren't really things to be compared. However, of all the extreme downsides of life chronicled in this section of the book, none is as big in scope, resonance, or number of victims as the subject of this entry, an atrocity known simply by two numbers: 9/11. Basically, that means it's going to be hard for me to joke around here. I'll try, though.

On the morning of September 11, 2011, 19 members from the Islamic terrorist sect al-Qaeda hijacked four passenger airliners as part of an elaborate mass murder/suicide mission. The terrorists took over the controls of these four jets midflight, sending one of the planes into each of New York City's Twin Towers, and a third into the massive Pentagon in Washington DC. The fourth was diverted from whatever its unknown DC target was, thanks to the brave response of its passengers and crew, a response that turned into a sacrifice as it crashed into an empty field in southwestern Pennsylvania.

All told, close to 3,000 people died from the brazen attacks, all but about 200 or so of them perishing at the New York site. That site, the World Trade Center, was a seven-building complex situated right in the middle of New York's Financial District. It was most often symbolized by the pair of boxy, 110-story skyscrapers that had dominated the New York skyline since their construction in the early 1970s and which took the hits directly from the two commercial planes.

Each of these once tallest buildings in the world burned for about an hour before collapsing straight down. The dramatic images were indelible to all who saw them in person or on the television—office workers plummeting to their death to escape the infernos, the massive towers collapsing into themselves as if girded by Tinkertoys, the giant thick clouds of gray and light brown smoke and debris propelled down the surrounding streets like special effects in some over-the-top alien invasion movie, people covered in ash as if they'd just exited a volcano.

Ground Zero, a generic term up to this point for most of the country, suddenly sprouted capital letters.

Although the actual attacks only lasted over the course of a single hour, the story protracted itself over the next decade with global effect, until only just in the past year earning some form of closure with the killing of al-Qaeda leader Osama bin Laden and the opening of the 9/11 memorial directly on the site of the Twin Towers.

That memorial opened on the 10th anniversary of the attacks. I visited about a month afterward.

At the time of our visit, the surrounding buildings were still under construction, with giant cranes looming around the site like defensive cannons. To visit the memorial, we had to reserve free tickets for a particular time slot and then pass through metal detectors, security officers, and a maze of temporary pathways lined by chain-link fence until finally arriving at the memorial proper.

In the exact spot where the two signature World Trade Center towers once stood were now two vast black pits diagonal from each other along a north–south axis and constructed to the exact dimensions of the footprints of the two skyscrapers. Each pit is about an acre across, and because of both their large scale and the fact that they are basically holes, you can't really get a view of both simultaneously from ground level, although many of the tall buildings in the area certainly afford that view.

The square pits are lined with black granite, and all four sides of the pits are veiled in massive waterfalls circulating a total of some 500,000 gallons of water that drain and are recycled below into a smaller, even darker central square of space. At the rim of the pits are brass plaques with the names of all the victims of the 9/11 attacks, including the Pennsylvania and DC victims, as well as those who died in the World Trade Center bombing of 1993. Nearby terminals enable visitors to look up specific names to find their location among the thousands etched into the memorial.

We visited at night, and the names were backlit, while the interiors of the pits were lighted so that the waterfalls glowed eerily and strikingly. Staring down into something simultaneously black with mourning and alive with lighted water was an experience in emotional contrast, alternately sobering and beautiful.

The entire 8-acre area that is the memorial is planted with hundreds of trees and back-dropped by all the surrounding high-rises, but also by the oblong metal and glass façade of the 9/11 museum, which should also give a good view of the memorial both literally and in abstract, although it wasn't yet open at the time of our visit.

To the more practical-minded, an easy thought might be that the $700 million memorial is a waste of valuable lower Manhattan real estate. Which is fine. Because hopefully then the phrase "what a waste" will take on a more accurate and profound meaning with what happened on that spot.

The vastness of the memorial and its specific relation to the actual foundations of the building are its most impressive and affecting features. To realize that the tragedy that most of the country witnessed on the small windows of our television screens fit into those two acres of vastness, which was then multiplied 110 times above our head, was dizzying.

Eventually, and probably by the time you read this, the surrounding construction will be completed and the museum will be opened for visitors. When that happens the area will also be opened up into a public park, where people can enter freely from all points to view these footprints of giants . . . giant skyscrapers, giant loss, giant changes in our culture and the world.

Wisteria Cottage

IRVINGTON

CRAP. ALBERT FISH. I have to write about this guy. True, he's not the only serial killer in this book, but, man, thinking about this one in particular makes my flesh want to crawl right off my body, flap down the street, and commit suicide in a tanner's shop.

As with most serial killers, Fish's final tally of victims is unknown. The courts only needed one to revoke his existence, but depending on who's recounting the story it can soar to the triple digits. What is known is that his victims were always children and that his crimes included rape, torture, mutilation, murder, and cannibalism, and that his most notorious crime was laid out in agonizing detail in an unsigned letter he sent to a victim's mother, the letter that finally led to his trial and execution at the unfortunately ripe age of 65. That's too many decades to do too much horrible stuff. How's your skin feeling?

Hamilton Howard Fish was born in 1870 in Washington DC. He went by "Albert," I assume, to avoid the name "Ham Fish." According to various accounts, his family was prone to mental illness but not, as far as we know, to raping and eating children. Due to the death of his father, who was 75 when Albert was born, and the financial straits of his mother, Fish spent a couple of his formative years in an orphanage.

By the time he turned 20, he had made the move to New York City, the land of massive loads of potential victims. At some point in his life that I'm sure he highlighted in some way in his diary, he began indulging in self-inflicted pain as sexual gratification. He would flog himself with nail-studded paddles, insert alcohol-soaked cotton balls into sunshine-deprived places and light them on fire, and stick needles into his pelvis so deep only X-rays could find them (when he was captured, they revealed close to 30 puncturing his guts). And that's just the stuff he would admit to.

All of that is sick and dangerous and screams for intervention, but is not illegal in a free country, I guess. However, at some point he started doing that kind of stuff to children, along with even more wicked things. No one's sure really sure why he committed the crimes nor why they were so varied, or really anything about the inside of this guy's head. But that's good. Probably shouldn't understand.

Meanwhile, in that other part of his life that doesn't make any sense, he got married and fathered six kids, meaning his direct line probably continues to this day. His wife left him for another man, but the kids remained in his, well, care, I guess.

Fish sought out his prey outside of his family, often in inner-city regions, garnering him the name "Brooklyn Vampire" at one point. He also worked as a traveling house painter to spread out his particular brand of victimization across the country. A red-stained pair of painter's coveralls doesn't elicit shock.

His most notorious crime, and the one he was eventually convicted of, garnered him the nickname "Were-wolf of Wisteria." It was committed when he was 58 years old, which went along with his previous nickname, "the Gray Man."

Fish answered a classified advertisement in Manhattan from an 18-year-old boy named Edward Budd, who was looking for work. Pretending to be a farmer looking for laborers, Fish visited the Budd family twice to "interview" the boy, and in the course of doing so noticed his 10-year-old sister, Grace.

On that second visit, he promised to hire the boy, but mentioned that he needed to attend the nearby birthday party of his niece before he could take the boy with him. He offered to take Grace to the party. Grace's parents allowed her to accompany the harmless-looking old man who held promise for their son's future.

Grace was never seen alive again, and Fish, who had given a pseudonym, got away with the crime for more than half a decade.

Six years after Grace's disappearance, the Budds received an anonymous letter explaining in an excruciatingly specific fashion how the writer had stripped, beaten, murdered, and eaten Grace over the course of nine days in a large, abandoned house. Sending vicious and obscene notes was something Fish did regularly, although usually to random women he found in the classifieds. The Budd letter, unlike those letters of depraved fantasy, admitted a depraved reality.

The full text of the note is all over the Internet, and if you want to ruin your day, certainly look it up. Today that note resides in the private collection of artist and collector Joe Coleman (see "Legends and Personalities of the Macabre").

There was one good thing about the note. Authorities were able to track Fish down, based on the stationery. He led authorities to the site of Grace Budd's horrible ordeal, a large ruin of his family's summer house in Irvington that they called Wisteria Cottage, a 40-minute train ride away from where the Budds lived. The little-girl-size bones that were found there affirmed the tale of the unsigned letter.

Fish was arrested, put on trial, attempted an insanity defense, received a verdict of "We don't care. Go to hell," and then obliged in a wooden chair wired to electric death in Sing Sing prison (see page 81).

Much of what is recorded about the details of Fish's life came from Fish himself during his interviews with police and psychiatrists. As a result, little of it is trustworthy. The atrocity of Wisteria Cottage, however, is documented with the bones of Grace Budd. Somehow, the building wasn't razed to ground. In fact, it still stands.

Today, the 150-year-old home with the distinctive wraparound porch has been refurbished into a million-dollar property, according to a recent Sotheby's listing. A few black-and-white photos of the house from Fish's days still float around for comparison, and the exterior seemingly retains all the same architectural elements from that dark part of the structure's life. The address of the cottage is 379 Mountain Road, a secluded residential road jutting off from the Saw Mill Parkway and lined with similarly pricey abodes of the type you'd expect in that area of the Hudson Valley.

When I passed it by, the house looked lived in and had a car in the driveway. I don't know whether the current residents know the history of where they brush their teeth and play Scrabble on family game night, but I wasn't going to be the one to ask them. Don't be the jerk to let them know, either, even if I'm the jerk to tell you the address.

Whew. Done. The next entry is about a pair of U.S. soldiers who were tortured and killed by Native Americans in the 1700s. It's a horrible story, but a relief to read by comparison.

Boyd-Parker Torture Tree
Leicester

Trees are often symbols of life. Here's one of torture and death. The year was 1779, four years into the Revolutionary War. A Continental Army expedition led by Major General John Sullivan was in the Finger Lakes region of New York to decimate the Native American villages of the Iroquois who had joined the British forces and were attacking settlers in the area.

At one point during this three-and-a-half-month campaign, Sullivan sent out a scouting group headed by Lieutenant Thomas Boyd. The scouts were ambushed in an area now known as Groveland, just southwest of the southern end of Conesus Lake. Most of the two dozen or so men in Boyd's company were killed, a few escaped, and two were captured. Those two men were Boyd himself and a Sergeant Michael Parker.

After being questioned by British military leaders, the two prisoners found themselves in the vengeful purview of Little Beard, chief of the Seneca people and a part of the Iroquois League which Sullivan was there to violently displace. This is the part of the movie where the protagonists say, "Uh-oh" if it's a PG-rated movie and "Shit" if it's an R. The outcome was all R, though.

The Native Americans, furious at what Sullivan's army was doing to their villages, tied Boyd and Parker to a tree and then commenced a series of drawn-out tortures, the details of which tradition—the same tradition that has forgotten the location of the Ark of the Covenant, the dying words of Albert Einstein, and the identity of the author of *Beowulf*—has carefully preserved and passed down over the past two centuries.

Judging by the condition of their cadavers, Boyd seemed to have gotten the worst of it. His torture involved everything one would [not want to] imagine: genital mutilation, finger- and toenail removal, sensory organ amputation, and, in one especially grisly detail that has probably done more than anybody will admit to perpetuating the story of Boyd and Parker, his entrails were fastened to the tree and he was forced to run around it in a macabre maypole dance before both men were finally beheaded.

Their mutilated bodies were found soon after by their comrades and were buried on the spot. Little Beard's village was then sought out and razed. Modern-day Cuylerville currently claims that zip code. In 1841, the remains of Boyd and Parker, along with those of some of their fallen mates, were transferred with much ceremony to a spot in the newly opened Mount Hope Cemetery in Rochester.

Today, monuments mark the various locations of this wartime atrocity. For instance, where the ambush took place is memorialized by the Groveland Ambuscade Monument. Set on a hill overlooking farmland and forest, the simple obelisk is inscribed with a verse about the spot's being baptized in Boyd and Parker's "patriot blood." The stone shaft can be found at 5434 David Gray Hill Road in Groveland. To get there, take the road until it ends at a seasonally open stretch and turn left at the Groveland Ambuscade Park sign. The short portion of road terminates in a small parking lot. From there, you should be able to see the

monument in the slight distance through a thin row of trees. A set of wooden steps leads up to it.

In Mount Hope Cemetery at 1133 Mount Hope Avenue, a boulder with a plaque affixed to it marks the plot where Boyd, Parker, and other of the ambushed party repose. It's in the back corner of the cemetery, in Section BB, right on one of the cemetery roads. In front of the boulder is a series of individual plaques set flush with the grass that mark the individual bodies, which includes that of the party's Oneida guide, Honyost Thaosagwat.

Of course, none of these memorials is as compelling as the Torture Tree itself, which, at least according to that fickle tradition already mentioned, still stands. Located in the small Boyd and Parker Memorial Park in Leicester, the massive monstrosity of a plant is immediately evident upon pulling into the parking lot.

The park is on Cuylerville Road between Barrett Road and Canal Street. The only things in the small grassy space are a couple of informational signs, two plaque-adorned stone memorials (one to Boyd and Parker and another to the Sullivan expedition in general), a small building housing a bathroom that was, when I visited, broken due to vandals' taking the handles, and in the corner overshadowing the road, the gigantic impromptu torture device itself.

I saw the tree in wintertime, in all its naked and gnarly, Ent-like glory. The at least 250-year-old bur oak is 70 feet high and 24 feet in circumference, a large girth under any circumstances, but an interminable one when a person is trailing his internal organs around it. It would take four people to wrap their arms all the way around its lumpy trunk. A plaque at its base that references a pair of impressive-sounding arborist societies validates the age of the tree as dating back to the Revolutionary War, but defers from officially designating it as the Torture Tree of legend.

There are memorials to plenty of tragedies all over the entire state of New York. Enough that, had I not been forced to be selective, this section of the book would have dwarfed the rest of it. However, these dead stone and metal monuments don't come close to the poignancy of being able to see an actual living organism that (may have) stoically played a central part in the Boyd-Parker tragedy.

Prison Ship Martyrs' Monument
BROOKLYN

S INGLE, FREESTANDING STONE COLUMNS are bland and extremely civic ways to honor a person or event. But if yours is grown from the bones of more than 11,500 men, women, and children, then you've got my attention.

Such is the case with the century-old, 149-foot-tall granite column in Fort Greene Park, a 1-square-mile tract of hills in northern Brooklyn that was the site of a fort for two wars, the Revolutionary War and the War of 1812.

And it's on the spines, skulls, and scapulae of Rev-olutionary War victims that this Doric column now stretches toward the sun.

Prison ships are a part of the Revolutionary War that's not often discussed, one of those nasty sidebars that we want to forget when commemorating historical victories with sky explosions or watching movies where men in tricorn hats and powdered wigs walk around speaking KJV English. But these floating POW camps are as much a part of the Revolutionary War story as were Paul Revere's ride and George Washington's Delaware River crossing.

After the British won the Battle of Brooklyn in August 1776 and took possession of New York, they stuffed as many Continental soldiers and civilian patriots into the local prisons as they could, but there just wasn't enough room. So they loaded the gigantic surplus onto about a dozen decommissioned ships, the most infamous of which being the HMS *Jersey*, anchored out in Wallabout Bay in the East River.

Life on an 18th-century ship was no party even if you chose to be there, but when you were both imprisoned and ill-treated in one, it was a circle of hell not even Dante dared to probe. Victims suffered from disease, starvation, over-crowding, inhuman living conditions, physical cruelty. People died daily en masse and were buried shallowly near the shore or were merely pushed off into the bay.

Eventually, of course, New York was taken back, but for years afterward, the bones of these unfortunates would be found unearthed at low tide or washed up on the beach. It's a tragedy that wouldn't let itself be forgotten

All told, 11,500 of these people died for refusing to swear loyalty to the British crown. What could be found of their remains was collected over the years and stored first in a tomb near the Brooklyn Navy Yard and then, in 1873, in a crypt at the 30-year-old Fort Greene Park.

It wasn't until 1908, almost 130 years after their death, that the Prison Ship Martyrs' Monument was erected in its current form over the crypt. Fifteen stories high, it is topped with a green-aged brass urn that, I can imagine, probably commands a view of the waters where floated their suffering and torment.

Once upon a time, I wouldn't have had to imagine. A rail around the urn, which can be lit up at night, and two doors in the base of the column testify that originally this was no mere column but an actual tower. It even had an elevator. The tower has long been closed to the public, though, as is generally the Spartan crypt beneath it, with its plain boxes of jumbled bones. The locked entrance to the crypt can be found set into the steps below the monument.

We prefer to give people a dignified end when we can, and because the ship's martyrs didn't get that, we can at least give them the tallest gravestone in the region.

William McKinley
Assassination Site and Gun
BUFFALO

YOU'D THINK THAT THE GUN used to kill a president would be kept in some secret, hermetically sealed chamber deep within the bowels of the Smithsonian, somewhere between the remains of the Roswell aliens and Betsy Ross's first attempt at a national flag (butterscotch plaid with a jubilant thumbs-up

centered on it). However, the gun that killed President William McKinley in 1901 is on humble public display at an annex building owned by Buffalo's historical society, about a mile from where the assassination occurred.

On September 6, 1901, President McKinley, about a year into his second term of office, was making an appearance at the Pan-American Exposition in Buffalo. The exposition was a six-month-long world's fair in a temporary, purpose-built city full of scientific and technical innovation, international culture, and dazzling entertainment spectacles. Throughout its 350 acres it exhibited the wonders of mankind's progress, including X-rays, electricity, and infant incubators. But it inadvertently exhibited man's degeneration in a mere 6 square feet of it all.

McKinley had given a speech at the expo the day before, but on this occasion was greeting members of the public at the event's extravagant concert hall known as the Temple of Music. A man with a handkerchief wrapped around his hand walked up to the president, ostensibly to greet him, but instead shot him twice in the abdomen at extreme close range with a revolver secreted in the obscured hand. McKinley would die eight days later.

The assassin was 28-year-old Leon Czolgosz, a Michigan-born man of Polish descent. More relevant to his crime, he was an anarchist, one who believed government to be an inherently immoral institution, one that elevated the rich and oppressed the poor. He was immediately subdued. A couple of weeks later he was tried and found guilty. He was then sent to the state facility in Auburn (see page 133), where he was executed by electric chair less than two months after promoting Vice President Theodore Roosevelt.

Almost the entire mini-city that was the Pan-American Exposition was razed after the event ended, per its original plan. Today, the spot where McKinley was killed is a residential street, Fordham Drive, and across from 30 Fordham Drive in the median is a small boulder with a plaque affixed to commemorate the ex-president.

The gun eventually fell into the purview of the Buffalo and Erie County Historical Society, which is headquartered in the only building still standing from the Pan-American Exposition. Located at 25 Nottingham Court, the Pan-Am Building is a large, white marble, Greek-inspired affair. The bronze front doors weight more than half a ton each and are inscribed with two female figures: one with a lamp, representing history, and the other holding a skull, representing ethnology. The building's south side features a large dais with a statue of Abraham Lincoln overlooking Hoyt Lake in Delaware Park. Inside are exhibits that explore just about every aspect of the region's culture and history, including its native and immigrated cultures, its art and industries, and its pivotal events and people. The gift shop has plush buffalos.

And, while it's an excellent place to visit, you won't find Czolgosz's gun there.

The society operates another building about a mile away, which it calls its Resource Center. And although it's not exactly a secret, hermetically sealed chamber, it is open to the public by appointment only and is completely dedicated to the Pan-American Exposition.

The Resource Center is at 459 Forest Avenue, right across from the old Buffalo State Asylum. You can't miss the annex building as its entrance is framed by the white, 30-foot-tall face of a woman, a replica of a sculpture called *Dreamland* from the original expo.

Inside are artifacts, images, and even video from the world's fair. Most helpful is a map of the original exposition, with an overlay of the contemporary streets.

The McKinley portion of the exhibit is located in a back corner. The gun is tiny, a .32 caliber Iver Johnson revolver, barely even dangerous looking, much less appearing capable of destroying someone who holds the highest office in the land. It's hung on the wall, protected by a transparent cover, but you can get within a noseprint of it. It's surrounded by other grisly mementos associated with the assassination: the handkerchief the gun was hidden in, bullets from the gun, handcuffs used to restrain the assassin, part of a bandage used to bind McKinley's wounds, surgical instruments used on the dying president. All in all, a ghastly but impressive little collection.

You can tell by the arrangement of the exhibits that the curators try to contextualize it within the wonders of the Pan-American Exposition, even though it darkly overshadows the fair. In fact, one of the placards wonders whether the murder of the president also killed the enthusiasm of the expo and started a downward spiral of the city that lasted throughout the 20th century. All because of a tiny piece of metal that makes loud noises.

Flight Crash Memorials

Brooklyn, Queens, Farmingdale, Center Moriches, Fire Island

I DON'T CARE if you've never been on a plane or have enough reward miles to get you to Neptune; we're all scared of dying in a plane crash. Heck, I even think pilots and flight attendants have just learned to live with their souls in permanent fetal positions inside them. I mean, having to endure those few moments of inexorableness as one's plane goes Icarus is what sets that particular fear of death apart from the rest. It's long enough to realize how much you really want to live, but not long enough to hold out any type of hope for reprieve.

Being one of the densest population centers in the world means that New York City also has one of the densest populations above it. It claims two major international airports within its borders, John F. Kennedy and LaGuardia, and is served by a third, Newark, which is just over the Hudson River in New Jersey. All together these aviation hubs throw more than 100 million passengers a year into the air—a large enough number that the skies should be perennially dark with flocks of metal birds.

And while the sky above New York City isn't quite all jet undercarriages, it's still full enough that the statistically inevitable crashes have occurred in that air space many times. On the occasions that it happens, it means a serious loss of life numbering in the hundreds, high enough that permanent memorialization is almost as inevitable as complete loss of life. I visited a handful of these memorials in researching the 1,500 words of this particular entry.

For the purposes here, I'll omit the terrorist plane crashes of 9/11, as I've dealt with that elsewhere in this section (see page 100). However, scattered throughout the city and the surrounding areas are plenty of monuments to people whose last day on earth was spent at an airport.

United Airlines Flight 826 and TWA Flight 266

T AKE THE FAMOUS GREEN-WOOD CEMETERY at 500 25th Street in Brooklyn (see "Notable Graves, Cemeteries, and Other Memento Mori"). In its northwest corner right across Sylvan Avenue from a pond is a plot of land with a simple bronze plaque stating that buried there are the unidentified human remains from an airplane crash in Brooklyn. Nearby, a recently erected 8-foot-tall granite memorial commemorates in a little bit more detail that midair collision.

The date was December 16, 1960. Christmas was coming, the Jet Age was here, and two flights were arriving in New York City, United Airlines 826 into LaGuardia and TWA 266 into what was then officially called International Airport, casually called Idlewild, and which is now called JFK.

Unfortunately, the United Airlines flight was having navigation problems due to inclement weather and malfunctioning navigation instruments. The plane strayed off course and collided with Flight 266 about a mile over Staten Island. The wreckage from the TWA flight hit a sparse area of the island, but the United Airlines Flight rained down metal and fire and bodies into the Park Slope neighborhood of Brooklyn.

Everybody died, including 84 on the United Airlines flight, 44 on the TWA flight, and half a dozen people on the ground, making for a total of 134. The image from the crash that always comes up on Internet searches is the black-and-white picture of the severed, United Airlines–branded tail fin of Flight 826, sitting in the middle of a snowy intersection, surrounded by dazed pedestrians and emergency responders.

Although everybody on the planes did die, one 11-year-old boy named Stephen Baltz lasted just a little bit longer than the rest. He was thrown, broken and burned, from the wreck into a nearby snow bank. There are heartrending pictures of him as well, staring blankly from the snow-covered ground as passersby shield him with an umbrella.

He was taken to nearby New York Methodist Hospital, at 506 6th Street, where he was able to give a brief account of the crash. He was traveling by himself, his mother and sister having taken an earlier flight and his father planning on taking a later one. Stephen said that he looked out the airplane window at the snowy tableau below and, "It looked like a picture out of a fairy book. It was a beautiful sight." He then said he heard a loud noise and remembered the plane falling. He died the next day and was buried in his home state of Illinois. Today, in the small Phillips Chapel of Methodist Hospital, is a small, rectangular, wall-mounted plaque dedicated to him that incorporates the actual loose change that they found in his pockets. It's one of the saddest things I have ever seen.

American Airlines Flight 587

A CRASH OF A MORE RECENT VINTAGE is commemorated on a beach in Rockaway Park in Queens. There, at the end of Beach 116th Street, is a freestanding curving wall made of brownish granite bricks. Some are missing and you can look out into the ocean through the holes. Inscribed into many of the bricks are names, those of the 265 victims of the American Airlines Flight 587 crash.

On November 12, 2001, just two months after 9/11, Flight 587 was on its way from JFK to the Dominican Republic, carrying 260 passengers and crew. It went down at 9:16 AM in Rockaway's residential area, around Beach 131st Street and Newport Avenue. Showing again that not even being on a plane is no protection from dying in a plane crash, at least five people on the ground were killed, as well. Video footage and pictures show a neighborhood engulfed in flames.

The cause of the malfunction was a combination of design flaws in the rudder system and the pilot's own

American Airlines Flight 587 Memorial

overreaction in using those rudders to combat turbulence—relatively undramatic but sufficient to result in the second-deadliest plane accident in the United States.

Eventually, the houses were rebuilt, and the memorial was dedicated more than a dozen blocks away and five years after the crash. Today, people still insert flowers into the spaces in the memorial.

TWA Flight 800

T WA IS NOT AROUND ANYMORE as a company, but the acronym for Trans World Airlines still yields a mental reaction of "Flight 800" to those who remember the third-deadliest U.S. plane accident (second at the time of the tragedy) and certainly the most mysterious.

On July 17, 1996, it took off for Paris, with a flight plan of continuing on to Rome afterward. It barely made it a few minutes over the Atlantic Ocean, however, when the entire jet exploded in a fireball, beheading the plane and killing all 230 passengers and crew. The plane went down just off the coast of Long Island, and immediately speculation ran rampant about missile attacks and terrorist bombs.

Eventually, after years of investigation, it was determined that a short circuit caused a spark to ignite a buildup of jet fuel vapors in one of the fuel tanks. The most common representative image of the disaster is the wreckage laid out in a warehouse for this investigation. However, to this day, there are those who don't accept such a minor explanation for such a horrible catastrophe and insist on believing in a government cover-up instead.

Regardless, no one argues about the massive tragedy of it all. On Long Island, they've commemorated it in a few ways.

Those passengers whose remains were never found have been memorialized at Pinelawn Memorial Park, at 2030 Wellwood Avenue in Farmingdale. In that sizeable cemetery's Garden of Freedom, between a large white colonnade bearing the name of the garden and a statue of Thomas Jefferson, is a tabletop-size bronze plaque set in the ground and engraved with the names of all the victims of the crash.

Surrounding this horizontal plate is a series of 12 smaller grave plaques, each marking the spot of a passenger whose remains were never recovered from the Atlantic. Buried beneath each of those plaques is a casket holding personal

TWA Flight 800 Memorial

mementos of the person whose name adorns the plaque. All share the same death date.

A little over 35 miles away, in Mount Pleasant Cemetery at 37-69 Montauk Highway in Center Moriches, is another memorial. This one can be found right through the gates on the left before even getting to the cemetery proper. There, a human-size granite obelisk mourns the deaths of the TWA 800 victims. An image of a plane is carved into the top of the monument, below which is inscribed a brief and simple dedication.

Southwest of Mount Pleasant, at Smith Point Park on Fire Island, is a more monumental memorial. Set at about the closest point of land to where TWA 800 went down is a large curving wall of black granite that faces Mastic Beach, right beside the park pavilion. On the beach side, the stone is carved with waves made up of 230 seagulls, giving an effect similar to Hokusai's *The Great Wave off Kanagawa* print and representing the crash victims. The interior side is inscribed with the story of the crash and bears all the names of the lost.

The whole edifice is set on and surrounded by a concrete stage with benches and 14 flags representing all the nationalities aboard the plane. Also present is a 10-foot-tall triangular shape in complementing black granite that is intended to convey the idea of a lighthouse. It marks the interment of personal effects of the victims.

Honestly, I'm sure there are more flight crash memorials scattered throughout the city that I didn't find in the course of my research and travels. I think we erect so many because of our empathy for those who suffer such horrifying deaths, and as a way to communally remember the enormous numbers of innocent lives lost in one stroke of a Grim Reaper scythe. Also perhaps as a counterbalance to having to refer to those deaths by their stark and impersonal flight numbers.

John Lennon Murder Site and Memorial
Manhattan

CELEBRITIES WILL TELL YOU that wealth and fame aren't always what they're cracked up to be, that the loss of privacy and the high expectations and pressures that come along with it temper all the good points. They're stupid wrong. They've just forgotten how cracked the alternative can be. With one exception. One possible outcome of celebrity that's not worth all the fame, all the recognition, all the wealth, all the leisure, all the freedom, all the exciting adventures to which privilege opens the door deranged fans.

But even then, it still might be worth it. John Lennon would be the one to ask.

After all, his celebrity is so stratospheric I don't even have to include an introductory bio on him. Heck, I barely have to state the word "Beatle." Lennon has a large and largely praised body of work, the continued adoration of more fans than Jesus, and, while alive, all the wealth and pleasures that came with all that already cool stuff. Then he was murdered by an admirer. I don't know if he'd trade it all for an 85-year life of obscurity and toil, but I suspect he'd at least rather his life ended in some way other than it did.

It happened on the evening of December 8, 1980, after what I assume is a typical day for such a celebrity. It started at his home in the Dakota apartment building on the edge of Central Park with a photo shoot by Annie Leibovitz for a *Rolling Stone* magazine cover (the one where he's naked and clinging to his wife,

Yoko Ono), continued with a radio show interview, was followed by an impromptu autograph session outside his home, and then ended with some music recording work for his wife at a nearby studio.

Actually, the end happened after that. Upon his returning home with Ono at 10:50 PM, a young man shot Lennon four times in the back with a .38, right at the entrance to the Dakota. Lennon died soon after at Roosevelt Hospital.

Lennon's murderer was a chubby, bespectacled, harmless-looking 25-year-old by the name of Mark David Chapman. As a turn of the screw, Lennon had signed a copy of his *Double Fantasy* album for Chapman a few hours earlier during the aforementioned autograph session, a moment eerily caught on film by a photographer.

In reading any of Chapman's biographical information, you don't immediately see someone ready for straitjacket measurements. He was born in Texas, traveled the world, was a caregiver (of everything from camp children to Vietnamese refugees to hospital patients) of a caliber that he got the opportunity to meet President Gerald Ford, and he was a married man. Sure, he had his downs with those ups: a broken engagement, childhood bullying, youthful experimentation with drugs, parent problems, a suicide attempt. But that's the bio of a million nonmurderers.

But the events leading up to Lennon's final day revealed mental imbalances that ranged from strange to absolute psycho. Chapman traveled twice all the way from Hawaii, where he was living at the time, to kill Lennon. The first time, in October, he changed his mind. The second time, he spent a bizarre few days offering cocaine to a taxi driver, accosting singer-songwriter James Taylor in the subway (for reasons other than "Shower the People"), and waited outside the Dakota for hours, even to the point of shaking the hand of Lennon's five-year-old son Sean at one point, when his nursemaid took him out for a walk.

After the murder, the crazy continued at a more muted level. Once he shot Lennon, he sat down and waited for the police, reading from a copy of J. D. Salinger's *Catcher in the Rye* in which he had scrawled, "To Holden Caulfield. From Holden Caulfield. This is my statement." The book had become a Bible to him. He read passages from it aloud as his statement at sentencing, sent a letter to the media exhorting everyone to read it, even reenacted scenes from it the day he shot Lennon. It's enough to make an author go into exile.

In fact, although crazy is motive enough, the shooting is often at least partially attributed to the antipathy that the main character of that story, the aforereferenced Holden Caulfield, has toward those he calls "phonies," a character defect that Chapman might have transferred to a popular musician who sang/preached about peace and social issues while living the unabashed platinum-record-plated multimillionaire life.

Chapman pleaded guilty to the murder, despite the fact that his lawyers wanted and probably could have won an insanity defense, and he was sentenced to 20 years to life in Attica Correctional Facility, just east of Buffalo. Since 2000, Chapman has been eligible for parole every two years, but he's been denied every time so far.

Lennon's body was cremated at Ferncliff Cemetery (see the entries on Basil Rathbone, Joan Crawford, and Conrad Veidt in "Legends and Personalities of the Macabre"). His wife maintains possession of the ashes.

The 150-year-old Dakota still stands at 1 West 72nd St. (for more information about it, see the *Rosemary's Baby* entry in "Horror Movie Filming Locales"), right across the street from Central Park. Its entrance hasn't changed much in the 20 years since the murder, except that the people frequently gathered around it these days are mourning Lennon instead of searching out his autograph.

Just across the street, only a few dozen steps from Lennon's last, a small area of Central Park has been turned into a John Lennon memorial. Called Strawberry Fields, it has been specially landscaped with tree, flowers, and benches dedicated to his memory. Its central feature is a circular black and white mosaic with the title of his signature song "Imagine" emblazoned in its center, donated by the city of Naples, Italy. It looks a lot like a petrified spotlight, a spotlight that for John Lennon, turned into a target.

But maybe it was worth it.

Love Canal
Niagara Falls

I KNOW. IT SOUNDS LIKE A EUPHEMISM for a part of the female anatomy. Truth is, it's one of the more disturbing examples of corporate and municipal irresponsibility in the history of the country. We're talking toxic sludge and deformed babies, here.

Love Canal began as the entrepreneurial vision of a man named William Love in the 1890s. His aim was to dig a canal in the Niagara Falls region of New York to divert water from the Niagara River to power a community that he was planning.

For various reasons that just slow the narrative from getting to the disturbing stuff, the project fell through and only about 3,000 feet of the canal were dug. Reported measurements vary, but it was anywhere from 50 to 100 feet wide and ranged in depth from 10 to 40 feet. Mostly, locals used the watery pit as a swimming hole.

Sometime around 1920, it was bought by the city of Niagara Falls, lined with clay, and used as an industrial waste dump. In the 1940s, it was taken over by Hooker Chemicals and Plastics Corporation, which continued to add barrels of toxic chemicals to the brew. Eventually, more than 20,000 tons of all kinds of Toxic Avenger—inducing sludge was dumped there, running a gamut of Twinkie ingredients from caustics to carcinogens.

In 1953, the pit was capped and covered. Eventually, grass grew over the spot and made the whole thing look a lot more appealing than something so poisonous should.

Meanwhile, the population of Niagara Falls began to rapidly expand. Houses and schools were needed, and that 16-acre plot and its surrounding land became extremely tempting for a city looking to raise such infrastructure. The school board in particular wanted Love Canal. Apparently, it seemed like a great place to teach children. And they were right, as long as the curriculum centered on the horrors of life.

Here's where the story gets kind of confusing. Apparently, Hooker, against all stereotypes of evil corporations, didn't want to sell the land, due to safety and/or legal concerns, but eventually acquiesced to pressure from the school board. The company sold it to the board for one symbolic dollar. The deed clearly outlined the dangers of the property, and representatives even took the purchasers out to the site and drilled holes to show them Love Canal's creamy filling.

Basically, Hooker did enough to play the Pontius Pilate role in this passion play. It washed its hands of the site, but not its culpability.

So the board constructed a couple of schools adjacent to the area, and the banks of the canal were sold off to residential developers who built entire neighborhoods for the growing populace. Apparently and somewhat symbolically, the only thing built directly on top of Love Canal was a playground.

Gradually all the setup shots from the horror movie this was shaping up to be began to occur. The cap on the site began to crack, various other infrastructure projects altered the land around the canal and punctured the clay barrier, and Nature itself jumped in to deteriorate the integrity of the site.

Sometime in the 1970s, people started noticing strange odors, and oily noxious liquids began oozing into their basements and lying in ominous puddles on the ground. Plants and trees turned colors only describable by H. P. Lovecraft. Strange metal barrels could be found protruding from the soil. People would burn their feet just walking around. The miscarriage rate increased to an improbable level, and kids seemed to be contracting lots of medical problems.

It didn't take long for tests to reveal toxic waste contaminating the entire area as if there was a, I don't know, badly maintained underground dump site nearby.

Granted, who knows what causes what, but certainly intimate proximity with hundreds of chemicals, from lead to dioxin, didn't help, and it certainly unsettled the area's residents. The story went national and reporters came in and filmed angry parents protesting with footage-conducive signs. The Environmental Protection Agency, which had only just been instituted earlier that decade, stepped in, and President Jimmy Carter basically designated it a disaster area and invested federal funds to clean it up, demolish the affected school buildings and houses, and relocate some 900 families.

That previous paragraph makes it sound as if it all happened pretty quickly, but it actually took years for everybody to figure out what was going on and what needed to be done and how to coordinate to get it done. Oh, and who to blame. The faceless corporation that was Hooker, which by this time had been purchased by another company, Occidental Petroleum, was held accountable for exactly $129 million worth of blame.

The event was so influential that it became the catalyst for the federal Superfund initiative, a strangely named project that to this day continues cleaning up neglected industrial waste sites throughout the country. Terrifyingly, Love Canal is not an isolated incident. It's not even that rare. Just one of the most infamous, mostly because it was the first to be brought to national attention, but also probably because of its incongruous name.

Today, most of the 16 acres of Love Canal proper are surrounded by a rectangle of 10-foot-tall chain-link fence. Inside, there's just a green stretch of land strewn with innocuous-looking wells and access pipes for testing the groundwater. A small water treatment plant sits on the site to help filter rainwater. Mostly, it's just an empty field, though.

You can drive all the way around the property, which I did. I was hoping for some photo ops with "Danger" or "Hazardous Chemicals" signs. I was even ready to settle for a Mr. Yuck sticker, but nothing adorned the fence. I also wanted to see whether anything was left over from the mass and massive demolition, but apparently the materials were buried right there in Love Canal, before the whole site was covered with layers of protective plastic and soil.

Honestly, the land looks somewhat serene, like the perfect place for a soccer field or a park. Or for a traveling carnival to set up on every year. Love Canal still sits in the middle of a residential area, and the houses, while not crowded around it as in past decades, are still pretty close, some a mere strip of road away and others just a couple of blocks, but all that is a testament to the work being done to keep the location safe, I guess.

Technically, Love Canal is more or less the area between 93rd and 102nd Streets. Not all of those streets exist anymore, so to get there just aim your GPS for either Frontier Avenue or Colvin Boulevard, which bookend the area.

And that's the story of, that's the story of Love Canal. No evil corporations. No power-mad politicians. No bad guys, really. Just a lot of regular people making a lot of bad decisions based on social pressures and self-interest. You know, everyday life.

Minus the toxic ingredients.

Renwick Smallpox Hospital
ROOSEVELT ISLAND

A HOSPITAL CAN BE A DAUNTING ENOUGH PLACE, but when you have one like Renwick Smallpox Hospital, which is named for a highly contagious fatal disease and is isolated on an island, you're just setting it up to be the backdrop for a thousand future horror stories.

Smallpox is a terrible and highly contagious virus that's basically transmitted

through eye contact. Its victims suffer every bit of bodily insurrection possible (fever, vomiting, aches, delirium, bleeding, sores, etc.), culminating in the ultimate mutiny of death in many cases. It was pretty much the bane of the prevaccine world. Heck, the long struggle against it is the reason that we have vaccines in general today.

In the large population center that was New York City, outbreaks were dealt with by quarantining the victims wherever they could. However, in the 1850s, the city got serious and built the Renwick Smallpox Hospital out on Roosevelt Island.

Back then, the 2-mile-long island in the East River was called Blackwell's Island, and the hospital just bore the generic description "smallpox hospital." It's known as the Renwick Smallpox Hospital today because its architect was James Renwick Jr., the same man who designed Saint Patrick's Cathedral in Manhattan and the Smithsonian Institution Building in DC.

At the time of the hospital's construction, the island was already the site of both a prison and a lunatic asylum. The addition of the smallpox hospital meant that the city could upgrade to hotels on its next turn. The hospital officially opened in 1856 as a three-floor, granite-faced Gothic brute with a 100-bed capacity, a veritable fortress against contagion.

In the 1870s, with the noninstitutionalized population of Blackwell's Island rising and the opening of quarantine facilities farther up the East River at North

Brother Island (see the entry on Typhoid Mary, page 84), two wings were added to Renwick, and it was converted to the Maternity and Charity Hospital Training School. But even that went its way, and in the 1950s, Renwick closed down for all purposes but decay, a mission which it has faithfully pursued brick by brick at the southern tip of the island.

Today, smallpox has been wiped out, Blackwell's Island has been renamed Roosevelt Island and is the home of a thriving community, and the ruins that were once a smallpox hospital are now a National Historic Landmark in the process of being converted into the centerpiece of a 14-acre park.

In fact, when I visited this island in the perpetual shadow of the Queensboro Bridge in the summer of 2011, I couldn't access any of the southern section of the park due to the construction and restoration efforts. A tall chain-link fence covered in a black tarplike material had been set up the short width of that end of the island. Through random holes in the material, the lay of the land only allowed small glimpses of the north side of the structure from a distance.

However, a few months later, while in Manhattan, I was able to find a great spot for viewing the building across the river. At the end of East 51st Street is a pedestrian bridge that stretches over a small park and the noisy highway that is FDR Drive. From there, the building is only 1,500 feet away across the water.

Soon, though, maybe even as of the moment that you're reading this, that information will be less valuable, as visitors to Roosevelt Island will be able to go directly to the southern end of the island and personally race among the smallpox hospital ruins as if they're in a Gordon Lightfoot song. Smallpox is that dim a memory, I guess.

Grave and Memorial of Leo Frank
QUEENS

THIS TRAGEDY IS NOT A NEW YORK ONE; it belongs to Georgia. However, the reverberations of the events of the spring of 1913 have spanned time and nation, and the central figure of infamy and tragedy has himself turned into New York soil and been memorialized here.

It's not the type of tale that's fun to hear, but here goes. We'll start gently.

Born in 1884 in Texas, Leo Frank lived much of his life in Brooklyn. After earning a mechanical engineering degree from Cornell University, he was offered the opportunity to oversee a pencil manufacturing plant in Atlanta, Georgia.

He moved to Atlanta in 1908, settled nicely into the local Jewish community, found a wife, and began what was supposed to be the "happily ever after" part of the story.

Here's where it starts getting rough.

In April 1913, a night watchman found the body of a murdered 13-year-old girl in the basement of Frank's pencil factory.

The girl's name was Mary Phagan, and she worked at the factory. A cord was wrapped around her neck and two semi-illiterate notes found nearby seemed to be a bad attempt at implicating the black man who was the night watchman.

Soon, it was determined that 29-year-old Leo Frank, who had given Mary her pay the previous day, was the last person to see her alive. That, combined with Frank's nervous reaction to police questioning and sudden rumors of his sexual predation, were enough to have the slim, neat, bespectacled man arrested for one of the worst crimes a person is capable of.

Then the janitor of the building, a black man named Jim Conley, was discovered washing what appeared to be bloodstains from his shirt. He was arrested as well, but the story he told implicated Leo Frank worse than any mere twine of suspicion before.

And thus began a horrible collision of prejudice, bias, and racism that has yet to be untangled today and out of which rose both the modern resurrection of the Ku Klux Klan and creation of the Jewish Anti-Defamation League. And there wasn't just anti-Semitism and anti-African Americanism. There was also a strong anti-industrialism and anti-North sentiment, as well, in this Southern city just two generations or so removed from the Civil War. It was whites against Jews, Jews against blacks, whites against whites. Mob mentalities, gawkerism, and inflammatory media attention. The whole thing was a gigantic mess.

According to Conley, Frank had often enlisted his help as a lookout while he had illicit trysts at the office, and on that day had come to him telling him that a young girl had accidentally been killed and that he needed help moving her body to the basement furnace. He offered Conley money and then coached the janitor into writing the notes. It was a strange sort of confidence Frank seemed to have in the man.

Despite being caught in a few lies early on, Conley's testimony was believed by the jury in a trial that many thought violated the tenets of due process. Frank was convicted of murder and sentenced to hanging. After a series of lengthy appeals that went all the way to the U.S. Supreme Court, the state governor finally commuted Frank's sentence in 1915 to life imprisonment. Apparently not everyone was that convinced of Frank's guilt.

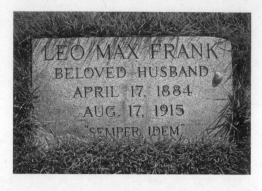

Some were, though, to an extreme degree. Despite how long it had been since the original crime, the people of Atlanta were sufficiently invested in it that the lighter sentence enraged a group of some of them, so much so that they stormed the prison where Frank was being held, took him to the town of Marietta where Mary had lived, and lynched him.

Far from its being a reactionary act on the part of an easily provoked and undesirable element of Atlanta society, pictures that were taken during the lynching revealed the mob to include some of the more prominent citizens of the city. In addition, they left Frank hanging from the tree, and tourists arrived in droves to see it and remove souvenirs from his corpse.

And that pretty much ends the story. Later evidence would seem to point to Conley as the murderer, including a statement from his own defense attorney and an after-the-fact eyewitness, but many to this day maintain that Frank was the right culprit, even if he was executed wrongly.

It's a wound in the Jewish community that never completely healed. In the 1980s, more than seven decades after the crime, the state of Georgia, upon the request of the Anti-Defamation League, posthumously pardoned Frank for its own failure to protect him. However, it stopped short of exonerating him of the crime for which he was convicted.

Georgia has its own memorials and markers of the tragedy, but it's in New York that Frank is buried, in his family plot in a Jewish cemetery in Queens by the name of Mount Carmel. The cemetery has multiple entrances at multiple street addresses, but Frank's grave is in Section 1 near the entrance of the office, at 83-45 Cypress Hills Street. His grave is in Block E of that section, to the right once you're inside the gates, right on Path 41 (maps can be found at the cemetery website). The inset stone merely gives his name, dates of existence, and the phrases "Beloved Husband" and "Semper Idem" ("always the same").

Just outside the office at a spot you'll have to pass to get to his grave is a small, polished stone pedestal that memorializes him. It was installed on the 90th anniversary of the founding of the Anti-Defamation League, and touts without equivocation his debatable innocence and emphasizes the undisputed injustice.

Like I said, a big mess. A real, big mess. Sometimes every side of humanity is an ugly one.

Joel Rifkin House
East Meadow

I'M HAVING A BIT OF TROUBLE coming up with an angle on this smear of human feculence. Sure, Joel Rifkin is a notorious serial killer with upward of 17 victims to his credit . . . er, detriment, but his story is pretty bland as far as serial killers go. I mean, look no further than his serial killer name, "Joel the Ripper," to see that not even the tabloids put much thought into him. Also keep in mind that he is here discussed in a section that features a cannibal of children, a murderer who got his instructions from a talking dog, and a serial killer nurse. Variety is the arsenic of life.

Aside from his murdering and dismembering prostitutes, Rifkin's life could have been anybody's. He was born in January of 1959, was adopted weeks after his birth, was brought up on Long Island, had a sister, ran track in high school, worked at a lawn-mowing business.

Sure, there were bumps on the way. He apparently had a less than ideal relationship with his adopted father, who committed suicide after suffering from cancer. Rifkin also dropped out of college, and was generally just an awkward outcast . . . which is usually the angle that people take on him. Still, those aren't the kind of bumps that jolt a person into abject inhumanity.

Still, inhumanity was where this man went with a cinderblock on the gas pedal. Interestingly though, despite killing a self-admitted dozen and a half women between 1989 and 1993, he didn't have a reign of terror. Nobody even knew there was a serial killer stalking the streets of New York during that time, because his victims were all drug-addicted streetwalkers in a city full of that kind of violence.

But it was also because he was apparently great at hiding bodies, cutting them

up into manageable pieces and distributing the parts hundreds of miles apart throughout New York and New Jersey. See, Dad? Good at something.

His arrest was even somewhat bland. In the early morning of the summer of 1993 he was driving his capped pickup truck on Long Island's Southern State Parkway, when his license plate fell off. A police officer tried to pull him over for it, but Rifkin took off at high speed, eventually crashing into a light pole. Before the cop could even get out a, "Geez, buddy, it was just a citation for license plate," he caught whiff of something bad. Turns out, Rifkin was traveling with a badly decomposing victim in the back that he was on his way to dispose of.

Rifkin was questioned and pretty much immediately admitted that the girl was number 17. His house was searched, and in a room completely filthy with stuff, the police found a cache of personal items belonging to his victims: jewelry, underwear, photo IDs, for goodness' sake. They were able to directly connect him to nine victims. He was found guilty on all counts and sentenced to a couple hundred years in prison. He still serves that sentence today in the Clinton Correctional Facility in Dannemora, the same prison where Richard Angelo is incarcerated (see Angel of Death Hospital, page 141).

Still, if the 17 that he admitted to is accurate, that makes this underachiever the most prolific serial killer in New York history, which I guess is the actual angle that I should've opened this entry with.

He committed most of those murders at 1492 Garden Street in East Meadow, where he lived at the time with his adopted mother and sister. It's a cozy-looking pink house on a nicely landscaped corner lot in a pleasant-looking Long Island neighborhood. Its number doesn't match up with the sequence of the three-digit addresses on Garden Street, but it's located at the end that intersects Spruce Lane.

As I stood in front of it, hoping that nobody would come out while I was loitering awkwardly on the sidewalk, it was hard to connect the darkness of Joel Rifkin's story with any palpable darkness about the place. I mean, in the end, it's just a house. But that affirmation doesn't make it less creepy. After all, Joel Rifkin is just a man. But somewhere in that simple statement is hidden the strange stuff that quickly makes living on this planet a bad time.

Brooklyn Theatre Fire Mass Grave
BROOKLYN

THANKS TO SUPREME COURT Justice Oliver Wendell Holmes Jr., the standard example for exceeding the bounds of free speech is shouting, "Fire!" in a crowded theater. I can't say for sure why he chose that particular venue and that particular emergency for his point, but I assume the idea stuck in culture because it's absolutely terrifying and absolutely plausible. The discombobulating darkness, the crushing crowds, the thin line between an enjoyable night of diversion and a hellish night of horror, the faces of actors looking down like indifferent gods . . .

And it's not such a hypothetical situation. Some of the most deadly building fires in the history of the country have happened in theaters, with one of the worst happening in New York on December 5, 1876, when close to 300 people met their fiery end for the mere reason of wanting to catch a play.

The Brooklyn Theatre was built in 1871 at the southeast corner of Washington and Johnson streets, on the site of an old church. On that fatal winter night only five years later, about a thousand people were in attendance to watch a stage production of *The Two Orphans,* a play where the titular characters are abducted into different and opposite destinies, and one that doesn't allow writers about the fire to play off any ironic underpinnings of the story.

Just after 11 PM, sometime before the last act, in both senses of the term, a piece of painted canvas used as a backdrop got too close to a gas flame backstage and caught fire. It was a small fire, noticed immediately by the stagehands and not conspicuous to the audience. Some of the actors saw it, but continued in character. When in doubt, act. As the stagehands attempted to put it out, fire did what it does best: be unpredictable, uncontrollable, and fast. Suddenly it tore through the many flammable items on the stage and in the building . . . including people.

The audience was seated in three tiers, and most of the attendees on the first and second floors escaped without injury. However, the cheap seats of the much more crowded and much more isolated third-floor gallery was where most of the deaths occurred.

Of course, dying in a fire at a public venue is more complicated than just dying in a fire. Besides being burned to death, it can also mean being trampled by panicking crowds, asphyxiating from smoke, getting smashed by falling debris, or falling through floors. And that's what happened. Lots of people died in ways that can make a person angry at the entire universe. The fire raged all night, destroying the entire building and leaving many of its victims unidentifiable.

Today the spot where the theater stood is an anonymous part of Cadman Plaza, but 3 miles away, a tall monument reaches to heaven as both a reminder of the tragedy and as a marker for the mass grave for 103 of the unidentified dead.

The memorial is a 30-foot-tall dark stone obelisk, the four sides of which tell the whole tragic story in about four sentences. The official death tally, according to the marker, is 278. It's found near the main entrance to Green-Wood Cemetery at 500 25th Street (see "Notable Graves, Cemeteries, and Other Memento Mori").

As follows most large-scale tragedies, we learned from this one and instituted better safety regulations and practices directly as a result of this fire. Still, the Grim Reaper isn't known for carrying a balance scale, and the whole thing just sucks bad. Death by fire, burial in anonymity, and they never got to see what would happen to the two orphans.

Triangle Shirtwaist Factory Fire Site and Memorials
MANHATTAN, QUEENS, BROOKLYN

FIRE MAY BE ONE OF THE CATALYSTS OF CIVILIZATION, but doggone if the stuff doesn't make us regret it sometimes. In the previous entry, we visited the mass grave of one of the worst building fires in the history of the country. Well, douse your candles and snuff out your cigarettes, because here's another one.

Although it killed fewer people than the Brooklyn Theatre Fire, the Triangle Shirtwaist Factory Fire of 1911 is often held in greater infamy. That's due to the details surrounding the tragedy. First, the victims were mostly women and teenage girls. Second, they were locked into the building by their employers. And third, the conflagration went on to incite important workplace reform. Oh, and fourth, two words: raining bodies.

Shirtwaists, also called simply waists, were a popular style of women's blouse at the turn of the century, and the Triangle Waist Company met that demand at its factory site in the top three floors of a 10-story building in Greenwich Village known as the Asch Building. Today, a Google search of that fashion reveals that it has become almost totally synonymous with the factory tragedy.

On March 25, 1911, a fire broke out on the eighth story of the building. The source is most often hypothesized as a wayward cigarette's igniting one of the many piles and bins full of clothes and cuttings.

There were hundreds of workers on the factory's three floors at the time, and very few options for escape. For instance, one of the doors was locked to prevent employee theft. Another opened inward instead of outward, a simple detail that becomes tragic when scores of bodies are pressing up against it. The elevator was limited and eventually crippled by the heat and the bodies falling down the shaft. The fire escape peeled off the wall from the sheer weight of people trying to use it.

As a result, many in the building were faced with two choices: stay inside to face death by burning or asphyxiation . . . or they could jump. Many chose that latter option, plummeting from the eighth and ninth floors, much to the horror of the massed and impotent onlookers.

The fire response was quick but inadequately supplied with ladders too short to service the top floors, water hoses with limited ranges, and everything complicated by the broken bodies surrounding the building and continuing to fall.

In the end, 146 people died as a result of the fire, all but about 20 of them women and girls.

The fire was eventually contained, and the resilient building still stands at 23 Washington Place, right beside Washington Square Park. Today, it's known as the Brown Building and is a part of New York University. On the Washington Place and Green Street corner of the building is a small plaque designating the place as both a National Historic Landmark and the site of the tragic fire.

But that's not the only commemoration of the calamity.

At the Jewish Mount Zion Cemetery, a crowded urban cemetery where some 20 of the victims are buried, are three distinct memorials all located in the Workmen's Circle, a section of the cemetery that can be found near path number 43, close to the corner where Tyler and Maurice Avenues intersect.

The section is demarcated by a pair of statues whose broken arms once formed an entrance arch of sorts. Beside those two statues is a short, white obelisk dedicated in 2004 to the memory of the victims. Just behind the statues is a small polished stone placed by the International Ladies Garment Workers Union that proclaims the deceased as martyrs to the cause of social and labor responsibility.

At the back of the Workmen's Circle, among the rows of closely packed tombstones, is a tall, older monument made of 14 white, stone pillars that further commemorates these unknowing martyrs. Mount Zion Cemetery itself is at 59–63 54th Street in the

Maspeth community of Queens.

Eight of the unidentified victims were interred at Evergreens Cemetery at 1629 Bushwick Avenue in Brooklyn, although one was eventually identified and transferred elsewhere. The rest have been memorialized under a single, tall, white slab bearing the image of a woman kneeling at a large urn above an epitaph that mourns the "women and children" who died in the fire. Recently, researchers were able to match these remaining victims with identities.

And while these are all the types of memorials that indicate that at one time somebody did remember, a fresher, living memorial was held on the centennial of the tragedy, in 2011. Gatherings and speeches occurred at the actual lower Manhattan site. Marches, photography exhibits, and other events were also held throughout the city, all grieving the horrible loss of life but also heralding it as the catalyst of significant workplace reform.

Auburn Correctional Facility
AUBURN

I T'S A POINT OF PRIDE for towns to be the first place for something to happen. Gives them something to be besides a McDonald's pit stop on the way to somewhere else. So, if you're the site of the first-ever use of an electric chair for capital punishment, how proud should you be? Like tourist brochure proud? Back of a quarter proud? Buried deep in the town records of the local historical society proud?

Turns out, Auburn, a city of 30,000 in the Finger Lakes region of the state, is historical sign proud. Granted, New York in general loves its blue-and-yellow historical signs, the ones shaped like flattened crosses (think Chevrolet logo). They're everywhere in the state. Heck, in front of the Auburn Correctional Facility at 135 State Street are three within 20 paces of one another, one about the Native American history of the area, another about the local silk trade, and the already mentioned one, which touts, "First Electrocution in the World." Also, inaccurately touts. It was the first *purposeful* electrocution in the world. Accidents had happened before then. In fact, it was an accidental death that led to the idea of using electrocution for executions in the first place.

That landmark event occurred at the Auburn Correctional Facility in 1890, when William Kemmler, convicted hatchet murderer, at least in regard to his lover (see the following entry, "The Electrified and Electrifying"), was the first person to take the mercy seat.

Built in 1816 and "welcoming" prisoners in 1817, Auburn Correctional Facility is one of the oldest continually operating prisons in the United States. It was built on a site that was previously a British prisoner-of-war camp during the War of 1812 and even more previously the location of a Cayuga Native American village.

Before becoming better known for the first state-sanctioned human electrocution, it was famous for its influential Auburn System of prison management, where inmates were housed in solitary cells and condemned to silence, even during group activities, to prevent convict collusion.

More jarring than the electrocution sign is the fact that this maximum security facility is right downtown, directly across from a gas station and adjacent to strips of restaurants and retail establishments. In other words, you could jail break, grab a bite to eat, and fill up your getaway car before the guards would even know there was a tunnel behind the Raquel Welch poster.

As a still-operating prison, the Auburn Correctional Facility has almost everything you'd think a jail should have, all viewable from the sidewalk in front of it: guard towers, barbed-wire-topped security fences, castlelike walls and turrets. No "Beware of Prisoners" sign, though.

Currently, all those security features keep close to 2,000 criminals at bay, which in the recent past has included such infamous fellows as Robert Chambers (a.k.a. "the Preppy Killer") and J. Frank Hickey (a.k.a. "the Postcard Killer"). Further back it time, it held (and electrocuted) Leon Czolgosz, the assassin of President William McKinley (see page 109), and early-20th-century murderer Chester Gillette.

All in all, it's a pretty intimidating place, even to us law-abiding . . . that is, except for the colorful little copper statue of a Revolutionary War soldier at its apex. That bit of Americana looks like it belongs staked in somebody's front lawn beside a flamingo and a wooden cutout of a woman bending over. His name is Copper John, and he has stood sentry on the rooftop there since the late 1840s.

Copper John was made by prison inmates. He weighs more than a quarter-ton and is over 8 feet tall (over 11 feet if you count his bayonet rifle). He's based on a wooden version that was carved by an Auburn local and which had held the rooftop post for two decades previously, although back then it was on an administration building that is no longer standing. Weather damage to the original statue prompted the changing of the guard.

Copper John's purpose these days is mainly historical for locals and aspirational for inmates, who only get to see him from the back until they are released and are free to walk the public streets he faces. Mostly, though, it seems to just detract from the crowds of human depravity and tragedy behind it.

Back to the grim place marker on the front gate turret of the building, it takes on an added significance when you realize that the last death by electric furniture was in the early 1960s, and all forms of the death penalty have been outlawed in the state of New York since the mid-2000s (after going back and forth about it for decades). As a result, the only New York locale where you'll find an electric chair these days is in a museum or at a Halloween attraction. The device is both worth preserving and worth being scared of.

The Electrified and the Electrifying
BUFFALO, AUBURN, BRONX

T HE STORY OF THE ELECTRIC CHAIR is a New York story. It was invented here, first used here, and many of the main characters in the story were born, electrocuted (where applicable), and buried here.

The story starts, as so few of them do, with a dentist. In the early 1880s, Dr. Alfred Southwick of Buffalo witnessed a man accidentally electrocute himself on a generator. Southwick was impressed by the efficiency of the killing. Far from being a random and perverse thought on Southwick's part, it was actually relevant to the times.

You see, public opinion had started to turn against the current gold standard of execution, the noose. Apparently watching twitching people suffocate at the end of a swinging line, when their head wasn't violently ripped off during the drop, was fun for a while, but got old. As a result, the state was looking for something to replace hanging as a means of capital punishment.

So in between tooth drilling, Southwick designed a device that incorporated lethal amounts of electricity. His being a dentist, the device took the form of a chair. After all, if it could be used to inflict pain, than why not death? After some lobbying, New York officially legalized its use in 1889.

The chair was built and first used the next year at the Auburn Correctional Facility in Auburn (see previous entry).

The man who ascended that first throne was 28-year-old William Kemmler, who murdered his girlfriend Tillie Ziegler in both Buffalo and a drunken rage, with a hatchet. For the classic crime, he was to get a cutting-edge sentence. After a few civil words, the placement of electrodes, and the fastening of restraints, the proverbial switch was proverbially flipped. One thousand volts later and a still (badly) living convict later, it was flipped again, this time delivering 2,000 volts of death. Accompanied by a bad smell and a death pronouncement, Kemmler took his dubious place in history for his eight minutes of fame.

Interestingly, there was a business and political subplot to Kemmler's electrocution. The sentence took place during the height of the AC/DC wars, when George Westinghouse and Nikola Tesla were pushing the much more efficient alternating current (AC) standard for electricity against rival Thomas Edison's already established direct current (DC) standard. For the electrocution, Edison made sure the prison used AC power, so that he could market how unsuitable and dangerous it was for everyday use.

Westinghouse knew this, so during the appeals process for Kemmler's sentence, Westinghouse supported the appeal, while Edison testified for the state. Edison won that particular battle, but, of course, eventually lost the war as AC eventually became the standard for most uses across the globe. After the execution, Westinghouse was quoted as saying, "They would have done better using an ax." It had, after all, worked on Ziegler.

The electric chair was also an equal-opportunity electrocutioner. The first woman to have her seat warmed in such a fashion was 44-year-old Martha Place in 1899, for killing her 17-year-old stepdaughter, apparently out of jealousy. The murder took place in Brooklyn, and Place's execution, at Sing Sing prison in Ossining.

The most famous female chair holder, however, was Ruth Brown Snyder,

Grave of Ruth Brown Snyder

who, along with a man she was having an affair with, strangled her husband, Albert, in Queens. She was also executed at Sing Sing, in 1928. Her posthumous infamy came about because a reporter smuggled a camera into the proceedings and took a picture of her strapped to the chair. It was subsequently published and circulated, and you can still see the terrifying image today on the Internet (go ahead and Google it . . . seeing this kind of stuff is one of the main reasons we have an Internet).

These days, many states have outlawed the death penalty in its entirety. For the rest, they have either outlawed the use of the electric chair particularly or offer alternatives, such as lethal injection.

However, you can still trace the early history of the electric chair in New York through the locations, artifacts, and gravestones relevant to the death machine. For instance, you can view Southwick's grave in Forest Lawn Cemetery in Buffalo (see "Notable Graves, Cemeteries, and Other Memento Mori"). His tombstone is marked on the cemetery maps, and can be found in Section 31. It's a small, loaf-size marker within a row of three or four identical ones for his family. His particular marker says "Father," on top, but not "of the Electric Chair."

Auburn Correctional Facility proudly bears a historic marker denoting its place in electrocution history, and if you're ever in Ossining, you can visit the

Sing Sing Prison exhibit (see page 81), where you'll find a replica electric chair made with loving care by inmates of the prison.

Although the first woman to be executed by electrocution was buried in her home state of New Jersey, the grave of Ruth Brown Snyder is in New York. She's interred in the Brown family plot in the Arbutus Section of Woodlawn Cemetery in the Bronx. The communal headstone is a plain rectangular one with the family surname carved in a simple font on its face. Her actual plot marker is the one labeled "May R.," which was her original name, back in the rosy premurderess days of her youth.

Now, with the era of the electric chair pretty much over, the dentist chair is that much closer to reclaiming its title as the scariest chair actively used by man.

General Slocum
Tragedy Site and Memorials
North Brother Island, Manhattan, Brooklyn, Queens

IT'S A COMMON HYPOTHETICAL QUESTION, "Would you rather burn to death or drown?" The correct answer, the only conceivable one at least, is, "Neither." Unfortunately, for the more than 1,000 poor souls aboard the steamboat *General Slocum* on June 15, 1904, that's exactly the decision they were forced to make.

The *General Slocum* first dipped its pair of 31-foot-diameter paddle wheels into the water in 1891. At 235 feet long and 37 feet wide, the three-deck wooden vessel was just big enough for a giant tragedy. On that dark day in June, the steamboat was commissioned by Saint Mark's German Lutheran church in lower Manhattan to take its passengers up the East River and across the sound to the Eatons Neck area of Long Island for a picnic. It was an annual tradition for the community, one that it had been doing for almost two decades. The party consisted of more than 1,300 visitors—mostly women and children, accounts (like this one) are always quick to add.

They never even made it to the sound. Somewhere past what is now known as Roosevelt Island, a fire broke out. No one is quite sure how, but where there's steam, there's fire. What is certain is that every other square inch of the boat and its cargo was extremely combustible. The fire took off as if it wasn't surrounded by water. However, what made the tragedy wasn't so much the fire, but the poor response. Bad decisions were made on the part of an unprepared captain and crew, and the life rafts and safety floatation devices were old and improperly cared for. They may also have been faultily and, and even fraudulently, manufactured.

The captain, William Van Schaick, eventually (some say after too long) grounded the ship on North Brother Island, a small island at the top of the East River and home to the Riverside Hospital, a quarantine facility for everything from smallpox to leprosy. A few years later, this island hospital would become the home and prison of Typhoid Mary (see page 84). The day of the grounding of the *General Slocum* was probably one of the few times that the patients at Riverside thought of themselves as the lucky ones.

By the time the burning hulk of the steamboat hit the shallows of the island, it was too late. At the end of the day, more than 1,000 of its original 1,300 passengers had died. Pictures from that day show bodies washing up and lining the shore of the island like sea foam.

As with every tragedy, blame was thrown everywhere it could be aimed. In fact, half a dozen or so people were indicted, from the owners of the boat to the captain to the safety inspectors. Captain Van Schaick was the only one convicted,

however, and he spent three years of a ten-year sentence in Sing Sing. He was pardoned by President Taft shortly thereafter. The company itself was fined, and what little remained of the *General Slocum* was refurbished into a barge called the *Maryland*, which then sank in a storm about seven years later.

The *General Slocum* is gone, North Brother Island and its hospital are now abandoned (although the ruins of the latter can be seen from the shores of southern Bronx), and the last survivor died in 2004 at the age of 100, but many monuments still keep the memory of that tragic day alive.

In Tompkins Square Park in Manhattan, at East Seventh and Avenue A, a 9-foot-tall, pink marble, gravestone-shaped monument was dedicated in 1906 to the tragedy. Located in a courtyard near the bathrooms, the memorial bears the peaceful image of a pair of children, above which is carved a line from Percy Bysshe Shelley's "Revolt of Islam": "They were earth's purest children, young and fair." Below them, a lion's head and basin form a small fountain. A picture of this memorial is included in the entry on the Butcher of Tompkins Square Park elsewhere in this section.

The dead were interred all over the city. Notably, 58 victims were buried in a mass grave in Evergreens Cemetery at 1629 Bushwick Avenue (see the Reed's Tomb entry in "Notable Graves, Cemeteries, and Other Memento Mori"). Almost half of these ill-fortuned were under the age of 15.

Others were buried in the Lutheran All Faiths Cemetery at 6729 Metropolitan Avenue in Queens. This mass grave features a large, elaborate memorial that was unveiled in 1905 in the presence of some of the survivors. It comprises three monuments; two angels on pedestals, one with a trumpet and the other with a child, flanking a central, 20-foot-tall, multilevel pedestal topped by a quartet of women. The pedestal tells the story of the *General Slocum* in both words and an engraving of the burning ship, shockingly complete with simply rendered victims hanging over the sides.

The cemetery straddles Metropolitan Avenue. To get to the monument, head to the southern section, the one on the opposite side from the office, and then continue parallel to Metropolitan until you get to Lawn Avenue on your right. Take that just for a little bit until Slocum Avenue branches off to the left. The monument is about halfway down that path. Maps and, in my experience, enthusiastic help are available at the office.

Incidentally, the *General Slocum* was named after Henry Slocum, a Civil War officer turned New York state congressman. He was alive at the time of the honor of the ship's christening, but fortunately, didn't live long enough to learn that he inadvertently lent his name to what was at the time the worst tragedy in the history of the city and which even now is only second to 9/11.

Angel of Death Hospital
West Islip

NOBODY WANTS TO GO TO THE HOSPITAL, for a long list of reasons, but absent on that list is the fear of being offed by a serial killer. However, in 1987, the patients of Good Samaritan Hospital on Long Island could add that reason to their list. It was probably above, "Hate being around sick people" but below, "It's going to cost a fortune."

The incident sounds like the plot of a hack thriller: A nurse kills the patients who trust him to care for them. Ironically, his name is Angel, and his serial killer name of course becomes, "Angel of Death." Sometimes real life is a hack thriller, although that still doesn't excuse hack thrillers.

Richard Angelo was in his mid-20s when he worked the night shift at the intensive care unit of Good Samaritan Hospital on the south shore of Long Island in the town of West Islip. Chubby, bespectacled, and bearded, he was a bit off-putting for those patients hoping for attractive, nubile candy stripers, but at least he didn't seem sinister.

But sinister is exactly what he was. He began injecting the powerful muscle-paralyzing drugs Pavulon and Anectine into the IVs of patients, telling them it would make them feel better. That's a loose definition of death, but still a technically correct one. The patients felt numbness followed by paralysis, and would then suffocate to death.

Angelo's patients were often older ones, with weaker constitutions, making their death less suspect. However, he slipped up when one of the patients, septuagenarian Gerolamo Kucich, managed to push the call button, was revived by responders, and then told them about the bearded man who had injected something into his IV. The unprescribed drugs were found in both Kucich's system and Angelo's apartment.

The hospital administrators then went through the records and noticed that the number of deaths and near-deaths during Angelo's shift were at ludicrous

levels (in hindsight). Bodies were exhumed and tested, and he was officially charged with six deaths that could potentially be traced to him, although estimates are as high as 25.

All serial killers are pathetic in their own way, but judging by Angelo's explanation for his crimes, he's probably the serial killer that other serial killers would pick on in the serial killer locker room. He claimed to have extremely low self-esteem and high aspirations to grandeur: He didn't mean to kill, just wanted to put the patients in life-threatening situations so that he could be the hero and save those lives he had just put in jeopardy.

He was apparently bad at it, though, despite having experience at multiple hospitals and being trained in emergency procedures. They often died, so the feelings of inadequacy were actually justified by his actions instead of expurgated.

His defense lawyers attempted a defense based on psychiatric disorder. And Angelo was ruled to have a disorder . . . that he killed people . . . one curable by 60-odd years in prison. He was convicted of four murders, and as of the writing of this entry, is still serving his sentence at the Clinton Correctional Facility in the northeast corner of the state in the village of Dannemora, where we can only assume his purported inferiority complex has intensified to the point that we wishes he at least had an inferiority complex. Incidentally, Clinton Correctional Facility is the same prison where serial killer Joe Rifkin is hidden from polite society (see page 127).

These days, the 50-year-old Good Samaritan Hospital still sits on its original 60-acre property at 1000 Montauk Highway. It's expanded and modernized a bit more in the past two decades, and its brief time as the hunting grounds of a serial killer are well behind them as the staff continues in its valiant mission of healing the sick and injured.

After all, hospitals are used to the real Angel of Death prowling their halls. He's just not supposed to be on the payroll.

Collyer Brothers Park
MANHATTAN

HOMER COLLYER and his younger brother Langley had it all . . . and it killed them. However, this isn't your typical story of wealthy overindulgence. It's a bit more literal than that. This is the infamous story of the hoarder brothers of Harlem.

Homer was born in 1881; his brother, Langley, four years later. Their family was affluent. Their parents made a fortune in body parts: their mother, by serenading the ears of aesthetes in her career as an opera singer; and their father, by probing the vaginas of Manhattan in his career as a gynecologist.

Both brothers went to Columbia University, Homer earning a degree in admiralty law, and Langley, in chemistry and mechanical engineering, although the latter concentrated more on his musical interests, going so far as to play the piano at Carnegie Hall. They had a life of open yellow brick roads ahead of them. Instead, they smashed into a wall of junk.

In 1909, the family moved to a four-story brownstone at 2078 Fifth Avenue, in the then-upscale neighborhood of Harlem. The brothers stayed there when their parents moved out years later, and continued to stay there after their parents died in the 1920s, as well as when Harlem changed to a predominately African American community.

That's kind of when the story gets weird. The Collyer brothers had a cen-

tipede's worth of legs-up in life—money, talent, skill, and family—yet, for some reason that no one is sure about except for the rats in their mansion, the siblings become extreme recluses. Further compounding matters, Homer eventually had a stroke that caused him to go as blind as his namesake, as well as becoming as paralyzed as all the statues of his namesake. Fortunately, he had Langley to take care of him. Unfortunately, he had Langley to take care of him.

The brothers started to become the neighborhood boogeymen. The house had no power, no water; Langley only left the house at night, and that was to forage for food and supplies. They started getting unwanted attention from neighbors, the press, and even vandals. Langley went so far as to set up booby traps throughout the house. But that's not all the weirdness that was going on inside, although it would take somebody's dying for the outside world to learn about it.

In April 1947, police received an anonymous tip that there was a dead body in the Collyer mansion. When police tried to get inside, they found themselves up against a mountain of boxes and newspapers and relics and all kinds of disgusting debris. The brothers had been accumulating random bits of trash and materials to the point that sometimes only tunnels went from one room to the next.

Finally, after playing miners more than policeman, the authorities found the body of Homer Collyer, sitting in a chair and dead for about half a day. Langley was nowhere to be found. The police followed various leads looking for Langley, as well as any reason why he would abandon his brother, while continuing to sort through rooms and rooms solid with junk.

About half a month later they found Langley. He was in the house, not too far away from the body of his brother, caught under a pile of rubbish that was the bad end of one of his homemade booby traps. He had died days before his brother, who, all alone, had then succumbed to starvation and dehydration.

The story was a macabre one, and therefore huge. Onlookers gathered to watch more than 100 tons of debris removed from the house, everything from newspapers to musical instruments to an entire car that Langley had moved in piece by piece and then reassembled (as a power generator, some speculate). The Collyers died as broke as their lives and were buried in unmarked graves in Cyprus Hill Cemetery at 833 Jamaica Avenue in Brooklyn. The house, rotting out from under the weight of a lifetime of superaccretion, was torn down before the year was out.

Today, the graves are still unmarked, but the spot where their house in Harlem stood is labeled for posterity. It's now Collyer Brothers Park, a tiny plot of grass and trees the size of the footprint of their house—the size of the footprint of almost their entire lives. Called a pocket park, it's located at its same Fifth Avenue address, between Malcolm X Boulevard and Madison Avenue. The park is adjacent to a row of houses, sharing the wall it shared as a house, in fact. The other three sides are surrounded by a tall, wrought-iron fence. The front gate was open when I visited, but didn't really need to be as you can experience the entire park with just a brief glance. A piece of paper tacked to a glass-fronted announcement board on the gate told the story of the Collyer brothers.

An immediate impulse is to treat their story as a cautionary one, but it's difficult to do so with so many unanswered questions. These were two men more than capable enough and more than funded enough to do solid things, and yet, at some point, for some reason—be it family secrets, private catastrophe, or mirrored mental breakdown—they took a hard left.

It's a mystery. A mystery marked only by a solitary little park.

National Shrine
of North American Martyrs

AURIESVILLE

Y OU KNOW WHAT THIS BOOK and Christianity have in common? An absolute obsession with death.

Deicide, holy wars, a worldwide flood, incorruptibility, blood sacrifice, resurrection, the End Times. Of course, it could be argued that the Christian focus is more on life after death, but when your Choose Your Own Adventure novel can end in eternal wormy fire, then you've still got a pretty macabre set of beliefs there. Basically, the Bible's a much better grimpendium than this one.

The particular bit of grimness at topic here is martyrdom—people who willingly take on death, often accompanied by humiliation and torture, for their beliefs: Joan of Arc in the flames. Peter upside down on a cross. Sebastian bristling with arrows. They died doing what they loved.

North America has had its share of Christian martyrs, as well, and one merely has to travel to the Mohawk Valley of New York to feel what a place "sanctified by the blood of martyrs" feels like.

The small hamlet of Auriesville is just south of the Adirondacks in the village of Fultonville, about 40 miles west of Albany. It is here, secluded among rolling hills and forests of that region, that you can find the National Shrine of North American Martyrs.

The North American Martyrs are eight French Jesuit missionaries tortured and killed at various times in New York and Canada by Iroquois in the mid-1600s. Three of them—Isaac Jogues, René Goupil, and John Lalande—achieved martyrdom in New York on the site of the National Shrine itself, and it is to those three that the site is primarily dedicated.

Back then, the area of Auriesville was a Mohawk village. The Mohawk were an Iroquois tribe and were at war with the Huron people, whom the Jesuits had been evangelizing in Quebec. Two Jesuit missionaries were captured during a supply trip and brought to the Mohawk village.

Father Isaac Jogues and his lay companion René Goupil were enslaved and tortured for weeks. Goupil was killed by a tomahawk to the skull after tracing the sign of the cross on the forehead of a child, but Father Jogues eventually escaped

and went back to France. Despite his experiences in the New World, he felt compelled by the power of Christ and stories of peace efforts between the warring tribes to return to help further the cause. He brought with him John Lalande, another Jesuit layman. The two were ambushed in the village and beheaded, joining Goupil in the North American Martyrs club four years after his death.

In the late 1880s, the land of their demise was purchased by the church and dubbed the Shrine of Our Lady of Martyrs, a name still used alongside National Shrine of North American Martyrs. The shrine became a popular spot of pilgrimage and continued to expand until its present-day holdings of 400 acres on which are some five chapels, a couple of museums, shrines, monuments, walking trails, and even a visitor center and gift shop.

The martyrs were canonized in 1930, and shortly afterward, a resulting surge in visitors to the area encouraged the church leaders to build on its grounds a large church called the Coliseum. This main building on the complex is round in shape and holds 10,000 people when factoring in standing room.

Inside the building, at its center, is a 12-foot-tall altar made to look like a colonial stockade, with vertical pointed logs arranged in a fencelike fashion. This main altar is complemented by statues, relics, and smaller altars and is dominated by a life-size statue of Christ on the cross.

Throughout the pleasantly wooded grounds are more statues and shrines, along with the Stations of the Cross, and visitors are encouraged to wander and meditate. Any random impulse I might have on an ordinary day to meditate gets mistranslated by my brain as, "Turn the TV on," but if any environment is conducive to religious meditation, this one certainly seems it. Few people were there when we visited, and most of them congregated in the Coliseum.

The shrine is on Shrine Road, in Fultonville, which cuts through the property from Noeltner Road on the western side to Route 5S to the north. At the Noeltner Road entrance are signs pointing to a short nature trail that leads down a ravine and to a clearing with further shrines and statues. This is the ravine where Father Jogues searched for the discarded and desecrated bones of his companion Goupil, eventually finding them and burying him thereabouts in an unmarked grave, the location of which is to this day unknown. The path is lined with placards showing excerpts from Father Jogues's harrowing account of the death of his friend and his quest to find and bury the body. It's probably the most affecting site on the entire grounds, even with all the crucified Saviors around.

Although much of the Shrine of the North American Martyrs is centered around death and torture, not all of it is. Apparently, the first Native American to be beatified belonged to the very tribe that killed the Jesuits. Her name was Kateri Tekakwitha, and she was born in 1656, about a decade after the events that resulted in eight new Catholic saints. She had poor health and only lived to the age of 24, but dedicated that short life to Christ. As of the writing of this work, she's just a miracle away from official sainthood. There are just about as many statues and memorials to her on the grounds of the shrine as there are for the martyrs.

They say that death brings peace, and while that's normally meant to be interpreted as peace for the deceased, anybody who's been to a cemetery knows death yields an exterior peace, as well. Some refer to that type of peace as sacred. Others, as creepy. And that's the Shrine of the North American Martyrs. Peaceful, sacred, creepy.

Van Nest Family Gravestone
FLEMING

THE VAN NEST GRAVESTONE in Sand Beach Cemetery in Fleming would be a unique one on its own, even if it didn't have the phrase "All Murdered" inscribed into its time-stained surface.

The marker is basically three gravestones cut into a single large rectangular

slab, which, instead of being laid horizontally or planted vertically into the ground, is angled back at about a 45-degree angle against a pair of stone wedges, like a ramp.

Not surprisingly, the surnames on all three sections are the same. Surprisingly, the date of death is also: March 12, 1846. Nearby, another more conventional gravestone bears the same date.

It was on that night that 41-year-old John Van Nest; his 30-year-old pregnant wife, Sarah; their two-year-old son, George Washington; and Sarah's mother, Phebe Wyckoff, were all brutally stabbed to death in their home in Fleming, a few miles outside of Auburn.

The killer was quickly caught. His name was William Freeman, and he was a 21-year-old Auburn man of mixed descent: his father was a freed slave and his mother was a Native American. Two nonfamily survivors of the rampage were able to identify Freeman, although he wasn't trying very hard to hide his bloody tracks anyway. It wasn't the only strange thing about William Freeman.

The fate of the Van Nests was sealed about five years earlier when Freeman was jailed in the Auburn Correctional Facility (see page 133) at the age of 16 for stealing a horse. It was a crime of which historical records seem to show him innocent. Either way, it was a strange starting point for such an unbalanced outcome as a family massacre, but Freeman was apparently an unbalanced outcome himself.

During his time in jail, Freeman suffered a blow to the head that permanently rendered him partially deaf and affected his mental state. That, on top of a five-year-incubated persecution complex, yielded a night of random violence on a family completely unconnected to the young man and his original jail sentence.

The case, naturally, was huge, with its violent nature, racial undertones, and a relatively uncommon defense tactic taken by Freeman's defense lawyer: not guilty by reason of insanity. That defense lawyer was William Seward, who would eventually go on to become secretary of state under Abraham Lincoln. He's also the guy that got us Alaska.

And although those are some mighty successes, his defense of Freeman couldn't be counted among them. Freeman was determined fit for trial, found guilty, and sentenced to be hanged. However, Seward didn't give up and won a new trial after an appeals court rejected the jury decision that Freeman was fit for trial. However, while waiting for that second trial, Freeman died in jail of tuberculosis.

Seward's defense of Freeman has been published and records the murderer's testimony, a chilling one that reveals he believed he was owed for being wrongly imprisoned for five years, that he chose the Van Nest family only because their light was on that night, and that it would have been the beginning of an even more violent rampage had he not cut his killing hand and had to flee, stealing a pair of horses to do so.

Today, you can still see the tombstones of the victims in the cemetery on the grounds of Sand Beach Church, at 2924 Sand Beach Road in Fleming, right at the top of Owasco Lake. Note that across the road is the large Saint Joseph Cemetery, but the Van Nests lie in the smaller Sand Beach Cemetery behind the church. The single large stone that marks the graves of Van Nest, his wife, and his son is close to the church and easy to spot because of its unique appearance. Phebe Wyckoff's tall, horizontal one is just a few gravestones over.

Usually, causes of death aren't included on headstones. However, in the case of the Van Nests, right under their names, is stated, "All Murdered on the Night of March 12, 1846." Below that is a long, four-stanza epitaph arranged horizontally. It doesn't mention any details about that night, instead starting out, "Mysterious providence indeed / That called us here to lie" and ends with "May we all meet in heaven again / A saved and happy time." It's a good balance. You shouldn't forget the "All Murdered" part, so state it quick and state it prominently, but dwell on the more hopeful bits, wherever you can get those.

Hook & Ladder Company No. 8, Ghostbusters Headquarters

THREE

Horror Movie Filming Locales

NEW YORK CITY might have lost to Chicago as the birthplace of the American horror film, thanks to the 1908 William Selig short, *The Strange Case of Dr. Jekyll and Mr. Hyde,* but New York was at least its childhood home. It was in 1910 at Edison Studios, located at the intersection of Decatur Avenue and Oliver Place in the Bronx, that the 16-minute *Frankenstein* was filmed. Ten years later, on an Astoria Studios soundstage in Long Island, what was possibly America's first feature-length horror film was made, which was again based on the Robert Louis Stevenson story. This time, its title was shortened to *Dr. Jekyll and Mr. Hyde,* and it starred John Barrymore as both titular characters. Sure, the original stories were British, but they became some of the first shambling steps of American horror cinema. And New York has been darkening both our screens and our nightmares with its movies ever since.

In fact, many non–New Yorkers have only experienced the state, and more specifically the city, through the movies that have been filmed here. In the case of horror fans, that means developing a pretty twisted view of the place.

After all, New York City is the spot in cinema where the child of Satan was born . . . where the world almost ended, due to a woman with a flat top and a giant marshmallow man ("Nice thinkin,' Ray") . . . where behemoths of every species are attracted to its landmarks, either to climb them or crush them . . . where ghost wolves roam its parks and ruins, vampires fit in perfectly with its night life, mutants hide in its sewers, and every neighborhood has its own serial killer like some kind of perverted mascot.

Of course, so many horror films have been filmed in New York, and especially in the focal point that is New York City, that, with the limited space of the book and the unlimited boundaries of my laziness, I had to narrow the number down. To that end, I used a formula developed by a hermitic Russian mathematician from the 16th century who liked to pickle and eat Karakurt spiders and sleep on a pillow case stuffed with rotting pears. Basically, I threw out any horror movie that just uses New York City for establishing shots. You know, helicopter footage of the Brooklyn Bridge or the city skyline, ferry shots of the Statue of Liberty, Times Square drive-bys. I also omitted movies that utilize their locations generically—anonymous gritty street here, random bit of sunny park there.

Then, to maximize the variety of locations in this section, I heavily weighted any movie that filmed in places outside of New York City, as well any film that creatively used its New York locales, featured a unique locale, or heavily focused on one locale in particular. I also tried to include a wide variety of horror movies, both by decade of release and by featured terrors, including serial killers, ghosts, mutants, monsters, giants, gremlins, zombies, demons, and, um, severed animated heads. I really tried to get *Vampire in Brooklyn* in here, as well, but that just didn't work out.

Finally, I ignored the formula at times and threw in some wild left turns in an attempt to keep it interesting.

So, after all that, what I've come up with is a completely arbitrary selection of close to 30 horror movies for this section. Heck, some aren't even technically horror. And some shouldn't even be watched, even if you need to for a book project.

Nevertheless, there are some great movies herein with sites definitely worth visiting, some good ones with sites worth reading about, and a smattering of questionable calls on my part.

People often use New York as a microcosm of the entire world. If that's an accurate usage of the state and its largest city, and if its horror movies are any indication, then the world is certainly a horrifying place.

King Kong (1933)
MANHATTAN

THE FIRST WHITE MAN to see a live adult gorilla was the French-American explorer Paul du Chaillu, during a West Africa expedition in the late 1850s. Before that time, the Western world had only bones and rumors. The discovery of this amazing creature enabled important insights into the zoological and evolutionary sciences. I'm pretty sure, anyway. Science always says that about everything it discovers. Most significantly, though, in 1933, it gave us *King Kong*. Of course, it also gave us *Congo* in 1995. Progress must take a few steps backward every once in a while to continue forward.

We're all privileged to eat popcorn in a movie era of advanced puppetry, costuming, and CGI, yet rarely do these often mind-boggling special effects ever reach the compelling heights that a 2-foot-tall articulated metal armature covered in rabbit fur did 80 years ago. Mostly, this is due to the genius of stop-motion animator Willis H. O'Brien. However, it can also be traced to the model's use in one of the most iconic stories in the history of cinema, one that multiple sequels and two remakes cannot dull, one that has become synonymous with New York City's signature skyscraper, the Empire State Building.

King Kong is one of those rare anti–love stories in a medium where a romance subplot is one of the minimum requirements to get a project green-lit. You know the story of the colossal ape like Fay Wray knows the back of its hand, but since your knowing the story won't fill up this entry page for me, here's a synopsis nevertheless.

Kong is a monster-size gorilla who lives out a happy existence of adoration, worship, and sacrifice from the local natives on his home of Skull Island. That is, until Ann Darrow (Fay Wray) enters the jungles of his home and the cockles of his heart. The royal primate falls so hard in love with this vixen from another world and another species that he wrestles dinosaurs and other large, vicious beasts to keep her safe. Eventually, though, she is rescued from Kong's all-consuming passion.

However, Kong, in the anguished throes of a love that we've dedicated entire song genres to follows her to the beach, where he is immediately gas bombed and captured, taken to New York City, and put on display. Of course, Kong escapes and finds the girl of his heart, only to have biplanes shoot machine gun ammo through that same heart, knocking him off the Empire State Building, where he dies thousands of miles away from his home amid people who treat him as a monster. The epitaph for this beguiled creature is the final line of the movie, spoken by his captor (a director who, by the way, hated putting girls in his movies), "Beauty killed the beast." For Kong, love (and a fall from a skyscraper) ruined his life.

And to this day, the Empire State Building stands as a gravestone for this magnificent monster.

Admittedly, it seems like a bit of a cheat to count the Empire State Building as a filming location for the movie. After all, basically the entire movie was filmed in California, and the Empire State Building was only featured in establishing shots or in a scale-model version on O'Brien's worktable. However, what makes the Empire State Building more relevant to this topic is that to this day the skyscraper treats the big ape as its mascot.

One of the most visited tourist attractions in the city and visible for miles in every direction from its location at 350 Fifth Avenue, the Empire State Building is 102 stories tall and more than 80 years old. On the way up, which involves ascending at least one escalator, walking through various roped-off hallways, and taking multiple elevators, the only clue about its monster movie past is a large, lighted, two-dimensional exhibit prominently placed on one of the upper floors, featuring posters and images from the movie underneath the heading "King Kong: Eighth Wonder of the World."

However, after marveling at the city from the vantage point of a gargantuan primate, you eventually descend, a course that naturally takes you through the gift shop on the 80th floor. Here, you'll see about 3,000 square feet of *Kong* memorabilia. It was like being at a zoo gift shop. There were *Kong*-themed T-shirts and posters and mugs and stuffed animals of various sizes. Little statuettes and snow globes and key chains and magnets. We were there close to Christmas, so the merchandise also included plush Kongs in Santa hats and statuettes of giant

Santa Clauses scaling the exterior of the building. Pretty much everything except for swatches of hair from the beast's hide.

And while I'm not much of a gift-shop souvenir guy myself, I couldn't help but take home an overpriced plush Kong of my own. Hail to the King.

The Beast from 20,000 Fathoms (1953)
MANHATTAN, BROOKLYN

A WAKENED FROM A 100-MILLION-YEAR icy slumber by an atomic bomb alarm clock, a giant reptile wreaks destruction on one of the world's largest cities. And it's not Godzilla.

But this monster is the inspiration for Godzilla, as well as every other Atomic Age giant monster that made the 1950s such a hard decade in which to get urban property insurance.

Basically doing what *King Kong* somehow didn't do 20 years earlier, the 1953 *The Beast from 20,000 Fathoms* unleashed the giant monster phase of cinema. I say that, but the 1950s monster movie craze is still often attributed to *King Kong*, because the movie was rereleased in 1952. However, it was the monkey's fourth theatrical release, so *Beast* seems to have been the actual catalyst. The research is preliminary, though, as scientists are still running tests.

Regardless of the cause, the end result was that every town and every city was besieged by giant ants and giant scorpions and giant octopuses and giant crabs and giant spiders and giant leeches and giant lizards. Even giant humans and, on one particularly unnerving occasion, giant shrews.

However, *Beast* is even more notable for the two Rays who are associated with the picture. The film is ostensibly based on a Ray Bradbury short story (the script was written before a connection with Bradbury's story was made) and features—no, stars—fantastic stop-motion creature animation from Ray Harryhausen.

Besides its giant lizard's tromping and chomping stuff, the movie is about a nuclear researcher who attempts to convince people that he saw a dinosaur in the Arctic during a bomb test, until he doesn't have to convince them anymore because being bitten in two and swallowed by the creature is pretty conclusive evidence in any court of law. They eventually discover that it's a 50-ton, 1,000 foot-long rhedosaurus, a fictional dinosaur you won't find in any natural history textbook, although knowing its name does little more than give victims something specific to scream when it picks up their car in its jaws and tosses it.

As in most of the movies in the genre, the dialogue is often bad and/or badly delivered. However, the rhedosaurus itself has aged remarkably well, thanks to the mastery of Harryhausen. In fact, this stop-motion dinosaur acts more real than much of today's cutting-edge CGI and most of our famous actors.

As to filming locations, because it was stop-motion, they filmed most of the New York City scenes (the ones that weren't stock footage, at least) on a model on a table top in Harryhausen's garage, but I included the film in this section because I really wanted to get both Rays in this book.

Just based on landmarks in the movie, you can pretty much trace the New York City route that the monster took in the model of the city and the frightened masses running from it took in the real thing. Most of its terrorizing occurs in lower Manhattan on Nassau and Wall Streets. Rhedosaurus Road, from here on out.

Eventually, though, the 20,000-fathom beast arrives at Coney Island in Brooklyn, where sharpshooter Corporal Stone (Lee Van Cleef) fires a radioactive isotope into it from the top of a roller coaster, for a pretty cool ending. Nothing like the image of a giant lizard corpse surrounded by a demolished roller coaster to throw your end credits over.

The Coney Island climax was actually filmed in Long Beach, California, but a model was made of the famous Coney Island Cyclone, located in Astroland, which still stands today, 60 years later, at the intersection of Surf Avenue and West 10th Street, despite the fact that Astroland was closed down a few years ago. These days, the working coaster is an official New York City landmark, as well as listed in the National Register of Historic Places. After all, this is where a dinosaur was taken down. Not many landmarks on the planet can claim that.

The Brain That Wouldn't Die (1962)
TARRYTOWN

SOMETIMES THE ONLY WAY TO GET a head in the world is to suffer a horrendous automobile accident that decapitates your fiancée. I have no segue between that sentence and the rest of this entry.

In the 1962 *The Brain That Wouldn't Die* a brilliant surgeon by the name of Dr. Bill Cortner is obsessed with the possibilities of transplantation and impatient with the plodding ethics of medicine. He'd rather steal body parts to animate than submit research to peer-reviewed journals. Usually, this personality trait would be endearing, as we all love a maverick, but that doesn't apply when it comes to medicine and science. The Fonz, after all, could never unleash a monster.

Of course, this movie tries to be a bit more, uh, cerebral, than just a monster smash flick, although in addition to the severed-head star, it does keep a more typical monster in its back pocket for the awkward climax. *Awkward*'s a pretty good descriptor for this movie, in general, actually, although it does alternate between that and harrowing at times. Well, more accurately, it's awkward punctuated by one or two harrowing scenes.

My favorite bit of awkwardness might be the ickier-than-a-living-severed-head moment when Cortner's fiancée, Jan, tells her future father-in-law, "I can promise you one thing . . . your grandchildren won't be test-tube babies." A statement that has added irony when she later loses her ovaries . . . and the rest of her body.

And she does that in a vicious car accident that is set up by about 10 minutes of extremely reckless POV car footage. After the wreck, Cortner is only able to

save Jan's head, which he pulls from the fiery wreckage over the still twitching arm of his fiancée and wraps in his sport coat—which is a use case for the article of clothing that is shamefully overlooked by garment marketers. Cortner then sits the severed head in a pan of solution and connects it to a vicelike apparatus. Jan awakes to find out she's no more than a pretty face to him now and immediately hates him for this. After all, as much as we all want to live, sometimes not dying is not all that great.

In some ways, *The Brain That Wouldn't Die* is a movie about male fantasy fulfillment, because while Jan's head sits and seethes, Cortner's on the prowl for her new body. It's kind of perfect: you fall in love with the girl for who she is, but then you get to pick her body . . . how tall she is, her bust size, whether she has an innie or an outie.

So of course, the first thing he does is visit a badly faked Moulin Rouge, which is one long scene of awkward foreplay that ends in a stripper fight. He also visits a swimsuit contest, which is the first time I've ever seen one of those so integral to a movie plot before. All in all, this is a film that turns the phrase "checking out her body" on its head. It also turns the phrase "on its head" on its head.

Anyway, a few philosophical arguments with Jan's severed head later, the film comes to its awkward climax, which involves the aforementioned monster, a failed experiment that Cortner and his assistant have locked in another room all this time and which telepathically teams up with Jan's head ("I'm only a head, and you're whatever you are. But together we're strong").

The title of the film actual misses its nomers a bit; actually, in a couple of ways. It's not so much about a brain that wouldn't die, as it's about a brain that wasn't allowed to die. Also, it's more about a head than a brain, and the original *The Head that Wouldn't Die* title can still be seen in the ending credits.

As to its filming locations, the movie was lensed predominantly in the New York City suburb of Tarrytown, adjacent to the town of Sleepy Hollow. However, only a few exterior shots were featured amid all the interior acts, including a couple of residential scenes and the anonymous patch of grass that was the inciting crash scene.

Most centrally used was the vacation house that Cortner's family owns, which is where he conducted his secret experiments and to where he was . . . headed . . . when the accident occurred. The single brief and partial shot of it used in the movie reveals it to be more castle than vacation house.

You'd think being a castle or castlelike mansion would make it pretty easy to track down in real life, but turns out that area of the Hudson Valley is absolutely medieval with castles.

As a result, I couldn't find this on my own recognizance and turned to Jim Logan, a local historian whose purview includes Sleepy Hollow Cemetery (see the Washington Irving entry in "Legends and Personalities of the Macabre"). Jim's someone with whom I've been glad to keep up since the first time I ever visited the Sleepy Hollow area years ago. It took him and his crack network of Hudson Valley experts just a couple of days and a couple of freeze frames to dig up not only the name and location of the castle, but the fact that it burned down, as well as the existence of an interesting artifact that allowed me to salvage this entry.

The small bit of edifice used briefly in the movie was known as Edgemont, and it was the 22-room home of Julian F. Detmer, a wealthy textile merchant who died only a few years before a bunch of people with a severed head prop and a film camera ran across his property. The estate was on Benedict Avenue. In 1971 it was damaged by fire, and then just a few years later it was later torn down completely to make room for the Edgemont Condominiums complex.

However, at least one item from the house was saved: the Detmer Panel. This massive, rectangular, wall-sized oak carving of a coat of arms has been on display in the Children's Section of the Warner Library at 121 North Broadway in

Tarrytown since 1979. It was originally set over a mantel in Detmer's living room and is a copy of the lion-and-unicorn coat of arms of King James I. I don't even want to edit this entry to see how we've arrived at ancient British royalty from a living severed head.

Anyway, the fact that the film featured a three-second shot of the exterior of a mansion that doesn't exist anymore really should have disqualified it from inclusion in this book, but I really wanted to spend some time with this movie. You probably shouldn't, though.

Just kidding. Watch it.

Rosemary's Baby (1968)
MANHATTAN

MOVIE MONSTERS like to stake out territories. Of the New York ones in this section of the book, you'll find a giant ape claiming the Empire State Building, a flying Aztec god nesting in the Chrysler tower, and a 100-million-year-old dinosaur making a stand at a Coney Island roller coaster. Every landmark should have a patron monster. Here, we have a famous building on the edge of Central Park that is the domain of the Devil himself.

The innocuously titled 1968 film *Rosemary's Baby* is frequently touted as among the best in the horror genre due to its well-crafted tension, its patience of plot, and its high level of creepiness. Based on a book by Ira Levin and directed by Roman Polanski, the film stars Mia Farrow and John Cassavetes as a young couple who move into a Manhattan building called the Bramford. There, they make a few senior citizen friends and have a baby, all while enduring Satan rape, old people nudity, and Vidal Sassoon haircuts.

The story centers mostly around Rosemary herself, as, over the course of her pregnancy, she becomes more and more convinced that everybody she knows is a Satan-worshipping witch and that, for some reason, they are after her baby. I'd wager it's probably in the top ten worst pregnancy side effects a woman can have.

Interestingly, this horror classic was produced by William Castle, the notorious B-movie director and general grand gimmicksman behind such films as *House on Haunted Hill* (1959), *The Tingler* (1959), and *13 Ghosts* (1960). He and his

trademark cigar even make a cameo in the movie, genially waiting his turn at a phone booth while the pregnant and panicked Rosemary makes a desperate call to a doctor to see whether modern medicine has yet invented a treatment for demonic manipulation.

Most of the movie takes place in the Bramford (nicknamed "the Black Bramford" because of certain unsavory happenings in its past), which is actually the distinctive 10-story Dakota apartment building at 1 West 72nd Street, on the western edge of Central Park. Built in the 1880s during a time when Manhattan had less of its first syllable about it, the lavishly decorated complex now seems shouldered out by all the high-rises surrounding it.

When I visited, a handful of other people were taking pictures of the building, as well. However, it was probably not because of its historical significance as the location of the advent of the Antichrist. For, even though this 130-year-old building is not overrun by witch covens in real life, it is infamous for being the site of John Lennon's assassination in 1980. He had been living at the Dakota at that time and was shot right at the entrance of the building (see "Infamous Crimes, Killers, and Tragedies").

However, *Rosemary's Baby* is still the second reason you'd point to it while strolling along the edge of the park. After all, this film is a classic of the genre that achieved mainstream success by skillfully unnerving its audience, not to mention popularizing the vodka blush (as of this writing, 40-odd years after the movie's debut, the number one search result for that drink is a Church of Satan page describing its less-than-sinister ingredients). Oh, and immortalizing the fashions and interior design philosophies of the late 1960s. Satan help us.

Dark Shadows Movies (1970/1971)
TARRYTOWN, SLEEPY HOLLOW

WE'VE ALWAYS KNOWN that monsters make for great story villains and metaphors, and over the years we've also learned that they make great cereal mascots and sitcom characters. Still, even with all that, who would have thought that they'd make great soap opera stars?

Apparently, the creators of *Dark Shadows*. In 1966, Dan Curtis and crew darkened daytime television with the story of the wealthy but decaying Collins family of Maine. Going thick with the gothic, the sudsy melodrama was also wormy with monsters . . . werewolves, ghosts, vampires, all of evil's greatest hits. The atmospheric show was popular enough to run more than 1,200 episodes over the course of five seasons, including twice being stretched to fit the big screen. Actually, make that three times, as during the editing phase of this book, the Collins family found themselves on the big screen again in a version directed by Tim Burton and starring Johnny Depp.

The first time, though, was in 1970. Titled *House of Dark Shadows*, it featured various stars of the television series, including Joan Bennett as the Collins matriarch Elizabeth Collins Stoddard and Jonathan Frid as Barnabas Collins, who reprised their roles from the television series while others took on brand-new ones according to the general practice of actor recycling that the show was known for.

Although the series was a mad monster party, the first movie only invited its resident vampire, Barnabas Collins, who just happened to be the show's most popular character. In this story, adapted and altered from his series story arc, Barnabas is accidentally released from imprisonment in a chain-wrapped coffin after hundreds of years of trying to decide whether he could detect a difference between the back of his eyelids and the underside of the coffin lid. Free to stretch his wings and cape, Barnabas starts making red holes in people until he's offered the opportunity to be cured of his vampirism, so that he can learn why everybody seems so obsessed with beach vacations.

The show managed to maintain the creepy atmosphere of its source material, which is most of the reason to watch a *Dark Shadows* project in the first place, and a sequel was called for. In fact, almost before the projectors showing the first one had stopped spinning, the creators were off onto another film.

In 1971, just after the series itself had ceased running, *Night of Dark Shadows* was released, featuring other characters and actors from the *Dark Shadows* universe.

This time around, the movie is a ghost/past-life possession story, in which husband and wife Quentin and Tracy Collins, played by David Selby and Kate Jackson, find themselves in, well, possession of Collinwood, the family estate, sometime after the death of Elizabeth Collins Stoddard.

Once there, Quentin finds himself having strange visions about another life that involves a blond woman, a hanging body, and himself with sideburns that gradually seem to be taking him over, driving him mad and making him a danger to his wife and friends. Overall, the film is more modern than its predecessor, but retains the general *Dark Shadows* ambiance.

And much of that, as is the case with *House of Dark Shadows* as well, can be attributed to its filming location.

The one character that stays the same in both movies is Collinwood itself. In the series, the exterior of the Maine estate that was Collinwood was a Newport, Rhode Island, mansion. However, for the movies, a New York site was used, the Lyndhurst mansion, to tower over all the supernatural soapery.

The 170-year-old mansion at 635 South Broadway in the Hudson Valley village of Tarrytown is much more castlelike than is its television counterpart, and unlike that counterpart, was used for interior scenes, as well.

Lyndhurst was built for a New York politico named William Paulding Jr., who, among other public and military offices, served as a U.S. representative for New York and mayor of New York City. The Gothic Revival edifice also eventually became the home of businessman George Merritt (who named the property after its linden trees) and then railroad tycoon Jay Gould.

Switching back from history to horror, the *Dark Shadows* movies were filmed all over the 67-acre grounds of Lyndhurst, even making use of outbuildings such as the derelict greenhouse and swimming pool building. Heck, the mansion was so important to the story that its image was used on the posters for both movies, and it was even given top billing. The Lyndhurst mansion was acknowledged by name in the blood-red opening credits of the first movie.

Today, it's still a gorgeous and Gothic-looking mansion and estate that retains most of the outbuildings used in the filming, with the most striking example of that being the nearby greenhouse. You can tour the mansion and walk the grounds, which feature a great view of the Hudson River and are especially elegant in autumn, and generally just pretend to be the last scion of a family cursed by its monsters.

Another interesting location, although it was only used in *House of Dark Shadows*, is the family mausoleum from which Barnabas is freed. For this unholy site, the creative team ventured just down the road to 540 North Broadway in adjacent Sleepy Hollow, home of the Headless Horseman (see the Washington Irving entry in "Legends and Personalities of the Macabre").

At that address is Sleepy Hollow Cemetery, where Barnabas's large, gray stone mausoleum can be found inside just beyond Washington Irving's well-marked plot. In real life (and death), the mausoleum is actually the cemetery's receiving vault, a temporary resting place for bodies before they reach their finale. For the movie, they covered up the "1900" that adorns its apex with the Collins family surname and then stuck a pair of small statues above the entrance for set dressing.

The Munsters and the Addams family might have made being a family of monsters look like a real good time, especially compared to the dreary old dysfunctional Collins family, but you can't visit their houses in real life. Collinwood is an amazing place to visit, whether you're a fan of the *Dark Shadows* movies or not.

Silent Night, Bloody Night (1974)
OYSTER BAY

H ORROR DOESN'T GET A CHRISTMAS BREAK. Heck, judging by Charles Dickens, it can actually reach its peak paired with curved peppermints and humanoid gingerbread. Of course, although the great novelist showed us how to do it with literature, we haven't quite done it in the horror movie genre yet. Sure, it's been tried. Horror movies have festooned their sets in red blood, green bile, and white bone, and attempted to set their horrors against a backdrop of indoor evergreens and sooty stockings as some sort of dissonance, the way they'll often use a cheery song or children's rhyme over a scene of horrendous brutality.

Too often, it's used as a gimmick, though—you know, psycho Santas and snowmen and whatnot. However, you'll find no killer Kringles in the 1974 *Silent Night, Bloody Night*. Actually, the Christmas backdrop of this low-budget movie is so wilted and drab it's easy to forget the time of year.

Some of that murkiness might be because it's hard to find a decent transfer of the movie to watch. Years ago, the movie slipped into the public domain, so anybody can haphazardly burn it onto a disc and sell it. Of course, with movies about the deranged, having too polished a print can be a bit of a distraction. Sometimes, you just want to believe that everybody who's making the movie is just as deranged as its story. Plus, the right kind of bad quality can be just plain creepy for a film.

The movie tells the story of the Butler mansion, a family homestead and ex-asylum that is being sold after decades of abandonment. The FOR SALE sign staked into the lawn unearths quite a few secrets, secrets straight out of the skeleton-crowded closets of both the Butler family and the town itself, secrets with clues that might only be held by the escaped lunatic who is murdering anybody who so much as talks about the property.

Portrayed by a wordless (and later handless) John Carradine and a handful of actors and actresses from Andy Warhol's casting troupe, the characters are about as murky as the print. In fact, if the acting is any indication, the entire cast was forced in front of the camera by a lunatic filmmaker with one hand on a knife and the other on a focus knob.

Still, somehow the director managed to achieve some intensely eerie scenes. It's the kind of movie you might laugh at during high noon and shrink from at midnight.

Silent Night, Bloody Night is set in New England but was filmed across the Long Island Sound, in the coastal town of Oyster Bay. Naturally, there's only one real filming location of interest here, the Butler mansion itself, the vortex of all the spooky and disturbing shenanigans that take place throughout the story.

The particular mansion used in the movie is in the Mill Neck area of Long Island's Gold Coast, on a 19th-century estate called The Cliffs, at 1026 West Shore Road, just south of where it intersects with Cleft Road.

The private estate is much better kept these days. A pair of security gates face the road and Oyster Bay Harbor just a few feet further. Only the upper floor of the building, with its distinctly sharp gables, can be seen from the road through the trees that surround the property and the large hill in front of it. The view from Google Earth reveals the shape of the house, some outbuildings, a garden area, and a swimming pool. If you take Cleft Road during winter, you can just make out the profile of the mansion through the leafless trees where it sits up on a hill.

I'm not sure whether the owners celebrate Christmas there, but if they do, here's wishing them peace on Earth, and good will toward madmen.

The Sentinel (1977)
BROOKLYN

WHEN LOOKING FOR AN APARTMENT in New York City, there are a few things to keep in mind. One, hiring a professional real estate broker could mean the difference between getting a great apartment and a mediocre one. Two, it's an extremely competitive market, so be sure to have all your paperwork in order so that you can immediately lock down a place when you're ready to buy. Three, and this is where hiring the real estate broker really pays off, don't rent one on the entrance to hell.

In the 1977 *The Sentinel,* Alison Parker, played by TV regular Cristina Raines, seems to have it pretty good. She's a beautiful model in a committed relationship with a wealthy, handsome lawyer (Chris Sarandon) who wants to marry her. Sure, she has some past baggage that she's dealing with, but who doesn't in a horror movie. Naturally, now that she's found herself in a great situation, she makes the logical decision to randomly exert her independence and get her own place.

She finds an unbelievably good deal on an unbelievably lavish flat in an ivy-covered brownstone apartment building in Brooklyn Heights. In real life, such a deal would make you suspicious of hidden vermin infestation or underemphasized flood plains. In horror movies, of course, you're risking so much more.

Eventually, strange noises, phantom neighbors, and the blind priest that lives above her unit begin to unnerve her. To the film's credit, she's not just dealing with demons or Satanists in that post-*Exorcist,* post–*Rosemary's Baby* world of the late 1970s, but instead with the diseased forms of the lascivious and murderous dead, many of whom were played by people with actual physical malformations. At one point she even attends a get-together with eight dead murderers. It's a birthday party. For a cat.

The film ends up being part horror movie, part detective movie, and part orgy. It does have some worthwhile creep scenes and a bit of intrigue, but the real joy of watching *The Sentinel* these days is for all the character roles.

For instance, Jeff Goldblum has a tiny recurring role as a photographer, Richard Dreyfuss appears in an easily missed and uncredited cameo, Ava Gardner plays a mere Realtor, and Christopher Walken has an almost silent role as a detective sidekick named Rizzo, although the camera does seem to linger incongruously on him in close-up a lot, as if it knew his future.

In addition, Burgess Meredith has a great little role as one of the neighbors, William Hickey plays a lock picker, Tom Berenger pops up briefly, Jerry Orbach and Eli Wallach are present and accounted for, Jose Ferrer and horror great John Carradine portray priests, and Beverly D'Angelo has a role that will make it hard for you to make eye contact with her the next time you watch *National Lampoon's Christmas Vacation*.

Overall, with all those familiar faces, *The Sentinel* is like a homecoming for all the movies you've ever seen . . . as long as you're homecomings usually feature an abundance of nontitillating nudity and creepy afterlives.

At the end of the story, the apartment building gets demolished and is replaced with a more modern-looking gate to hell. But in real life, the original still stands. Turns out, it really is in the wealthy neighborhood of Brooklyn Heights. The address is 10 Montague Terrace, and the windows of the distinc-

tive-looking building face out on the dead end of Remsen Street, right above the Brooklyn-Queens Expressway and offering a view of the Statue of Liberty in the distance.

These days, all the ivy that gave the building a lot of its character is gone, I didn't see any silhouettes of priests in the top-floor window, and none of the minor passersby in the street around me was a famous movie star; but, on the other hand, the naked, deformed dead weren't trying to make me kill myself, either.

He Knows You're Alone (1980)
STATEN ISLAND

THE HORROR MOVIE GENRE is a regularly disparaged one and, more often than not, it's for reasons that are its own fault. Still, without it, the film universe would be devoid of many of its favorite actors and actresses who might otherwise have never seen the light of a spotlight. Would Jennifer Aniston have been so lucky if she hadn't gotten her shot on *Leprechaun?* Without *Critters 3*, Leonardo DiCaprio might just have been a television actor. *A Nightmare on Elm Street* unleashed both Freddy Krueger and Johnny Depp on an unsuspecting world. And the 1980 slasher flick *He Knows You're Alone*? Well, that gave us Tom Hanks.

Unfortunately, it didn't give us much else.

This movie's name is one of those "tested well" titles that has nothing to do with its plot. Hardly anybody is ever alone in this film. However, that's the least of its faults. After starting out with a rather clever scene that has since been copied elsewhere, most famously in Wes Craven's *Scream 2,* it ends up being a dull, lifeless slasher right at the beginning of the dull lifeless slasher phase of horror movies that *Halloween* inspired.

In this movie, it's not babysitters that the killer hates, but brides. It's never explained why. He just thinks that blushing brides are just not, I don't know, red enough, I guess. Something borrowed something blue, something bloody something cruel. So he kills them before they get married, and anybody who is helping them get married.

Strangely, the killer's face is shown pretty much from the beginning of the movie. Some of the death scenes are even inverted from the usual formula,

which, granted wasn't a usual formula yet, and we're given the victim's perspective instead of the conventional killer's perspective. Also strange for the genre, this is a no-gore movie, other than maybe a head in an aquarium. Which I guess is gore. I'm a bit jaded. (Just check out the table of contents for this section.)

The film was shot in a quick and dirty 15 days on Staten Island, with a low budget and plenty of volunteer help from friends. To find most of its locales, you merely have to walk New Dorp Lane.

Starting at the intersection of New Dorp and Third Street, just southeast of High Rock Park, where the jogging scene was filmed (and where we first see Tom Hanks in the movie), is Our Lady Queen of Peace Catholic Church. It was here that Amy, the main bride-and-victim-to-be, goes to deal with one or two of her cold feet regarding marriage.

Continuing down the road in a southeasterly direction, you'll next encounter Miss Rosemary's Dance Studio at 5 New Dorp Plaza. It was here that Amy and her friends show off what they look like in leotards and then, outside, run into the professor with whom one of Amy's friends is having an affair. It's a less awkward encounter than the previous dance studio scene, actually.

Next, at 314, is Sedutto's Happiness House, an ice-cream parlor where we get to see the killer practice his now-you-see-me-now-you-don't trick and where we meet Amy's ex, a morgue attendant who somehow couldn't parlay that august profession into being the love of Amy's life.

After that, at 365, is Theresa's Bridal. Back when the movie was filmed it was called Renaissance Fashions, and it was here that Amy gets fitted for her wedding dress by a balding, cigar-smoking guy named Ralph—"Think of me as your father." If her father died horribly in the back room of a bridal shop, then that should be easy for her to do.

The last location on this strip is the theater exterior from the opening scene. It's found near the intersection of Hylan Boulevard and New Dorp, at 107 Mill Road. Back then it was the Fox Theatre. These days, it's a United Artists. The exterior was only shown briefly, though, and is now, of course, unrecognizable. The much more substantial interiors were filmed at the then 50-year-old and then decrepit Saint George Theater at 25 Hyatt Street, which has since been refurbished into a posh live venue.

Tom Hanks has basically one scene, at the now defunct and now apartments South Beach Amusement Park, east of New Dorp Lane. The arcade featured in the same scene was nearby at 300 Sand Lane. It lasted longer than the amusement park, but was still shuttered a few years ago and remains abandoned (and graffitied) today. Nobody thought to spray-paint, "Tom Hanks wuz here" on it, though, and I left my cans at home, unfortunately.

It was at these locations that Tom Hanks, with the best hairdo of his life, philosophized about Hitchcock's *Psycho* and fear, rode a Scrambler, and used backgammon as a euphemism for sex. Apparently, he was supposed to have a death scene in the movie, but it was never filmed, which means he missed out on what an arrow through the throat in *Friday the 13th* did for Kevin Bacon's career. Hanks's storyline just ends abruptly, as if he suddenly got cast in a sitcom where two men dress up as women so as to get the apartment they want.

The morgue scenes at the end of the film were shot at Seaview Hospital at 460 Brielle Avenue, which is famous for its history as a tuberculosis and psychiatric hospital, as well as for the old, abandoned buildings on its property.

I couldn't find the location for the main house in the film, the one where Amy lived and where we get treated to the head in the aquarium. Usually I'd just brush my failure under the rug and not even mention it, but for some reason I can't let this omission go. The place was a large, building with a two-story wraparound porch and a back turret room with a conical roof. If you happen to know the address, do me a favor and jot it down in this blank for me _____. Thanks.

Basically, *He Knows You're Alone* works less as a horror film and more as a Staten Island time capsule, one that we only dig up because of the fact that one of the most popular actors in recent decades got his start there.

Fear No Evil (1981)

ROCHESTER, ALEXANDRIA BAY

DEATH BY DODGEBALL; Satan leading an army of zombies; a guy growing breasts; and a soundtrack that features the Talking Heads, Sex Pistols, and Ramones. I'm surprised this film isn't more notorious and/or loved in horror movie circles.

The 1981 film *Fear No Evil* is a strange one for a number of reasons that have to do with plot and filming specifics, but beyond such things as the use of actual dead dogs as props and the inclusion of more male nudity than I've seen in my entire life (counting every time I've undressed in the past three decades or so) is its overall sense of schizophrenia, to continue the traditional misuse of that term.

For instance, it's an obviously independent and amateurish movie that somehow manages to live up to the ambitiousness of its story and feature solid production value. Second, it's as if two different films were spliced together, a film about teenage life on the edge of the 1980s and another about a cosmic battle between Lucifer and a trio of archangels. I mean, screen time is divvied up between a 60-year-old woman who likes to garden and battle the forces of evil, and a 17-year-old boy in a leather jacket who bullies other boys by kissing them in the shower, for goodness' sake.

Frank LaLoggia was only in his mid- to late twenties at the time that he wrote and directed this, the first feature film of his career. Later, at the end of that decade, he would go on to garner fame for his 1988 movie *Lady in White* (which I cover on page 191).

Far more interesting than the

movie, though, is its central filming location, which is why I've double-dipped into LaLoggia's film oeuvre for this book: It gave me a tax-deductible excuse to visit a 100-year-old island castle.

LaLoggia is from Rochester, and he shot a good portion of the film in that area, including at Spry Middle School at 119 South Avenue in Webster. However, most of the movie was shot just around the bend of Lake Ontario, in the Thousand Islands Region, an archipelago of islands forming a boundary between the United States and Canada. Filming locations here include a couple of churches in the town of Clayton, Depauville United Methodist Church at 324 John Street and Christ Episcopal Church at 412 Hugunin Street, as well as the most important location, out in the middle of Alexandria Bay on Heart Island.

It's on that tiny island where the central and most atmospheric scenes of *Fear No Evil* were shot, in Boldt Castle.

Boldt Castle was originally intended as a monument to love, but ended up being one to tragedy. It was built as an elaborate testament of devotion for his wife by millionaire George Boldt, manager of the Waldorf-Astoria Hotel in New York City. Work began in 1900 on what would become a six-story, 120-room castle complete with outbuildings worth living in themselves.

However, in 1904, Boldt's wife died, and he stopped all construction on the massive edifice. It was left to ruin until 1977, when the Thousand Islands Bridge Authority took it over and turned it into a tourist destination.

We found the easiest way to get there was to buy tickets in advance on the Internet, drive to Boldt Castle's yacht house at 22252 Boat House Road on Wellesley Island, and then take the short shuttle ferry from there. We were there in the summer and found the island itself to be pretty crowded, although it's a big enough mansion and island that the crowds didn't matter too much. You're free to wander through the many rooms of the castle on your own, from its basement to its balconies. Some of the rooms are unfinished, while others are extravagantly appointed. As you wander the grounds, you'll see Alster Tower, a medieval-looking outbuilding that was used heavily in the film. The large stone entry arch for the island, topped by a pair of deer statues, bookended the movie. Also keep an eye out for the large stone fountain with its demon-head spigot, which made a cameo.

So cringe at the dead dogs, cringe at the skill level of the locals who acted in the film, cringe at the excessive male nudity . . . but marvel at the overall strangeness of *Fear No Evil*, as well as the majesty of Boldt Castle itself.

Wolfen (1981)
MANHATTAN, BRONX

H EY, PSST . . . wanna see Gregory Hines get mauled by a ghost wolf? Or Native Americans dance atop the bridge tower of the Brooklyn Bridge? Or South Bronx back when it looked postapocalyptic? The 1981 film *Wolfen* is your window into all of that. And it's not a werewolf movie.

Also starring Albert Finney and Edward James Olmos and based on a book by Whitley Strieber, *Wolfen* tells the tale of a series of vicious murders of seemingly unrelated victims and of the alcoholic ex-cop, hip coroner, cute psychiatrist, and beyond-state-of-the-art security corporation that try to solve the murder.

Of course, "solving the murder" takes on whole different connotations when the killer isn't a mugger or a terrorist or a psycho. When it's instead a pack of hyperintelligent wolflike creatures somewhere just under spirit, just above man, and way past animal (even while they're played by wolves in the movie)—creatures that can "see two looks away . . . hear clouds pass overhead" . . . oh, and decapitate a man with one scissor of their jaws. And it's not a werewolf movie.

The strangest thing about this strange little movie is that it's not at all filmed like it's a strange little movie. Featuring a solid production budget and directed by Michael Wadleigh of *Woodstock* fame, the film treats its offbeat premise in a straightforward, urban cop story kind of way. You know, plenty of shots of naked cadavers treated casually by jaded morgue staff, a cranky police chief, the ever-present city always taking up more frame space than the characters. The story's admittedly a bit weak, but the characters are intriguing and the New York City setting is masterfully utilized, even if you find the idea of superintelligent ghost wolves prowling downtown Manhattan to be not enough of a draw for you. And it's not a werewolf movie.

The major location is the South Bronx, where the Wolfen den in an abandoned ruin of a church, a building that was built and ruined expressly for the movie. It was somewhere in the area of the intersection of East 172nd Street and Seabury Place, and surrounded by an incredible urban devastation the causes of which analysts are still sorting through today. However, even though enormous piles of rubbish, burnt wreckage, and abandoned hulks of apartment buildings make for a sad social commentary, they do make for an excellent place to film. These days, the area where this was shot looks way better, almost suburban, in fact.

Another major location is Battery Park, at the southern tip of Manhattan right on New York Harbor. It was here that the first victims of the Wolfen are attacked: a wealthy and coked-up couple and their Haitian voodoo bodyguard, all of which added up to no match for ghost wolves. But that's what they get, I guess, for attempting to revitalize the Wolfen's South Bronx hunting grounds.

The climax of the movie starts in front of and on the steps of the Federal Hall National Memorial at the corner of Wall and Nassau Streets—a giant, Grecian-style, colonnaded building fronted by a statue of George Washington, who got no credit for being in the movie despite being surrounded by black wolves. It was here that the Wolfen began their final attack of the film, and where we get the payoff for the Gregory Hines line earlier in the movie about one in five decapitations during the French Revolution yielding severed craniums that stayed alive for more than a minute.

Oh, and it's not a werewolf movie.

The New York Ripper (1982)
MANHATTAN

YOU KNOW THE OLD CLICHÉ. If it quacks like a duck, it must be a serial killer. Well, that's how it apparently translates into Italian, because that was exactly the premise that Lucio Fulci ran with in *The New York Ripper.*

In this 1982 film, a serial killer in downtown New York is targeting women with 1980s-era Time Square morals. While so engaged, the murderer quacks and talks in a Donald Duck voice, the same voice he uses to call and taunt the police detective who is trying to solve the murders. I assume with this gimmick, Fulci was going for a shocking contrast of the innocent and the depraved. Instead, it's as annoying as you'd think it would be.

The New York Ripper is a grimy little film nevertheless, with more blood and uncomfortable nudity than a major hospital, the kind of flick where a shot of a naked girl portends the slashing of an eyeball or the splitting of an abdomen. It's enough to make a guy not want to see a naked woman, actually. In addition, it has all the tropes of the gritty police procedural . . . wire taps where the cops need to keep the killer talking, a world-weary detective, and badly dubbed dialogue. Wait—that last element should be part of the next paragraph.

Fulci's is not the first *giallo* (an Italian film genre characterized by extravagant murder scenes) to take place in New York, but most of those other films

simply feature a few establishing shots of the New York skyline and some of its iconic sites. Fulci really tries to make *The New York Ripper* a genuine New York movie. You can tell because he put "New York" in the title. Even though all the interiors were filmed in Italy, all the exteriors were shot on location, especially the sections of the city that, like the decade-equivalent films of Frank Henenlotter (see *Basket Case,* page 181), made the city seem like a circle of hell.

All the usual New York filming locales are featured: the Staten Island Ferry, the subway, porno-era Times Square, all of which have been cleaned up to be almost unrecognizable these days. Others are now defunct, including the site of the Cavalier Hotel at 200 East 34th Street, which became an infamous crack house but still survived up until a few years ago. The house where the duck-billed ripper lived is on the west side of Bedford Street between where it intersects Barrow and Grove Streets, although a solid door has replaced the gate in the courtyard wall, preventing a view of the entrance.

The only location that really looks the same is Columbia University at 116th Street and Broadway in Manhattan. The college's Low Plaza, with its massive Grecian-style buildings, makes a couple of appearances. It was here that the detective enlists the services of a professor who doesn't end up helping to solve the crime but does provide lots of psychological exposition.

If you can't tell already, *The New York Ripper* is one of those movies that are entirely for people who like to dare themselves to watch movies instead of enjoying them. I've seen it three times.

Q (1982)
MANHATTAN

IN 1928, WALTER P. CHRYSLER, founder of the Chrysler Corporation, spent $20 million to erect a 77-floor, 1,047-foot-tall skyscraper headquarters for his company in the middle of Manhattan. With its art deco crown, its stainless steel gargoyles in the shape of Chrysler hood ornaments, and its various other auto-inspired embellishments, it was meant to be a shining monument to enterprise, the automobile industry, and Chrysler him/itself. Unless you're a monster movie fan. Then it's a $20 million, 77-floor, 1,047-foot-tall nesting place of an Aztec god in the form of a giant winged serpent named Q.

Well, actually it's Quetzalcoatl, but, as the tagline for the 1982 movie says, "Just call it Q . . . that's all you'll be able to say before it tears you apart!"

Also called *Q: The Winged Serpent* for those in the demographic who are uncomfortable with one-letter titles, *Q* was the brainchild of Larry Cohen, a well-known B-movie director and screenplay writer, otherwise famous for writing and directing the 1974 *It's Alive* about a killer infant and for writing the 1988 *Maniac Cop* about a maniac cop.

In *Q*, a giant lizard flies around Manhattan ripping the heads off window washers and cherry-picking topless sunbathers from rooftops. Meanwhile, in this city of people who never look up unless it's raining blood, a pair of detectives played by David Carradine and Richard Roundtree try to solve a series of ritualistic murders that involve flaying and organ stealing that might be connected to the appearance of the giant lizard god currently fouling up their skyline. In movie summaries, *might* almost always means *is definitely*.

Honestly, I had a lot of fun with this movie, despite enough bad dialogue and acting to have even its B-movie status demoted. I mean, when an ex-junkie jazz piano player can hold the city of New York hostage for a million dollars by not revealing where the nest of an ancient Aztec god is, I'm all in. Especially when that ex-junkie jazz piano player is Michael Moriarty, in one of the performances of his life.

The movie also features lots of terrific extended aerial footage that really lets you examine the upper metal canopy of New York City in some detail. In addition, the stop-motion monster Q overlaid on that metal canopy seems less a cheap effect and more a pleasant throwback to the movie monsters of old.

Most of the exteriors for *Q* were filmed guerrilla style, without filming permits, meaning the actors ran out into the streets and did the scene surrounded by an oblivious public, while the cameraman filmed surreptitiously and the producer looked around in worry. The cast and crew did end up at a few major New York City landmarks, though, including Columbia University and the American Museum of Natural History. They even filmed at and on the roof of the now condominiums Liberty Storage and Warehouse building on 43 West 64th Street, which for about a century was famous for its 30-foot metal Statue of Liberty replica on its roof. These days, the statue is situated in the Steinberg Family Sculpture Garden of the Brooklyn Museum of Art on 200 Eastern Parkway, where it's been restored and is no longer the dingy woman seen in the movie.

And while the first scene of the movie takes place at the Empire State Building, it's the Chrysler Building at 405 Lexington Avenue that takes costar credit with the monster. The filmmakers use it well, shooting scenes in its elaborately distinctive lobby, and most impressively, in the extreme attic space that is the topmost part of the spire, where Q roosts with its giant egg amid partially digested bodies. I'm not quite sure how Cohen pulled that off, considering his budget, but I assume his main tactic went something like, "We could do for your structure what Kong did for the Empire State Building."

The building is filled with an army of business tenants and isn't open to the public, nor are there any tours, but you can check it out from the street or enter the lobby for a quick peek at its art deco interior. You can also get a better look at the crown of the tower from the nearby (as the skyscraper flies) observation deck of the Empire State Building.

With this bit of film art firmly lodged in the timeline of its history, Chrysler needs to one day come out with a car that features a Q hood ornament. When that happens, I'll know that all the best parts of the world are finally starting to align themselves.

Basket Case (1982)
MANHATTAN

A FRESH-FACED YOUNG MAN with a 1970s rock-star haircut carries a large wicker basket down the smut-ridden sidewalks of a grimy 1980s-era Times Square. You can name that Frank Henenlotter film in three notes.

Basket Case tells the touching story of two closely knit (at the abdomen) brothers, Duane and Belial Bradley. These telepathically linked ex-Siamese twins have simple needs that include large amounts of foil-wrapped hamburgers, the

touch of a woman, and bloody revenge on the doctors who separated them against their will.

Oh, and Belial is a deformed, wicker-basket-size, flesh-colored blob of mostly head and arms with amazing strength and the apparent lethality of an army of wolverine-riding serial killers with dynamite strapped to their chests, which he whips out whenever his brother gets aroused. Definitely watch this one with the kids.

Duane and his brother-in-a-basket, being new in town, end up at the Hotel Broslin, the type of place that'll rent by the hour and throw in the bedbugs for free. In between murder scenes (where the victims thrash around with the soccer-ball-size Belial prop in a way that you can just hear Henenlotter offstage in his best Ed Wood voice, shouting, "Shake his arms around, make it look like he's killing you!"), Duane walks around putting up with a lot of "What's in the basket?" queries while attempting to balance his own happiness with loyalty to his monstrous brother.

Not that Duane doesn't legitimately care for Belial, of course. Amid all the carnage and bizarrerie in the movie are quite a few scenes of tenderness, or more accurately, tender creepiness, such as when Duane finds his brother hiding from the authorities in the commode of the hotel room and sweetly comforts him while cradling and gently drying the toilet water off him. It's the kind of scene that Norman Rockwell would have painted had he lived into that decade.

Belial is animated mostly through puppetry, with a few jarring stop motion scenes. In puppet form, though, if you can ignore the fact that his fingers sometimes bend backward like empty gloves, Belial can be pretty terrifying, with his dead eyes and inarticulate screams of existential agony and rage . . . although usually in a "beat it with a stick until it's out of his misery" kind of way.

The city itself takes third billing to the brothers, but just barely, and is represented mostly by Times Square back when it was seedy . . . which is a word we don't use too often nowadays, but which we always use for Times Square past. In fact, Henenlotter kind of made his own alternate universe New York City with such films as this one, *Brain Damage* (1988), and *Frankenhooker* (1990), in which New York is a harrowing place from all angles, full of inhuman humans and human inhumans. Heck, movies like these made me terrified of the city for longer than I care to admit, to the point that when I realized that *The New York Grimpendium* was my next book project, I lifted my arms to the sky and yelled "Henenlotter" while lightning crashed and rain poured around me.

In addition to some residential backstory shot upstate in Glens Falls, *Basket Case* was filmed all over the city, pretty much anywhere the independent and slimly funded production could easily and cheaply set up a camera, including 42nd Street, Franklin Street, the Statue of Liberty, and a few clubs. However, the main portion took place at the fictitious Hotel Broslin.

An office building at 80 Franklin Street stood in for the lobby of the hotel. For the exterior, the crew hung a red neon sign off a fire escape on a random building a few blocks away. It was at this latter location where the climax of the movie was filmed, when Duane and his brother dangle from the fire escape above a bunch of aghast hookers before falling to their death/injury, depending on if you've seen *Basket Case 2* or not. That exterior can be found at 2 Hubert Street, right where it intersects with Hudson. Today, the building looks the same, and there's still a fire escape. I didn't see any aghast hookers. Not that day.

Sleepaway Camp (1983)
ARGYLE

W HEN YOU'RE A MOVIE that's a rip-off of a rip-off of a rip-off, you need to bring something new to the table, er, screen. And that's pretty much what the 1983 slasher *Sleepaway Camp* was, and did.

In 1978, John Carpenter's *Halloween* showed that horror could be done well with a simple idea and a small budget. The lesson that a lot of people took away from the movie, though, was that horror could be done cheaply and uncreatively. So a lot of *Halloween* rip-offs polluted theater screens for decades after. Most were forgotten, but a few managed to stake out a bit of blood-soaked ground for themselves.

Like the 1980 *Friday the 13th*, for instance, which took most of the formula and gave it a different backdrop, summer camp, and found its own success.

Naturally, its success got ripped off as well. In fact, the 1980s almost had a whole sub-sub-genre of summer camp slasher movies, including *Cheerleader Camp* (1988), *Madman* (1982), and *The Burning* (1981), the latter two of which were filmed in New York but aren't featured in this book due to vague filming locations.

And, of course, most prominent on that list is *Sleepaway Camp*. The only reason that *Sleepaway Camp* stuck so viciously in the horror lexicon is because of a 30-second scene at the end, which I'll be describing here in a few paragraphs. So be warned . . . both about the ending and about the fact that I'll be spoiling it here . . . if you count relating the ending of a 30-year-old bad slasher film as spoiling.

I'm not sure whether kids even go to camp anymore, but it's always been the perfect location for a horror movie, especially of the teenage slasher variety. Secluded. Not a parent to be seen. Lots of places to hide. Lots of victims to choose from. Lots of ways to die.

In *Sleepaway Camp* alone, there is boiling, drowning, neck-arrowing, spine-slicing, hot curling iron inserting, and wasp nesting. Actually, that's the entire plot in a list. Kids and camp workers are murdered by an unknown killer in these various ways.

Then, the ending.

There's no way the next few sentences will shock anybody, but on the screen, when you find out that the shy, tragic, innocent-looking Angela is actually a boy, when you see her/him full frontal, covered in blood, with a feral, frozen expression as her boyfriend's strangely peaceful severed head rolls away, it'll stick with you. No matter how bad the previous hour and 20 minutes are, and despite the fact that you might have to sit through it all for the last scene to work, it'll stick with you.

Pretty much the entire film took place at the camp, minus a few flashbacks involving a gay dad, a crazy aunt, and a boating accident. In the film, it was called Camp Arawak, but in real life the camp was Camp Algonquin, in the town of Argyle at the northeastern corner of Summit Lake, a tiny body of water between the southeast edge of the Adirondacks and the Vermont border.

Camp Algonquin was torn down years ago, not because of its history of killers with confused sexuality, but just because, again, I'm not sure kids go to camp anymore. Now, the area around the small lake is basically all houses. No traces of the camp itself remain, except maybe a few overgrown tennis courts that, judging by the construction going on beside them when I visited, might not be around by the time you read this.

Seriously, though, the scene'll stick with you.

Ghostbusters I and *Ghostbusters II*
(1984/1989)
MANHATTAN

I MIGHT, MIGHT, MIGHT just have pitched this entire *New York Grimpendium* project to my publisher so that I could have an excuse to visit Ghostbusters headquarters.

I mean, what can I say about *Ghostbusters*? It's a movie that needs no introduction, no synopsis, no writing angle. It doesn't matter whether you were too young, too old, or nonexistent when it came out in 1984. It's *Ghostbusters*, man. We all get it, we all dig it, we're all that much cooler as a species for having produced it. There's nothing really that needs to be said about it. But here's a wall of text, anyway.

Say what you want about any of the films of Woody Allen or Spike Lee or

Sydney Lumet, I posit that there is no more New York a movie than Ivan Reitman's *Ghostbusters*. If New York City were incarnated into flesh and then split into four people, you'd get Peter Venkman, Egon Spengler, Ray Stantz, and Winston Zeddemore, with maybe a Slimer by-product.

In Peter, we find the bravado and cynicism that comes from being one of the world's largest cities, which is both a burden and a point of pride. Relevant quote: "Maybe now you'll never slime a guy with a positron collider, huh?"

In Egon, we find the serious, academic side that comes from being home to a staggering number of world-class museums, institutions, colleges, and libraries. This is the city that raised Isaac Asimov, Carl Sagan, Robert Oppenheimer, and Richard Feynman, and has produced scores of Nobel laureates. Relevant quote: "I collect spores, molds, and fungus."

In Ray, we see the childish wonder that still revels (although sometimes it pretends not to) in the bright lights of Times Square, the majesty of the Statue of Liberty, the beauty of multiple skyscrapers holding up the roof of the world. Relevant quote: "Hey, does this pole still work?"

In Winston is personified the everyday blue-collar worker who is the foundation of this grand city—the hard hat behind the jackhammer, the apron behind the hot-dog stand, the driver behind the delivery truck. These are the men and women without whom the wonders of New York City would never have existed. Relevant quote: "If there's a steady paycheck in it, I'll believe anything you say."

Even when it seems that the city has turned against them, when it's overrun by ghosts, when their work has been doubted and they've been thrown in jail, it's never Ghostbusters versus the city (although I think that's how the lower-quality but still enjoyable 1989 sequel starts out). Heck, the last line of the movie is Winston's: "I love this town." And obviously this idea comes to a culmination in the already mentioned *Ghostbusters II* when the Ghostbusters animate the symbol of the city, the Statue of Liberty, to attack Vigo the Carpathian and his slimy pink menace that threatens the world.

So that's what I can say about *Ghostbusters*.

But on to the filming locations.

Believe it or not, *Ghostbusters* was actually filmed in Chicago. Ha. Joking. Some of the exteriors and most of the interiors were, of course, filmed in Los Angeles, but all the important exteriors were in New York. For instance, the exteriors for the opening sequence were filmed at the Stephen A. Schwarzman Building, which is the main branch of the New York Public Library at 455 Fifth Avenue ("You're right. No human being would stack books like this."). The names of the lions that guard its main entrance are "Patience" and "Fortitude," the latter having the honor of being the focus of the very first shot of the film.

Another central location for the film was character Dana Barrett's apartment building, where the Ghostbusters first learned of Zuul through a refrigerator and where the climactic battle with that flat-topped female spook took place. The building, at 55 Central Park West, is just 20 stories high, although special effects were used to double its height and give it a more ominous and distinctive crown. Adjacent to the building is the church that the Stay Puft Marshmallow Man crushes. ("Nobody steps on a church in my town.")

The bank exterior for the brief but funny "My parents left me that house. I was born there" scene is at 489 Fifth Avenue, right across the street from the already mentioned main branch of New York Public Library.

Of course, before they were Ghostbusters, they were mere university-funded paranormal researchers. Columbia University at Broadway and 116th Street was the college that kicked them out ("But the kids love us!"), forcing them to privatize and offer their expertise to the common haunted man.

The restaurant where Louis finally succumbs to Vinz Clortho, the Keymaster, after being chased by its demon dog form, was Tavern on the Green, at the intersection of West 67th Street and Central Park West. These days, it's a New York gift shop. In addition, the fountain where Peter is introduced to "the stiff" by Dana and in front of which he does his little dance is at Lincoln Center, at 140 West 65th Street.

Well, you've made it this far, and I'm proud of you, especially because you can get all this information on every site on the web. Anyway, the most important filming locale for the entire movie was Ghostbusters headquarters, GBHQ.

It fits in with the whole "I Heart New York" theme of *Ghostbusters* that they would choose a firehouse for a headquarters, as well as the fact that it was a building that should be condemned ("There's serious metal fatigue in all the load-bearing members, the wiring is substandard, it's completely inadequate for our power needs, and the neighborhood is like a demilitarized zone").

The interiors were filmed at a Los Angeles fire station, but the more important exterior for GBHQ is Hook and Ladder Company No. 8 at 14 North Moore Street. Growing up in a suburban area hours and state lines away from New York City, I was used to fire departments looking much different than the tall, red brick and gray block edifice, embedding the building that much more in my mind as GBHQ. When I finally got to visit it, after decades of watching the movie, the iconic red door was shut, so after taking a few pictures, I hung around at a bar and restaurant called Walker's across the street. Finally, the door opened (for nonemergency reasons) and I was able to peek inside to see, hung prominently on the wall, the *Ghostbusters II* sign left over from when they filmed the sequel there in 1989.

Speaking of that sequel, I've neglected it so far in the entry, but let me remedy that right quick. Many of the same New York locations were used (for instance, GBHQ and Columbia University), but also featured in the sequel were the Washington Square Park arch (for a brief shot involving a giant ghost), the Statue of Liberty (of course), and the U.S. Customs House at 1 Bowling Green near Battery Park, at the southern end of Manhattan. That building played the role of the Manhattan Museum of Art, which was this movie's "spook central."

I've been to quite a few movie filming locations, both for this book and in my life in general. Often, there's a bit of a letdown at seeing too much behind the curtain. But with *Ghostbusters,* where the filming locations are as integral to the movie as the characters themselves, it feels a lot more like meeting a celebrity.

So when New York gets you down, which it can whether you live here, visit here, or just see it on the movie screen, all you have to do is watch *Ghostbusters.* Bustin'll make you feel good.

C.H.U.D. (1984)
MANHATTAN

MAN, I CAN TOTALLY IMAGINE what happened at the pitch for this flick. Guy walks into a room full of businessmen, a large briefcase (it's the early 1980s, remember) under his arm stuffed with conceptual art, script copies, casting notes, and marketing concepts, all carefully crafted and arranged to convince these men to finance his movie. After a few awkward moments of fumbling with his materials, he begins.

"Thank you for your time today, gentleman. I think you'll be excited about the great potential for the movie by the end of this presentation."

Silence. A few in his small audience spend too much time staring at the large metal dials on their wrists (again, it's the early 1980s).

A couple of nervous coughs later, he says, "Well, the movie we'd like to make is called *C.H.U.D.*, and it's . . ."

"Sold. We'll pay for it," says the leader of the group, while the rest nod their head in vigorous agreement.

And, seriously, what even apathetic movie watcher isn't going to pay attention to a movie with a title like *C.H.U.D.*, much less the dedicated horror movie fan. How can anybody resist the urge to reference the title at random but regularly occurring occasions, further perpetuating its legacy? Who cares about the movie itself? The title is the reward.

The acronym stands for "Cannibalistic Humanoid Underground Dwellers,"

as well as "Contamination Hazardous Underground Disposal." And those two phrases tell the entire story of the movie.

As to the quality of the movie itself, it's better than it should be. As in the best B movies, the actors didn't seem to realize that's what they were making (although judging by its entertaining DVD commentary track, they certainly do now). Featuring sincere performances by Jonathan Heard and Daniel Stern, as well as one of John Goodman's first movie appearances, the 1984 film (the same year that *Ghostbusters* came out, to give you some context) is about a bunch of mutated creatures in the sewers of New York City that are preying on its citizens while the government tries to cover up the whole radioactive mess.

According to the end credits, the movie was filmed, "in and under New York City." Mostly, that meant Manhattan, although there was some hazardous spillage over the Hudson into New Jersey.

Within all the random streets and sewers used in the movie, the climactic scene offers the best chance to visit a filming location from the movie. Fortunately it's an important one. It takes place at (and under . . . there's always an "under" in this film) a diner. This is the spot where the C.H.U.D. go full out against New York City. This is the spot where the filmmakers get to spend budget on flashing police cars and barricades and crowds of extras. This is where John Goodman gets enough exposure that he might have to attribute his career to slimy monsters with large, glowing eyes. This is where everything gets tied up but the loose ends.

The diner's still there, has been for about 80 years in fact, and pops up here and there in other New York–based movies. Today, it looks like it has recovered well from the *C.H.U.D.* attack. Called both the Corner Deli and La Esquina, according to its sign, it's at 114 Kenmore, where it intersects with Cleveland Place, right at the base of the small triangle called Petrosino Square. The exterior has changed a little bit, but not too much. It still features a long, horizontal lighted marquee wrapped around the top of the restaurant. Inside, the small eatery has completely changed from the counter-based diner it was in its *C.H.U.D.* days, to a Mexican restaurant.

Honestly, it could do with some *C.H.U.D.* rebranding, in my opinion.

Anyway, *C.H.U.D.* is a movie you need to watch to get all your horror movie merit badges. Plus, it officially gives you license to use the term "C.H.U.D." as much as you want. At the very least, you'll never look at a New York City manhole cover the same ever again. Or John Goodman, either.

Lady in White (1988)

SOUTH BRISTOL, LYONS, PHELPS

A T FIRST, THE 1988 FILM *Lady in White* seems like a delightfully nostalgic Halloween ghost story. However, if you set your kids in front of it and go off to the store to replenish your stash of mini candy bars, don't be surprised if you come back and their fingers have sunk death grips into the white flesh of their popcorn balls and their candy apples are all fuzzy from having been dropped on the carpet in horror. You see, about half an hour in, the movie elevates the drama a bit by turning into a mystery about a serial child killer, as well as featuring a rather heavy civil rights subplot. It does keep the ghosts throughout, though.

Written and directed by Frank LaLoggia (who also directed the 1981 *Fear No Evil*; see page 174), this personal and independent film is based both on LaLoggia's memories of his childhood and on a Rochester-area legend of the pale ghost of a woman eternally looking for her daughter's murderer (see "Classic Monsters"). He even covertly cameos as the horror author narrator of the film.

LaLoggia himself grew up in Rochester but wanted a smaller-town feel for his film, so he chose a few towns south and east of the city to collectively represent the fictional town of Willowpoint Falls, where the story takes place.

The first real location (after an establishing plane arrival shot in Buffalo) is the Willowpoint Falls Cemetery. It is here, where the narrator (and protagonist all grown up), waxes nostalgic, jumpstarting a formative story from his childhood. The cemetery is actually Coye Cemetery, situated at the top of Bopple Hill at the intersection of Route 21 and Bopple Hill Road, in the town of South Bristol. The tiny cemetery dates back to the 1800s, is adjacent to a couple of old farm buildings, and features a nice view of Canandaigua Lake. The entrance is on Route 21, but in the movie they installed a fake gate at the side, where there's a slight pull-off.

The town that represented the downtown area of Willowpoint Falls was Lyons, especially the area around the Wayne County Courthouse at 26 Church Street, with its silver dome and the Village Square Park that it faces. The four-pronged clock tower of the nearby United Methodist Church at 93 William Street was also used for town overview shots.

Incidentally, Lyons was also the location for all the exteriors shot for another 1988 horror film, *Slugs*. You can probably guess from the five letters of its title,

but *Slugs* was about a slimy infestation of black carnivorous slugs that somehow manage to be as lethal as a park full of cloned dinosaurs.

Back to *Lady in White,* the inciting incident of the film occurs when the main character, a young boy, gets locked in the school cloakroom on Halloween. There, he watches the ghost of a little girl pantomime her murder from a decade before, after which the boy is then attacked by the real-life murderer.

That school building where it takes place was Midlakes Middle School in the town of Phelps, at 144 Main Street, right beside Resthaven Cemetery, an aspect that the film makers take advantage of for a few of the scenes. These days, the school has been turned into a retirement home called Vienna Gardens. The cemetery is still there (the dead are notoriously sessile).

In the movie, a small, semicircular window in the cloakroom overlooked the cemetery and was used for the movie poster, the video cover, the DVD cover, and, these days, the small photo on the relevant Netflix page. You can kind of tell from the way it was filmed that the window was a mere cinematic embellishment. Although some of the windows in the building do overlook the cemetery, they are the large, rectangular sort.

Other than a few houses featured here and there in the area, the only other major locale is the cliffs in the movie's climax. In movies, every town no matter where it's situated has amazing cliffs from which to drop its villains. In real life, there are only a few good locations for that. In this case, the filmmakers went all the way to Hawaii for those scenes.

So if you're in the mood for a Halloween movie with lots of great childhood scenes to watch with your kids, plus a few that make you wonder whether you really should be watching this with your kids, there really is only one movie for you. And it's not *Slugs*.

Gremlins 2: The New Batch (1990)
Manhattan

A<small>H, *GREMLINS*.</small> What a great little movie. Unfortunately it was filmed in California. New York got the 1990 sequel *Gremlins 2: The New Batch*.

Although the Steven Spielberg–produced and Joe Dante–directed sequel is not as much of a nostalgia trigger as its predecessor, it does have something to recommend it. There's Christopher Lee, for instance. Also, Christopher Lee. And let us not forget, Christopher Lee.

Gone is the fake snow and small-town Christmas charm of the Universal Studios back lot where they filmed the exteriors of the first movie, replaced this time by the glass Babels of Manhattan. In fact, almost the entire movie takes place inside a single skyscraper, the Clamp Center, the symbol of which is a vice-like letter *C* squashing the planet.

However, fortunately, the filmmakers avoided the evil corporation cliché . . . but they couldn't avoid the gremlins. This time around, Billy Peltzer (Zach Galligan) and Kate Beringer (Phoebe Cates) find themselves working together in a way past state-of-the art building in New York City as they attempt to start their postgremlins lives together. However, nearby, in Chinatown, Gizmo is mogwai-napped by a pair of twin geneticists whose laboratory rents space in the same tower.

The rules are the same: Avoid bright sunlight, never get them wet, and never feed them after midnight. But now there's a fourth rule: Never inject them with experimental genetic serums.

Of course, Gizmo gets wet, thanks to a cameo by John Astin of Gomez Addams fame (see the Charles Addams entry in "Legends and Personalities of the Macabre"), and you can guess how the rest of the movie unspools.

More or less, anyway. The movie widely differs from its predecessor in two ways. First, because of the genetic laboratory story threat, we're treated, maybe mistreated, to bat gremlins and spider gremlins, intelligent gremlins and vegetable gremlins, electric gremlins and gender-bender gremlins.

Second, the tone is way more over the top than the first one, spoofing its way through skits almost, with its largest target being its predecessor movie. And while not really a horror movie exactly, *Gremlins 2* does pay homage to plenty of them, including *Invasion of the Body Snatchers, Phantom of the Opera, Donovan's Brain, Octaman, The Quatermass Xperiment, The Beast from 20,000 Fathoms* (see page 157), and *King Kong* (see page 155). And I've already mentioned John Astin as a janitor and Christopher Lee as Dr. Catheter, whose first line is, "Ah, splendid. This must be my malaria." Heck, one of the main characters is a vampire-makeup-wearing horror host.

As to exterior filming locations, there are basically only two, not counting some generic Chinatown shots. The Clamp Center is actually a 50-story glass skyscraper at 101 Park Avenue in Manhattan, just a building over from Grand Central Station. The plaza in front of the building where the rotating Clamp symbol stood in the movie is just a blank polygon of granite accented by a fountain. The other exterior location used in the film was the area outside of Saint Patrick's Cathedral on Fifth Avenue between 50th and 51st Streets, where they filmed the Dick Miller vs. the gargoyle gremlin scene.

Apparently, *Gremlins 2* satiated our desire for tiny, malicious reptilian creatures and the fuzzy merchandise machines from which they spawn, as there was no *Gremlins 3*. However, as popular as those creatures continue to be, that's probably going to be the statement that really dates this book.

Jacob's Ladder (1990)
Brooklyn

A LTHOUGH I'VE BEEN INVOLVED in some pretty intense Call of Duty campaigns in my time, I know very little about the horrors of war. In fact, most in my generation have had it pretty comfy when it comes to that kind of stuff. Sure, we've had enlisted peers warring on distant sands here and there for decades, but most of us know war only through video games and, for the more cultured among us, *M*A*S*H* reruns.

And that's where horror movies come in. I mean, you'll never find fictional horrors that'll top real-life ones, but you'll never come to grips with any of the real-life horrors without the fictional ones. The 1990 film *Jacob's Ladder* seems a decent example of that, as far as war movies go.

All that said, it's not totally a war movie. Not in the way that *Apocalypse Now* or *Full Metal Jacket* or *In the Army Now* is, anyway.

Starring Tim Robbins and Elizabeth Pena, it's about a Vietnam veteran named Jacob who's just trying to live a normal civilian life, delivering Brooklyn's mail. However, what's stopping him from doing that isn't neighborhood dogs or the daily trial of big catalogs and small mailboxes. Instead, Jacob finds himself haunted by demons that include a broken family, the death of his son—played by Macaulay Culkin—and, well, literal demons. Or hallucinations. Neither he nor we are sure until the end of the movie. Either way, lizard-tailed creatures and strange, eyeless beings whose heads move at otherworldly rhythms seem to be trying to kill him and/or make his life a whole lot spookier than he really wants it to be.

These demons/hallucinations are the central mystery and drama of the movie: What are they, and why are they haunting Jacob and his troop-mates? You can tell my ignorance in matters of war because I use terms like troop-mates.

Speaking of those oddly rhythmed demons, *Jacob's Ladder* is the movie that introduced us to a unique in-camera special effect that has been copied by about one in three horror movies since. It's hard to describe on paper, but it's a simple yet clever technique that involves actors moving their head and keeping their body still while being filmed at, like, four frames per second, and then playing the film back at the usual 24 frames per second, meaning that the head moves independently in an eerie, rapid way that just screams demonic activity.

The end credits of the movie name the filming locations as New York and

Puerto Rico, the latter of which I assume to be where the war scenes were shot. There aren't too many New York scenes that really stick out, though, except for maybe the first one.

In it, Jacob finds himself locked in an empty subway stop. It's here that he first sees his demon pursuers and here that we as the audience realize that this isn't going to be a tender, heart-warming, healing power of love kind of movie.

The tiled signs in the scene clearly denote the scene as taking place at the Bergen Street station in Brooklyn, and that's exactly where it was filmed. However, it was in a lower, unused section of that subway stop. Basically, the filmmakers refurbished an abandoned tunnel there specifically so that we can watch Tim Robbins almost get run over by a train full of demons.

There are actually two Bergen Street stations, a few blocks from each other. The *Jacob's Ladder* station is the one at the intersection of Bergen and Smith Streets that is served by the F and G lines, not the one at the intersection of Bergen Street and Flatbush Avenue, through which run the 2, 3, and 4 trains. There are no demons there.

Heading down into just about any subway in any city is pretty much a netherworldly experience, full of strange denizens lurking in corners and doomed souls

being eaten alive by giant metallic worms. In *Jacob's Ladder*, the scene becomes a metaphor for the entire movie, a metaphor that were I to explore here would ruin the ending of this compelling if depressing experience for anyone who hasn't yet seen it. Sometimes death really is the only way to get out of life alive.

Wolf (1994)
Manhattan, Old Westbury

B EWARE WOLVES in Jack Nicholson's clothing. That's what I got out of the 1994 film *Wolf*. What I didn't get, unfortunately, was a new addition to my list of favorite werewolf movies.

It's your typical typical [*sic*] werewolf movie. Man gets bit. Becomes virile and virtually superpowered. Starts really getting into life until the blackouts begin and he finds himself waking up all bloody in the forest with pieces of raw meat stuck between his teeth. The variation this time is (spoiler) the main characters all work in the publishing business.

Reuniting Nicholson and Michelle Pfeiffer from their *Witches of Eastwick* days, and also starring James Spader, the film has some elegance to it, but overall comes off as rather pedestrian. Which really shouldn't happen with a movie about ravaging man-beasts. Even famous makeup artist Rick Baker's facial effects were underused and basically came off as clumps of hair strategically placed to not obscure the faces that the moviemakers were paying millions of dollars to feature.

In a way, it almost seems *Wolf* plays out as if it's too good for its own subject matter. For instance, it's a werewolf movie that never uses the word *werewolf*. *Werewolf*'s a good word, man. Strong. The kind of word that can rip out your throat or convert you to its cause.

The film is set in New York but was filmed mostly in California, including the Bradbury Building in downtown L.A., with its amazing Victorian-style interior featuring a five-floor-tall open courtyard, iron filigree rails and elevator, and a skylight.

Central Park is featured, of course, because that's where New York City's monsters always end up. The mugging scene took place beneath the 150-year-old Greyshot Arch, a bridge near Merchant's Gate between 61st and 62nd Streets in the southwest area of the park. Incidentally, this bridge was also where the last

scene in the 2008 monster movie *Cloverfield* takes place, where the footage is found in that "found footage" film. I didn't include an entry on *Cloverfield* in this book because the few actual New York filming locations are already featured throughout this section, a lot of it is mocked up in CGI so that they can destroy it, and I've already included three giant monster movies. Those guys take up a lot of space.

However, the one big New York locale where the werewolf's share of the film takes place is the mansion estate where Pfeiffer's character lives. The house and grounds are a main location for the film. It's where Nicholson's character goes, at various points throughout the movie, to get fired, get laid, get away, and get into a fight. That's the whole plot of the movie, actually.

The mansion estate used for this was Old Westbury Gardens, the 100-year-old, 200-acre estate in the town of Old Westbury, on the west end of Long Island. Situated at 71 Old Westbury Road, the British-style estate was originally the mansion home of the wealthy Phipps family and is now a historic attraction opened to the public seasonally (closed during winter and werewolf seasons). At least a dozen movies have been filmed on its grounds, including Alfred Hitchcock's *North by Northwest*.

If I had to review *Wolf* in six words, they'd be, "Too much Nicholson, not enough werewolf." I guess the actors didn't want to be upstaged. You know, that whole showbiz rule about never working with kids, animals, or monsters.

The Devil's Advocate (1997)

MANHATTAN

T HE 1997 FILM *The Devil's Advocate* isn't the first movie to cast Satan as a lawyer. Vincent Price played Beelzebub, Esq., in the 1957 *The Story of Mankind.* Walter Huston presented his case as Mr. Scratch in the 1941 *The Devil and Daniel Webster,* based on the Stephen Vincent Benét story of the same name. There are probably others. It's a pretty easy idea to get to. Lawyers are paid to argue over questions of right and wrong. They've also been stereotyped as sneaky, greedy bastards.

Also, at some point in these types of movies, the Devil has to give a passionate closing statement on why he's so evil and why he tries against an all-powerful god and a preordained Judgment Day. That bit of accepted dogma is okay in the religious world, but a giant plot hole in the movie one.

In *The Devil's Advocate,* Al Pacino tried on his horns in the role of the Devil, who goes by the name John Milton, while Keanu Reeves played Kevin Lomax, the small-time Southern lawyer whom Milton is trying to corrupt. Overall, it's a pretty color-by-numbers Faust story, actually much more pedestrian than the traditional Faust story. Then again, I'm not a big fan of seeing the Devil on screen. He rarely lives up to the hype promulgated by thousands of years of folklore (and Sunday school stories). Still, if you're going to have Satan in your film, Al Pacino might as well play him. He's pretty much the sole reason why the movie is watchable.

In the 1980s and '90s, probably even now but it was at least more obvious back then, there were two main ways to portray New York. The first was as a grimy cesspit, examples of which proliferate in this section and basically include anything involving a serial killer and a small budget. The other perspective was as an opulent and exclusive empire where people live and work on the highest, most expensive floors of skyscrapers and are fueled by bank account totals and egos that soar even higher. *The Devil's Advocate* is mostly the latter. . . . plus a few subway scenes.

The movie starts out in Gainesville, Florida, both in plot and filming location, but the rest was shot in Manhattan. And there is a lot of Manhattan in this movie.

It's a movie about high-dollar lawyers, so of course Foley Square is represented, which is where all the grand, historic New York courthouses are found.

It is in this area that we are first introduced to Al Pacino's John Milton, who in
the midst of all the glamour and deca-
dence of his life, just loves the subway. In
fact, he's first shown backdropped by the
vaulted, tiled ceilings at the entrance to
the Chambers Street subway station in the
south arcade of the Manhattan Municipal
building, at the intersection of Chambers
and Centre Streets.

Penta Plaza, where the law offices of
Milton, Chadwick, and Waters are headquartered, is actually the Continental
Tower at 180 Maiden Lane. The rooftop
scene with the infinity pool was filmed
atop this building, with the water digitally added later and a hefty insurance policy
added earlier, I'm sure, for shoving A-list actors out onto a 500-foot rooftop.

At one point the law firm finds itself having to defend one of its top clients,
played by Craig T. Nelson, in the murder of his family. His extravagant apartment was actually Donald Trump's own apartment at the top of Trump Tower on
725 Fifth Avenue.

It's a movie about the Devil, so of course there's a church scene; a couple,
actually. For the funeral scene where Milton boils the holy water with his finger,
the filmmakers used the Gothic-looking Central Presbyterian Church at 593 Park
Avenue for the exteriors and Most Holy Redeemer Church at 173 East Third Street
for the interior. For the scene where Lomax's wife, played by Charlize Theron,
dramatically reveals that she was attacked by Milton, they used Church of the
Heavenly Rest at 2 East 90th Street.

Finally, but not exhaustively, much of the action takes place at a posh residential building owned, lived in, and reigned over by Milton, and where the most
important firm employees reside, including Lomax. That's at Fifth Avenue and
94th Street, but the unique clock tower apex was digitally added to make it look
more like a place where the Devil would choose to rest his hooves.

As you can tell, I have a lot more to say about its locations than about the
movie itself, partly because they are so well documented and so easily verifiable.
But mostly, that's because of the movie itself.

Wendigo (2001)
PHOENICIA, KINGSTON

COMING-OF-AGE STORIES are pretty common, but when they're used within the framework of a horror movie, things can get a bit more complicated. Sure, the young protagonists still have to come to certain difficult realizations about the world. Sure, they have to overcome adult-size obstacles. Sure, they gain a better sense of self at some point. But in horror movies, they also have to deal with monsters. Admit it, puberty was a lot easier than that for you.

Larry Fessenden's *Wendigo* is such a story, although in many ways it defies classification, even as a horror movie. Fessenden is known for being involved with strange little independent films, whether in a writing, directing, producing, or acting capacity, and sometimes all at once. And in *Wendigo,* he does it all except for appear in it (for an example of him in acting mode, see the entry for *I Sell the Dead*, page 207).

I'll pretty much watch anything Fessenden's involved with, including anything produced by his company Glass Eye Pix, which usually turns out unique and authentic horror pictures, even when they're largely flawed. And *Wendigo* pretty much fits right into that critique.

This movie opens with a family from New York City played by Jake Weber, Patricia Clarkson, and Erik Per Sullivan (Dewey from *Malcolm in the Middle*) on their way upstate for a winter weekend in the snow-clad small-town ambiance of the Catskill Mountains. The movie's peculiar tone is set right away when they hit a deer, career off the road, and then tangle with the local hunters who had been chasing the animal.

It's a strange, long scene that leaves the characters and the audience inexplicably unsettled, a feeling that continues throughout the film and pervades every scene. And although there is some city-folk-versus-country-folk friction underlying the plot, the tense atmosphere goes deeper than that.

The titular monster of the film is a Native American myth, and in Fessenden's version is a shape-changing creature made of trees and animals and wind, but it mostly appears as a man-deer hybrid in both fleshed and skeletal forms. With the exception of maybe one scene, Fessenden doesn't use the Wendigo in conventional monster-movie ways. Instead, the creature is used more like an omen or some sort of extension of what Miles, the young boy played by Erik Per Sullivan, is experiencing in the movie.

The whole thing was filmed on location in the Catskills, in towns and villages all around the Ashokan Reservoir. Many of the local residents still remember the movie, and I was able to talk to Anne-Marie Johansson, who owns the Ashokan Dreams B&B at 111 High Point Mountain Road in West Shokan, where the sledding scene was filmed. She directed me to most of the locations for the movie.

For example, according to her, the house where most of the film takes place either is or was actually owned by Larry Fessenden, who used it again briefly in his 2011 *The Last Winter.* It is on Moonhaw Road, across a private bridge and past the Glen Atty Farm sign featured in the movie. You can't get close to the house because it's back a bit on the property and separated from the road by a stream, but you can still see it from Moonhaw Road.

Other locations in West Shokan are the 100-year-old and terrifyingly dilapidated Snyder's Tavern at 4161 New York 28A and a private property on Whispell Road. In addition, about 30 miles away from West Shokan, is Margaretville Memorial Hospital, which is used in the movie's ending scenes.

A central element in the film happens when the family goes downtown for some supplies. That town is Phoenicia, where they spend most of their time at the Phoenicia Pharmacy. Here the young boy meets a mysterious Native American,

learns the legend of the Wendigo, and procures the Wendigo totem that he carries around during the rest of the movie. The pharmacy is still there at 41 Main Street, just down the road from a Daniel Boone–like statue that was also featured in the movie, beside a fascinating-looking junk store called Homer and Langley's Mystery Spot.

The ancient pharmacy didn't seem to have changed much since the filming, and probably hadn't for many decades previously. Postcards that had been sunbleached blue were still for sale in the window, and the case that in the film held the Wendigo totem stocked a miscellany of picture frames and pens and soaps and electric shavers.

I visited the area in deep winter, hoping for the same snow cover that was used so well in the movie. Unfortunately, it was a rather snowless winter in general for the northeastern parts of the United States. There wasn't even any ominous Wendigo wind.

Still the area was just as rustic as in the movie . . . if a little more scenic than scary.

Poultrygeist:
Night of the Chicken Dead (2006)
Buffalo

"IT'S A TROMA FILM," is everything you need to know about this movie. You see, I don't care whether you're a bowtie–wearing movie critic for a preeminent culture magazine or a thirteen-year-old boy in a Misfits T-shirt; this is how you discuss it: "Holy crap, do you remember that one scene?" "Crazy. I can't believe they did that." "What the heck?" "I need to change my eyeballs." Except that you curse a lot more.

Basically, Troma films are unreviewable. And not in the "not worth wasting one's time to review" but in the "this word has no meaning in this sphere" kind of way. As to the audience for a Troma film, you're either already an initiate or you don't want to be. Although, I will say that if you want to see your first Troma film, *Poultrygeist: Night of the Chicken Dead* might be the one you should try.

Starring people you'll either never hear of again or who will change their name before you hear of them again, and directed by the fiercely incomparable

Lloyd Kaufman, president and cofounder of Troma Entertainment (who I interviewed for "*Legends and Personalities of the Macabre*"), *Poultrygeist* is . . . well, what it is. Like I said, a Troma film.

By this time in its august history, Troma Entertainment has done every possible gross thing with sex, gore, and bodily processes, as well as having exposed the body of just about every wannabe actress in the state of New York. How do you up an ante like that?

By taking all of that and adding a fast-food restaurant, of course.

The story concerns a military-themed fast-food fried chicken restaurant called American Chicken Bunker that was built on top of a sacred Native American burial ground. As a result, the angered Native American spirits possess the food, causing whoever eats it to become Native American chicken zombies. Oh, and it's a musical. Your film horizons have just been broadened.

The protagonist of the movie is Arbie, a young man who has missed out on college and gets a job at the ACB to piss off his lesbian ex-girlfriend Wendy (most of the characters are named after fast-food restaurants), who is part of a large protest against the corporate greed, inhumane chicken-handling practices, and Native American burial ground desecration of the fast-food chain. ("Revenge is a dish best served fried.")

It's a film that might make you want to stop eating fast food. You'll certainly stop watching movies.

Poultrygeist was filmed during the summer of 2005 in the city of Buffalo, almost solely in and around an abandoned restaurant at 3230 Bailey Avenue. In 2010, the building was torn down and replaced with a firehouse, so who knows what ghosts those emergency responders will have to face for erecting their firehouse on the site of a horror picture set.

Since I was braving this wasteland area of Buffalo, I figured I might as well check out a second site related to the movie. About three and a half miles away from this restaurant set, at the intersection of Linwood Avenue and West Ferry

Street, is an abandoned church. It was here that the cast and crew say horrors worse than Native American–possessed chicken zombies occurred. Apparently, some 50 of them were bivouacked for the months-long duration of the shoot with only one cold shower . . . cast and crew that were daily covered with fake blood, slime, feathers, and not-even-God-knows-what-else as they painted set pieces and built zombie chicken costumes and all other manner of movie alchemy.

When I interviewed Kaufman, he told me that part of their contract with the fast-food property prohibited them from filming any nudity on the site . . . so they had to film all that type of gratuity in that church instead. "Which is fantastic. Life is so weird," he said.

So to summarize, *Poultrygeist* is gross, crass, offensive, amateurish, and basically a taunt of a film to watch . . . if you're not chicken. And, honestly, it's only in this book because I liked Lloyd when I met him and needed another Buffalo site.

It's a Troma film.

1408 (2007)

MANHATTAN

I N 1977, STEPHEN KING made famous Room 217 of the Overlook Hotel by featuring it in his popular book *The Shining*. The Overlook was a fictional luxury establishment ostensibly based on the Stanley Hotel in Estes Park, Colorado, where King is supposed to have stayed before writing the book (in room 217, natch). Thirty-five years later, the Stanley Hotel continues to use the "haunted room" as part of its marketing efforts. In 2002, King tried it again, this time with a ghost story featuring Room 1408 of the Dolphin Hotel in New York City and more directly titled *1408*. Inevitably, since it's a Stephen King story, there's been a movie based on it.

The 2007 film stars John Cusack as a writer who pays his bills by traveling to and writing about haunted sites while privately not believing in the supernatural. Soon, an anonymous postcard draws him to Room 1408 in the Dolphin Hotel, an upscale high-rise in Manhattan managed by a character played by Samuel L. Jackson. In what is pretty much the most compelling scene in the

movie, the manager attempts to talk Cusack's character out of staying in the room. Of course, our protagonist doesn't listen, so things get ghosty. Or "fucking evil," as Jackson's character eloquently elucidates.

The first 40 minutes of the movie are some of the most excellent buildup a ghost story can have, but then the rest becomes less creepy and almost more like an action movie. However, in the filmmakers' and every other ghost storyteller in the history of the genre's defense, it's devilishly hard to end a ghost story satisfactorily. Technically, every one of them should just end in an ellipsis.

Still, it's an interesting concept, being trapped in a room while surrounded by thousands of other people in a hotel in the middle of the City That Never Sleeps and still being unable to escape or get help. It's the opposite of *The Shining*.

The downtown address of the Dolphin Hotel is given in the movie as 2254 Lexington Avenue at 45th Street, an address that doesn't exist in this reality and two roadways that, while they do intersect, don't have a hotel at the spot. The exterior of the Dolphin Hotel was filmed in Manhattan, though, at the Roosevelt Hotel at 45 East 45th Street, at Madison Avenue, two blocks west of Lexington.

The 90-year-old Roosevelt still retains its historic Roaring Twenties feel, thanks to a $65 million restoration in the late 1990s, although the moviemakers

CGI'd up the exterior architecture a bit. Instead of the three-towered construct of the Roosevelt, they inserted a single monolithic building above the ground floor entrance. The lobbies also don't match up.

The Roosevelt has 1,015 guest rooms on 19 floors, and there actually is a room 1408. However, from what I can tell from the Internet and my own visit, the Roosevelt isn't cashing in on its Stephen King ties. Like most historic New York buildings, it has a cinematic past that extends beyond any one random movie, so its bellhops are used to carrying that kind of baggage.

I Sell the Dead (2008)
STATEN ISLAND, MANHATTAN

THERE'S SOMETHING ABOUT PHYSICAL LABOR, the kind that yields an achy back, a sweaty brow, and dirty hands, that's satisfying beyond the triumphs of any mere desk job. It's as if the human body was made for that kind of work. Just ask any grave robber.

Better yet, ask Willie Grimes and Arthur Black, the two main characters from the great little 2008 film *I Sell the Dead,* written and directed by Glenn McQuaid. Actually, they're not so much grave robbers, which is technically defined as people who steal the pretty things we bury with the dead, but body snatchers . . . takers of the actual dead, stealers from worms, hijackers of Charon.

Starring Dominic Monaghan from *The Lord of the Rings* and *Lost* and Larry Fessenden from Glass Eye Pix (see the entry for *Wendigo,* page 201) as the two body snatchers, and featuring Angus Scrimm of *Phantasm* fame and Rod Pearlman of Rod Pearlman fame, the movie tells the hilarious and atmospheric tale of a pair of body snatchers who diversify to become occult body snatchers.

That's right, occult body snatchers. At first, the raggedy duo steals human bodies for doctors in the time-honored tradition of cadaver research, but eventually they find it more lucrative to harvest, well, monster corpses for the unknowable purposes of their various occult employers. You know, vampires, zombies, etc. (and there's a really clever "etc."). They soon find out, though, that these types of corpses are rarely as inert as the human kind that they're used to unearthing. An excellent conceit of the movie is that the thieves never know exactly what it is they're snatching, so there are no big clichés or monster baggage to have to contort the story around. They never once, to my admittedly porous memory, say words like *zombie* or *vampire*. They're just uncooperative bodies to Grimes and Black.

It's a novel concept that avoids gimmickry while still being rooted in the classic movie monster tradition. It also manages to be funny while still maintaining a creepy feel, thanks to great set design and effects.

Besides creating a funny, clever, and visually spooky film, the moviemakers also managed to make 2000-era New York look like 18th-century London on a pretty small budget. Here's how they did it.

For the opening-scene guillotine execution, the filmmakers used the Battery Weed section of Fort Wadsworth, a 200-year-old military base at the edge of Staten Island under the Verrazano-Narrows Bridge. The military base was actually active up until the mid-1990s, when it was opened to the public as a historic attraction.

They filmed the woodland scenes in Caumsett State Park in Lloyd Harbor on

Long Island, and the Fortune of War pub scenes in an East Village basement bar called The Scratcher, at 209 East Fifth Street in Manhattan.

In a movie filled to the top of the film canister (or hard drive, these days) with graveyards, they used Woodland Cemetery on Staten Island when they didn't just fake a cemetery on their own. It's at 982 Victory Boulevard, where it intersects with Highland Avenue. The cemetery is almost completely overgrown and forest-covered and looks as if it's been abandoned for about 100 of its 150 years of existence. Currently, efforts are underway to restore it, but it looks really cool as is, even if there are multiple places where a car can get stuck in the wilderness of the grounds.

The movie was released by the aforementioned Glass Eye Pix, an independent and New York–based production house run by the also aforementioned Larry Fessenden. I'd definitely recommend watching any horror movie this guy is connected with, whether he's directing, producing, starring, or cameo-ing. Chances are, you'll be in for a good, and sometimes great, time. *I Sell the Dead* certainly falls into the latter.

The Skeptic (2009)
SARATOGA SPRINGS

WHEN A MOVIE IS CALLED *The Skeptic,* and you find it in among horror titles, you can pretty much predict the plot arc. If there was only some way to predict the quality.

Starring Tim Daly, Tom Arnold, and Zoe Saldana, this haunted-house flick is about a smug lawyer played by Daly (the titular skeptic) who, to fix a few problems he's having with his wife, moves into the empty mansion of a recently deceased aunt. Of course, he ends up just trading his personal life problems for afterlife ones, because spooky stuff soon starts happening. Skeptics don't stand a chance in movies.

It's a pretty gentle little horror story, which isn't a criticism. That it's a rather poorly made one is, though. The moments of tension are diffused too quickly to be very effective, the dialogue is melodramatic, it oversells the main character's skepticism to the point of a drinking game, and then it ends way too abruptly.

However, *The Skeptic* has a nice autumn feel to it, with plenty of red and gold foliage, orange pumpkins, and a toilet-paper tree, the kind that blooms every October 31.

The moviemakers captured that feel by filming upstate, in the Saratoga Springs area. In fact, for a haunted-house movie, there are a ton of locations. It's almost as if the title character is never actually in the house.

Sites include Saratoga Springs City Court at 474 Broadway, the 240-year-old Olde Bryan Inn at 123 Maple Avenue, the Union Gables Inn at 55 Union Avenue, and Greenridge Cemetery at 17 Green-ridge Place as the token horror movie cemetery. Outside of Saratoga Springs, the movie was filmed at Union College at 807 Union Street in Schenectady and at the Buskirk covered bridge at the inter-section of Buskirk Road and Buskirk-West Hoosick Road in Hoosick.

Of course, this is a haunted-house movie, so that's pretty much the only location that matters (that is, if you buy at all into the overarching philosophy of this section that filming locations matter). In this case, the haunted house was the Batcheller Mansion at 20 Circular Street in Saratoga Springs.

The 140-year-old Batcheller Mansion is eccentric looking and extravagant. It's completely asymmetrical, with a roof that appears as if it were allowed to grow wild on its own, and features a conical tower topped by a cupola, a widow's walk, decorated dormer windows, and scalelike roof tiles that alternate colors. Every side of the house is dramatic and different, with various porches, windows, bal-conies, and ledges arranged and ornamented to the point of tactility. If it were a dollhouse, you'd want to run your fingers all over it.

The three-story mansion was commissioned by a judge and diplomat named George Batcheller. He called the place Kaser-el-Nouzha, which is apparently Arabic for "palace of pleasure." Through the years, it's been a private residence, a Jewish retirement home, a rooming house, and vacant to the point of condemned. These days, it's the Batcheller Mansion Inn, a posh bed and breakfast.

Both the exterior and interior of the mansion were used for *The Skeptic*. In the movie, it appears to be part of a secluded neighborhood full of mansions, when in reality it's right in the middle of town, surrounded by more mundane residences and businesses.

It's a gorgeous place, the kind of house that looks custom-made for lawns covered in brown leaves and windowpanes full of ghost faces. In fact, it's probably worth watching the movie just to learn about its existence.

FOR · OF · SUCH · IS · 𝔱𝔥𝔢
𝔎𝔦𝔫𝔤𝔡𝔬𝔪 · 𝔬𝔣 · 𝔥𝔢𝔞𝔳𝔢𝔫

Tonkin Mausoleum

Notable Graves, Cemeteries, and Other Memento Mori

MY FAVORITE THING ABOUT DEATH might be the getting buried part. I mean, I marvel daily at our technological and scientific achievements, at our feats of architecture and art, at our vast range of breakfast cereal textures. But I don't think we've ever done anything more fascinating than sticking a carved stone above a dead body.

Do I need to defend that statement? Yeah, I guess.

The truth is, we kind of have no good reason to label the spot where we plant our dead. We often call it an act of closure (even though "X marks the spot" is the exact opposite of closure). Or an act of remembrance (even though the memorial is nowhere near our everyday lives, where it could fulfill that purpose). We call it a tribute (though if you ask the living, having a stone above their grave is probably 103rd on their list of ways they'd want to be honored after death). Or a tradition (that one I can buy, but "we've always done it that way" is inherently a nonreason).

Signposting a dead body is just a weird thing to do . . . and I totally love that we do it. And if you can somehow make that tradition even weirder, then I'm going to visit your grave.

And those are the types of New York graves and cemeteries focused on in this section. Death spots in the state that are a bit different from their peers because of who is buried there, how they are buried, or because they have a story connected to their grave beyond "we threw dirt on him." In this section are the elaborate graves of presidents, strange epitaphs and placements, cemeteries that are more tourist attraction than private decay destinations, even a couple of pet cemeteries and one for ships.

Unfortunately, cemeteries themselves are probably a dying thing. Today we have much more economical and convenient options of disposing and memorializing our dead, we're much more practical about the whole death thing, and eventually we might even figure out an ideal way to deal with earthly remains. A society that has 40 types of grain flakes for dousing in milk can certainly expect that. Fields of crumbling stones seem so, well, Stone Age.

Of course, when that happens, we'll have lost the biggest benefit of cemeteries and gravestones. Not as remembrances of those who have passed on, not as spaces to grieve, not even as places to "ditch the body," but as memento mori: to remind us that we, too, shall die. Every gravestone is a pointing finger, every collection of them a chorus of, "We're waiting for you."

And that's why I've also included in this section other types of memento mori besides the usual marble-marked morbidity, death mementos that include giant statues of carrion birds, scientific collections of human brains, even a library dedicated to the macabre. They share in common with gravestones the acknowledgement of our mortality—and sometimes due to their uniqueness can be better at it—along with all the paradoxes inherent in that admission. For instance, that although death is the most unmovable fact of our existence, it's the one we seem to have to be reminded about constantly. Also, that we need to think about it to gain perspective on life, while simultaneously forgetting about it so that we can actually live.

I guess the whole thing comes down to the notion that death itself is just weird. We might as well do weird things such as weighting down corpses with stones, to keep in that spirit.

Grave of Chester A. Arthur

MENANDS

CHESTER ALAN ARTHUR doesn't have a memorial anywhere near the National Mall in Washington DC, but that just means he gets to be a big fish in a small pond, if that's a phrase I'm allowed to apply to a corpse and a graveyard.

Most of us can name more actors that have played U.S. presidents than we can actual U.S. presidents, and Arthur is one of those presidents who is easy to forget. He's like the Iowa of the "Name All the States" game. Heck, even the official Whitehouse.gov entry on his presidency opens with a sentence about his side whiskers, not any of his presidential achievements.

Nevertheless, he was the 21st president of the United States, even if he obtained the position in 1881 not by his own achievements but thanks to a crazy job-seeker who assassinated number 20, James Garfield, just six months or so into his term. Arthur just happened to be the vice president at the time.

Arthur was born in Vermont in 1829 but spent most of his youth in New York. Before getting into public service he was a teacher and a lawyer, and then held

various important state-level positions in New York, including during the Civil War. In fact, he got the vice presidency under Garfield as a result of his New York background and influence.

A few things did happen under the less-than-full term that Arthur got to serve as president (1881–1885). He passed the first federal immigration law, which outlawed the entry of the crazy, the moneyless, and the criminal (as well as, in a different legislative act, the Chinese). He also established a Civil Service commission, modernized the U.S Navy, and was in office during the first diplomatic forays into Korea.

In fact, both in his own time and in the hindsight of history, he has been credited with serving a pretty capable presidency, one that rose above partisanship politics. Even Mark Twain found little to ridicule about Arthur's term and went on record extolling the fairness of his presidency . . . and that guy made fun of small children.

Some credit Arthur's even handling of politics with the fact that shortly after he gained the presidency, he learned that he had Bright's disease, a fatal kidney malady. Imminent death puts a lot of things in perspective. Some also credit his illness with his lackluster attempt at earning a second term, which he lost to Grover Cleveland. Arthur died the next year, in 1886.

The small pond that he's buried in is Albany Rural Cemetery at the west end of Cemetery Road in Menands, the same graveyard where Charles Fort decomposes (see "Legends and Personalities of the Macabre").

Established in 1841, Albany Rural Cemetery is actually a large cemetery, although it's pretty easy to find Arthur's grave. Just look for the tall flagpole with the American flag. It can be found in Section 24, and is certainly the most impressive dead spot in the place.

Arthur is interred in a black, above-ground sarcophagus, with a human-size green-aged bronze angel guarding his head and eternally laying a palm frond across his stone casket. For some reason it reminds me of the story in the book of Jude where the Archangel Michael and Satan fight over the body of Moses. Except there's no devil crouching at the other end of Arthur's sarcophagus. That would be cool, though.

Anyway, like I said, Arthur apparently wasn't National Mall–worthy, but he did get a cool resting place and a nice word from posterity. In addition, the state of New York honors him with a bronze statue at the East 26th Street side of Madison Square Park in New York City, where you can see an artist's impression of his side whiskers firsthand.

Green-Wood Cemetery
BROOKLYN

BROOKLYN HAS BEEN SYMBOLIZED by various features over the past two centuries or so. Its bridge. Its brownstones. Coney Island. Spike Lee movies, I guess. Once upon a time, though, it was internationally famous . . . for one of its graveyards.

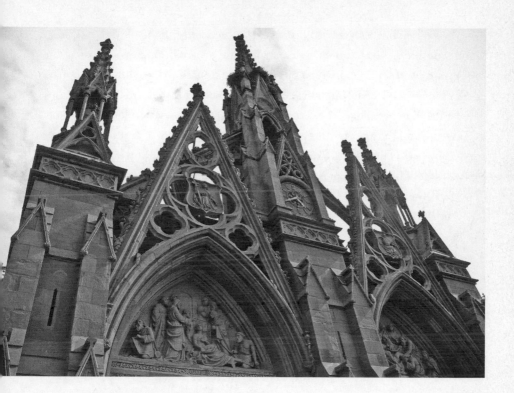

If you look at a satellite image of the borough, two large, adjacent green spots just northwest of center immediately stick out from the clustered urbanity that is Brooklyn. One is the 585 acres of Prospect Park. The other is Green-Wood Cemetery.

Green-Wood, located at 500 25th Street at Fifth Avenue, comprises 478 acres of precious city real estate that contains the remains of more than half a million people. That's an insanely rich stratum for future archaeologists to discover.

Established in 1838, it was one of the first American cemeteries to be designed both for the entombment of the dead and the enjoyment of the living. Beautiful works of art and architecture were erected there, and it was carefully landscaped to preserve, cultivate, and embellish the natural features of the large tract of land. The effort was successful, and in the mid-1800s, it was said that Green-Wood rivaled the mighty Niagara Falls as a North American tourist destination.

I'm not sure whether it's appropriate for me to call the highlights of a cemetery *highlights*. But it's at least safe to call them points of interest. And Green-Wood has some intense ones.

The gates of heaven are usually the gates associated with the dead, but Green-Wood's Gothic Revival arches give it a run. The brownstone entrance soars to more than 100 feet at its highest point and consists of three connected spires covered in an array of architectural flourishes of the sort that I'm not at all educated enough to describe. The central and tallest tower bears a clock face about halfway up, and the apex of the spire is fluffy with the nests of green monk parrots. Above each entrance are stone panels carved in various Biblical scenes, two on each side. The gatehouse facilities spread out on both sides from the arches.

The cemetery has a magnificent chapel and is full of elaborate mausoleums (the interiors of which are often more elaborate than the exteriors, and which can be seen on official cemetery tours), as well as funereal art and statuary. The Altar to Liberty is probably the most famous of the latter. The squat square of stone is flanked by a 9-foot-tall bronze statue of the Roman goddess Minerva. The altar and statue are set on the highest point of the cemetery, purposely built within sight of the Statue of Liberty, to which the helmeted Minerva raises a salute.

The monument was built to commemorate the Battle of Brooklyn, the first major battle of the American Revolution. Part of it was actually fought on the very land where the cemetery was founded. As a result, the ground was accustomed to the dead more than half a century before it became the official keeper of them.

There are other memorials to more recent large losses of life. Just inside the aforementioned gates is a tall, dark obelisk marking the mass grave of the 103 unidentified victims of the Brooklyn Theatre Fire (see "Infamous Crimes, Killers, and Tragedies"). In the northwest part of the cemetery, on Sylvan Avenue near a large pond, are remains of the victims of the United Airlines Flight 826 and TWA Flight 266 collision (Ibid.). This tragedy is also memorialized by a monument, an 8-foot-tall granite tablet.

Of course, Green-Wood has its famous dead as well, as it was a fashionable cemetery for the rich. Leonard Bernstein is there. Henry Ward Beecher. Both Currier and Ives. Samuel Morse. Boss Tweed. Strangely, the cemetery lacks a famous dead person with the mass appeal along the lines of Harry Houdini (in Machpelah Cemetery in Queens) or Herman Melville (in Woodlawn Cemetery in the Bronx), but it still contains a high number of personages whose names glow on our computer screens every so often.

A unique feature in this cemetery is its catacombs, at Lot 74 at the intersection of Locust and Grove Avenues, just south of the center of the cemetery. During one of the official cemetery tours, you can enter this underground corridor, where you'll find 30 different family-owned vaults off a central and very plain hallway running about 150 feet within the hillside. However, anytime the cemetery is open you can walk right above the crypts and see the three rows of skylights aligned along its roof. The middle row is above the main hallway and the row to either side is the skylight for each individual vault.

Even though its dominance in New York tourism is over, Green-Wood still has a thriving visitor presence with hundreds of thousands dropping by to say hi to the dead. Its calendar is jammed with tours, events, and restoration projects. In fact, it's probably the most undead dead place in the state.

Murder of Crows
Auburn

WHEN CROWS GET TOGETHER, their collective noun is a *murder*. However, every winter the city of Auburn has so many of these black carrion birds that *massacre* might be a better term.

Auburn is located at the tip of Owasco Lake, about 25 miles southwest of Syracuse. Since the early 1990s, an enormous crow population has swooped in to claim the city as its roost every time the seasons shift to cold weather. Estimates of the number vary wildly, but other than a few six-digit hyperboles, the number seems to be in the tens of thousands in this city of 30,000 humans.

The glossy black birds congregate in the downtown area and along the Owasco River, which cuts through the city. Sorting through local newspaper accounts of the phenomenon, you'll come across anecdotes about black skies, people carrying umbrellas on sunny days, and tons of Hitchcock jokes, which makes it all sounds like a party I'd want an invitation to.

Of course, despite how much a city overrun by crows appeals to my aesthetic sense, it doesn't take much empathy to realize what a huge public nuisance and health hazard this situation is for Auburn. As a result, in 2005, the city launched a program against these non-tax-paying residents, using laser lights, fireworks, and recorded crow distress calls for several weeks per year to annoy this cawing, crapping infestation enough to go elsewhere. Such as to Syracuse, I guess.

And it's sort of working. According to the newspaper accounts, the number of crows infesting the city each year seems to be decreasing somewhat, and they don't stick around as long . . . but they still come, and they still come in large numbers. Apparently Auburn is just naturally selecting for the most tenacious crows.

Not counting past lives and extended blackouts, I've only been to Auburn in winter once. It was mid-February, so past the peak time for the birds, but still cold enough to hope to see what makes this city the "murder" capital of the United States.

It was a Sunday, and driving through the downtown, the streets were eerily bare of both crows and people, enough to make one think that the annual war finally mutually exterminated both sides. However, I've never been to a graveyard that doesn't have crows, so I headed to one in the middle of town.

Established in 1851, Fort Hill is an 83-acre cemetery at 19 Fort Street. It's famous for being the site of the grave of Harriet Tubman, the former slave renowned for her daring and caring Underground Railroad exploits. It also has plenty of large trees, and sure enough, right in the center of the cemetery, the bare winter branches of a clump of trees were absolutely leaved with ebony foul. Anytime I got close they took to flight in raucous swarms. There could only have been a few hundred of them, though, so I can only imagine what Auburn's like at its most tar-feathered.

Other than drastic use of poisons and firearms or having all the human residents go about their daily business dressed as scarecrows, there's not much more Auburn can do to get rid of its crows. Some believe that, instead, the city should embrace its crows as a natural resource for tourism. After all, San Juan Capistrano, California, loves its swallows; Austin, Texas, loves its bats. Maybe Auburn should love its crows. And only park in covered garages.

The Three Crows
ALEXANDRIA

IT MIGHT SEEM ANTICLIMACTIC to follow up an entry on tens of thousands of crows that annually terrify a town with a mere trio of them, but that's because I haven't yet told you that these three crows are each 11 feet tall. Granted, they're also statues. And while that makes them less terrifying, it doesn't make them any less cool. Actually, wait. I really wrote myself into a corner with this intro. Eleven-foot-tall living crows are kind of hard to beat.

With all due deference to the raven, it's more often the crow that is the state bird of the grim, the ghastly, and the ominous. Rare is the horror story, be it on movie or e-reader screen, that doesn't feature their presence blackening the eye of a scene, or their eerie cawing unsettling the senses on a soundtrack.

As I mentioned in the last entry, the best place to find these carrion birds is your local cemetery, eating the worms that are eating your grandfather . . . but only because they can't get to your grandfather. That apparently doesn't hold true with giant statues of crows.

The Three Crows can be found in a field off I-81 in Alexandria, a northern New York town only a few miles from the Canadian border (as the crow flies, of course). Surprisingly, the birds aren't actually intended to be morbid, really. When I talked with William Salisbury, the artist who created these massive works, he said that the birds were installed about a decade ago and were meant to somewhat humorously invoke the premillennial fears of doom rampant (or at least rampantly discussed) before Y2K.

Made of welded metal and painted black, each of the three giant crows is a separate structure and positioned differently. They also each weigh an average of 1,500 pounds. That's a lot of crow to eat.

The artwork is located on Salisbury's own property and is just visible in the distance from the southbound lanes of I-81 just below Exit 50. However, if you want to see them at less than interstate speeds, you can drop by Salisbury's workshop on County Road 13, just down the road from Omar Cemetery. When I was there, a large banner out front advertised the presence of the birds. Salisbury had mown a path from there back into the overgrown field where the crows sit, and had even installed a bench for hanging out with them. Tuppence a bag, and all that. Certainly, being close enough to cool off in their shadows and see the rust stains on their monster flanks redefined the phrase *bird's-eye view* for me.

For more information about *The Three Crows,* you can visit the artist's web-site, willsalisbury.com. However, there honestly isn't a whole lot more to add about them, and there doesn't really need to be. There are three gigantic crows anchored into the bedrock of a field in northern New York like an illustrated page from H. G. Wells's *Food of the Gods.* It's enough that they just exist.

Grave of a Boy Killed by Kisses

BRONX

THE FIRST THING we want to know when we hear that someone has died is the how. Yet when we enter any given graveyard, we rarely get answers to that question. It's just not information traditionally considered epitaph-worthy. I've always kind of wanted it to be there, though. I mean, we'd get mostly *heart attack* and *cancer* inscribed in the stones of our cemeteries, but that would be worth it for the one *strangled by tight rope wire after accidentally skydiving over a circus.*

Still, every once in a while, someone dies in a way that his or her bereaved feels as if posterity should know more than that the deceased was a kind father or a loving son or a dedicated mother. Like 15-year-old George Spencer Millet.

His grave is in the amazing Woodlawn Cemetery at 501 East 233rd Street in the Bronx. There, the teenager's atoms mingle with the likes of Herman Melville, Duke Ellington, Bat Masterson, and Frank Belknap Long (see "Legends and Personalities of the Macabre").

Situated in the Lakeside section of the cemetery, near the intersection of Spruce and Observatory Avenues and near the western shore of the lake, the white, blocky, breadbox-size stone is a humble one. But that might be because his parents invested the funeral money in the long epitaph.

On the top side of the stone it gives his name; the names of his parents, Cornelius and Carrie; and the dates of the short span of his life, February 15, 1894, to February 15, 1909. That's right. He died on his birthday. Actually, because of it.

On the front-facing side of the tombstone, it tells this story:

> Lost life by stab in falling on ink eraser, evading six young women trying to give him birthday kisses in office Metropolitan Life Building.

The story is actually a well-documented one, and not just on a gravestone. George was an office boy at the original Madison Avenue headquarters of that famous insurance company. Newspaper accounts differ on whether he had worked there for eight months or two, but either way, he was apparently popular enough that on the day of his 15th birthday (just one day after Valentine's Day) several of his female co-workers threatened to take advantage of it by showering him with kisses.

As soon as work was over that afternoon, they struck. In the ensuing playful

scuffle, before they could even give him one to grow on, George fell and then shouted out, "I'm stabbed." He then went unconscious, bleeding profusely from his chest and dying soon afterward in an ambulance.

There followed a lot of confusion. The police initially thought it was a homicide and briefly detained one of the office stenographers. Turns out, George had an ink eraser in his pocket,

224 THE NEW YORK GRIMPENDIUM

which in those days meant a pointed blade for scraping ink off paper. Somehow in all the well-meaning shenanigans, he had fallen on it and it had pierced his heart. That simple. That sucky.

And his parents wanted all of us to know. Sometimes you should just take the cooties.

Arthur Kill Ship Graveyard
STATEN ISLAND

FEW THINGS ARE AS SPOOKY as an old graveyard, but one of them might just be an old ship graveyard.

For the past 60 years, whenever a ship outlived its usefulness in the New York/New Jersey area, its final resting place has often been the Arthur Kill Ship Graveyard, a marine scrap yard on the western edge of Staten Island run by the former Witte Marine Equipment Company, currently known as Donjon Marine, at 2453 Arthur Kill Road.

The name shared by the road and the ship graveyard is another name for Staten Island Sound, that thin body of water separating Staten Island from New Jersey and on which the ship graveyard is located. The term is an Anglicization of a Dutch phrase meaning "back channel" and is much more dramatic sounding than the alternative, especially when paired with the phrase *ship graveyard,* which is itself evocative enough to not need much elaboration. Here's some, anyway.

In the past, this amazing site featured the rotting and rusting remains of about 400 or so tugs, barges, ferries, and other watercraft towed here by water hearses and then stuck in the shallow water and muck of the channel shore to sink up to their naked masts at the pace of decay.

Today, there are still about 100 wrecks abandoned to molder in the brackish water. Satellite pictures offer a pretty good overview of the area, but up close you can see wooden beams jutting out like broken rib cages, glassless portholes staring like empty eye sockets, and rusty flanks peeling and splitting like no biological alternative that I can think of. Sometimes the piles of wood and metal are unrecognizable as ships. Other times they seem more like ghosts of their former physical selves.

It's both an awful and an awe-inspiring sight.

However, catching that sight can be problematic. The best land-based access is through the private property of the junkyard, which itself is a treacherous strip of land full of heavy equipment and hard-hatted men moving hazardous chunks of metal and wood. Basically, getting to the ship graveyard that way is both illegal and dangerous. Kayakers often paddle down the waterway for a more legal, if still somewhat dangerous, excursion, slipping in, out, and around the wrecks and getting all the best pictures that you'll see on the Internet.

For those of us who are allured by the water as long as our feet are dry-docked, there's a relatively safe and accessible spot up the road from Donjon Marine . . . through another old cemetery, this one for people. Right around 2298 Arthur Kill Road is a tiny, slightly elevated graveyard across the street from a small strip of businesses. Heading southwest, it'll be on the right before you get to Donjon Marine.

The graveyard is known as the Blazing Star Burial Ground, "Blazing Star" being a former name of the area, which was itself named after a local tavern. The cemetery has only about a couple dozen or so still-standing stones, the oldest of which that I could find dating back to the late 1700s, although some are probably even older. A large white and blue sign marks the graveyard, but when I visited it was overgrown almost to the point of the sign's not being visible.

From the graveyard, you'll be able to see some of the ships from afar, but a

vague path leads down an embankment and through grasses that have grown past human heights to a marshy area that will put you, depending on the tide, within camera distance of a sampling of these decaying hulks.

Standing there on the uncertain terra firma of the marsh grass, it seems as if the fabled locker of Davy Jones has been reclaimed from the sea. You can almost imagine doomed sailors staring forlornly from the crooked bridges and broken portholes of these dead ships.

Historic Pet Cemeteries
HARTSDALE, WEST SENECA

DESPITE DOING IT IN THE TITLE of this entry, I'm not exactly sure what it would take to accurately call a pet cemetery *historic*. I'm assuming if it were located on an ex-battlefield or if it were filled with presidential pets it might qualify. But these two New York patches of pet putrescence come the closest otherwise, I think, as one claims to be the first animal cemetery in the country and the other one isn't too far behind.

Hartsdale Pet Cemetery and Crematory can be found just north of Manhattan in Hartsdale. The front entrance is at 75 North Central Park Avenue, along the side of a highway. Its tall black gates are easy to miss, being that the entrance is sunk below ground level and somewhat hemmed in by thick bushes.

Those iron gates name the cemetery in white letters as Hartsdale Canine Cemetery (its name before it went multidenominational), and its date of incorporation, 1896, is similarly and proudly emblazoned. Besides considering itself the first pet cemetery in the country, Hartsdale also claims to be the second in the world and the oldest operating one in the world.

Once you descend the short flight of concrete steps from street level and pass through the gates, you'll find yourself at the bottom of a hill blooming with tiny gravestones. The cemetery is small, about 5 acres, but plenty large enough to handle the 70,000 or so interments (few animals need the 4 by 8-foot plot that humans do, and the place is also a crematorium) that range from the usual dogs, cats, birds, and reptiles, to horses, monkeys, and even, according to its website, a lion cub.

Its centerpiece is the War Dog Memorial, a bronze German shepherd

Hartsdale Pet Cemetery and Crematory

perched on a large rock dedicated to all the dogs that were used in the service during World War I. In a corner of the cemetery is another statue, whimsical this time, of four cats and a rabbit playing instruments and singing.

The cemetery began in the late 1800s when a veterinarian named Samuel Johnson allowed a woman from the city to bury her dog in his apple orchard. A human-animal interest story about it was printed in the newspaper, and suddenly everybody had a pet that needed a more human sendoff than a black garbage bag at the curb or a hole behind the shed.

The cemetery has a "secret garden" type of feel due to its location, the fact that it has no car access, and because the paths pleasantly meander around the hill and trees. The headstones have a surprising amount of variety both in shape and decoration. Pictures of pets adorn many of the small graves, as do heartfelt epitaphs and silly names. Some are "family" plots, meaning every time a family goes through another pet, it ends up buried with its predecessors, so some have half a dozen or so names inscribed in the tombstones. There was even a low mausoleum of some sort for "Toodles" and "Sally." The oldest burial I found in the half hour I was there was from 1908.

The length of the state away from Hartsdale (about 360 miles as Google Maps

flies), near Buffalo, is Pine Rest Cemetery, at 757 Seneca Creek Road in the town
of West Seneca.

Pine Rest goes back to 1919 at its present location, although who started it and
how long ago exactly nobody knows. It's a
much different type of place than Hartsdale, despite having the rather large commonality of atrophied animals 6 feet
beneath its lawn.

Pine Rest is located in a residential
area and is more like a park than a cemetery, with wide-open spaces, a stream,
and colorful animal statues scattered

Pine Rest Cemetery

around the perimeter of its 18,000 interments. Basically, it's the type of place
you'd bring a live pet to on a Saturday—and many do. Heck, I even ran across a
rafter of wild turkeys while visiting. I assume they were shopping for plots.

Pine Rest is a full-service cemetery and advertises various burial packages:
caskets, funeral services, ambulance services, viewing rooms, embalming, cremation, and other forms of extravagance that I'd probably not even lavish on a
deceased family member.

In my stroll through this cemetery, I saw plots where dogs and cats lie
together, a section reserved for greyhounds, and a headstone for a pig named
Buddha. The oldest burial I could find here was from 1929.

Even though the two cemeteries are vastly different from each other, both
seem to maintain a surreal aura that I assume every pet cemetery must have.
Maybe it's because the somber gravestones bear such names as Strippy, Nookie,
and High Hat Bob. Maybe it's the dissonance of seeing animals given what is traditionally a human ritual.

Most likely, though, it's because these cemeteries can make us feel the opposite of what we experience from their human analogues. Graveyards containing
people make us feel our own mortality acutely, which is rarely a nice sensation.
Further, anyone and everyone, from the bland to the rottenest, is buried there.
An animal's headstone, on the other hand, provides proof that the creature definitely gave somebody a lot of joy.

However, though Stephen King might've given the whole lot a bad name, at a basic level there's no difference between a pet cemetery and a human one. In the end, they're just plots of extremely rich dirt and extremely luxurious grass . . . and fascinating places to visit.

Morbid Anatomy Library
BROOKLYN

IT BOASTS A FASCINATING COLLECTION OF BOOKS, but it's not exactly a library. Its walls and shelves are covered in compelling artifacts and artwork, but it's not exactly a museum. My best attempt at encapsulating the small Brooklyn studio known as the Morbid Anatomy Library is to just call it a space, albeit a space dedicated to the morbid.

Actually, I could go one further and describe it as the exterior manifestation of what's inside one Joanna Ebenstein.

Ebenstein is the person behind the Morbid Anatomy blog, a website dedicated to all things medical and morbid (*morbid anatomy* is basically an older medical term for the study of the diseased body). The website tidily describes itself as a survey of the "interstices of art and medicine, death and culture," and the physical library came about as an extension of the blog . . . or an incarnation of it, I guess.

The library is at 534 Union Street in Brooklyn; you can enter by pressing the buzzer for 1E and awaiting a response. You can also go around the corner, down an alley, and enter the library through Proteus Gowanus, an art gallery and reading room of which the Morbid Anatomy Library is a "project in residence." I entered through the art gallery, and was directed to a door with a wooden sign marked "Observatory." Observatory was a more-or-less empty room on the other side of which was a door bearing a sign for the Morbid Anatomy Library, with a friendly admonition to enter.

I later found out that Observatory is a shared space used by Morbid Anatomy and others for art exhibits, presentations, and classes on such things as Anthropomorphic Mouse Taxidermy, Dissection as Studio Practice, and Animal Mummification. All the stuff that our schools neglected to offer as electives.

Inside the Morbid Anatomy Library proper, it's cramped, cozy, and basically like walking into a cabinet of curiosities.

Along one wall was a human skeleton lying horizontal in a wood-framed vitrine. A ceiling-high shelf of
books dedicated to death and medicine towered in a
corner. A taxidermied crow perched on a branch that
jutted out from the wall. A pair of freshly mummified
frogs dangled from nails beside a pair of severed emu
feet. There were photographs of medical displays from
around the world and paintings of skulls and other
similar themes. Small cabinets and drawers and
shelves held animals in formaldehyde jars, medical
implements, and religious icons (the latter being
always relevant for any contemplation of human atti-
tudes toward death).

As much as I wanted to just rifle through Ebenstein's collection, we sat down and talked first, one
undertaker of a death-related project to another.

Her history is similar to many of us death-obsessed: that childhood fascination that compels us to poke dead squirrel carcasses without repulsion or to
read gravestones as if they're short stories stuck with her and evolved into an
adult interest—in her case, in "the way beauty intersects with death."

I asked her to clarify what she meant. "I'm not interested in gore or crime
scene photos or serial killers." I pretended the book didn't have an entire chapter
dedicated to exactly that. "More the aesthetic quality of death."

In talking to her, it seems as if one of her favorite examples of that intersection is La Specola in Florence, the 240-year-old Italian museum famous for its
18th-century life-size wax cadaver models. A large photograph that Ebenstein
had taken herself of La Specola's so-called Anatomical Venus, a naked young
woman with highly detailed and removable interior organs, was displayed
prominently on one of the walls of the library.

The line she draws in her investigation into the morbid is understandable.
There's a difference between the qualities of an isolated brain in a jar and seeing
said brain spread all over the sidewalk. And while violent death is certainly an
important element to any definition of the morbid, she leaves that to others to
wrestle with.

In fact, the purpose of taking her collection public, she said, was to "rebrand
morbid." According to her, "I've been called morbid all my life. Am I the morbid

one for being fascinated by a skeleton or are you the morbid one for pretending we don't have such things in our bodies?"

By *you* she meant American society in general. While other cultures dedicate entire holidays to visiting dead relatives in cemeteries and practice religious rites in ossuaries, we push off thoughts of death (and anything that sparks those thoughts) as disturbing and inappropriate, even though it's one of our fundamental commonalities with each other and one of our most defining features.

After we talked, I took a closer look at her collection. There actually wasn't much, if anything, that could be construed as off-putting to more sensitive constitutions. There were natural artifacts such as snake skins and bird nests, plenty of animal taxidermy, and medically related objects. The photographs and books were worth sitting down with and perusing uninterruptedly for days. And that's pretty much exactly what you're supposed to do there. Meanwhile, a few people came in apprehensive, but curious, although they left quickly. The Morbid Anatomy Library can be daunting, as the size of the room can make you feel as if you're intruding.

But you're not, so don't let that stop you. The place can keep somewhat irregular hours, so contact Ebenstein by email through the Morbid Anatomy blog (morbidanatomy.blogspot.com) if you're making a special trip. To get the most out of your visit, I certainly suggest engaging in conversation with whoever's there (especially if it's Ebenstein), as I found our conversation the most worthwhile part of my Morbid Anatomy Library experience. Otherwise, browse the books, examine the artifacts, and just marvel at that inextricable part of life we call death.

Ripley's Shrunken Head Collection
Manhattan

CRAWLING WITH HUMAN BODIES, throbbing with light, vibrating with noise—Manhattan's Times Square is almost a living thing these days. However, it does harbor within its busy blocks some serious death . . . all thanks to Robert Ripley.

Robert Ripley, of course, is the founder of the Ripley's Believe It or Not! empire, a collection of oddities that includes strange feats, unique artifacts, and obscure facts. Ripley was born in California but lived much of his life in the global media hub that is New York City, and he always kept at least one residence in the state during all his worldwide travel adventures. In fact, he died in Manhattan itself in 1949, of a heart attack at the age of 58.

After his death, his empire of oddities continued to empire oddly on with television shows, books, and museums called odditoriums. The latter are located all over the planet and anywhere money-laden tourists are—Orlando, Niagara Falls, Hollywood, London, Bangalore. Basically, if it's an urban wonder, a Ripley's odditorium is usually there to add its own peculiar brand of wonders to the mix.

The Ripley's Believe It or Not! Times Square Odditorium is at 234 West 42nd Street, next door to Madame Tussaud's, the famous wax museum chain. Incidentally, Madame Tussaud's has a trio of great monsters for us macabre-interested amid its waxy pop stars, actors, and historical figures, namely, Bela Lugosi as Dracula and Boris Karloff as both Frankenstein's monster and the Mummy. I mean, by themselves they're probably not worth the hefty price of admission, but they're worth checking out if you find yourself Times Square drunk enough to go inside.

Ripley's Odditorium also has a pretty big entrance fee, about $30 per anybody over the age of 13, but it contains a bit more of interest than simulacra of Johnny Depp and Pope John Paul II. The entrance is a party in itself, with statues and lights and animatronics to entice the borderline curious. Inside are (a) a lot of cool things, (b) a lot of cool macabre things, and (c) a lot of extremely cool macabre things that the title of the entry has already given away.

Some of the death-related items you'll find in the museum include a cast of Napoleon Bonaparte's death mask, along with an actual lock of his hair; a vampire-killing kit; mummy parts; the cross-section of the head of an 18th-century French criminal; various medieval torture devices; and a series of wearable and/or decorative skulls from the native peoples of such exotic locales as Vanuatu, Tibet, New Guinea, and Borneo, places where what we'd consider Edward Gein levels of perversity are actually signs of respect and cultural norms.

Still, as much as those objects were a few of my favorite things, they were just grisly appetizers. At the end of the museum was a relatively small room with walls covered in bamboo and completely dedicated to one type of artifact: genuine shrunken heads.

The collection was displayed in a series of glass cases scattered about the room to make the best use of space and to spread out the crowds that would obviously be thronging them. It was a well-done arrangement, although in my

own naturally shrunken head I'd imagined them strung up on a Christmas tree.

By my count, there were close to 6 billion of them, but I was a bit overwhelmed at being surrounded by the tiny, preserved heads. The official tally is 24.

Still, Ripley's claims that it owns the largest collection of shrunken heads on the planet, and that this particular odditorium showcases the largest single exhibit of them and even includes specimens from Ripley's personal collection. It's at least certain that their collection is larger than my own. Probably yours, too. If not, e-mail me. We should hang out.

Now, the idea of primitive tribes' shrinking the severed heads of their enemies and then wearing them has permeated modern culture to the point that it's easy to think it was a widespread practice among indigenous peoples. However, interestingly enough, there was only one group to ever really practice the custom, the Jivaro of South America.

Located on the jungle slopes of the Andes in Peru and Ecuador and calling themselves the Shuar, this still-extant tribe has assimilated somewhat into the modern era, but back in its fighting days, its peoples were considered some of the fiercest warriors around. Wearing the miniaturized, decapitated heads of their foes was one way to maintain that rep, I guess.

One particularly gruesome story is told about their revolt against the Spanish empire. They killed 30,000 Spaniards, captured the avaricious governor who had cheated them in a trade deal, and then poured molten gold down his throat. He died. And I only say that last bit because I want to be credited as having written the most unnecessary sentence ever.

Still, the Shuar are most famous for the shrunken heads, which they referred to as *tsantsa*. By most indications they gave up the practice decades ago, but the details of the process are well documented. Basically, they would shrink the heads by removing the skull, sewing up the facial orifices, boiling the skin, and inserting and shaking around hot stones and sand to treat the interior. It's almost too obvious to say that it's extremely similar to throwing a wet wool sweater in the dryer. Actually, the Ripley's exhibit posted handy, detailed instructions for how to shrink a head yourself. Looking at them, you can apparently do this easier than putting together a coffee table.

The heads are about fist size, decorated with hair and sometimes feathers, and make me lean toward the "Believe It" in the dare of the museum's name. The features of the faces are so well preserved that I'm pretty sure I'd recognize the faces if they were expanded to original size and replaced on the bodies of their original owners.

At the very least, each head had its own personality (collect them all!), both due to the original features and the, uh, craftsman's decorating skills. Disconcertingly, there were even specimens from small children, apparently killed to ensure that the offspring of a victim didn't grow up to seek revenge. And, between you and me, I did in fact look around to see whether any of the tiny craniums belonged to white men. It's hard to tell because the process of shrinking usually darkens the skin, but one actually did bear the helpful label of "Caucasian." Not that I would've been disappointed otherwise. It's impossible to be so when you're surrounded by such crazy artifacts.

In the end, you can call the Ripley's Believe It or Not! Times Square Odditorium a tourist trap if you want, but it has an entire room dedicated to shrunken heads. Take that, Metropolitan Museum.

Reed's Tomb
BROOKLYN

WHEN WE LOSE A LOVED ONE, we're told that we must eventually move on. Jonathan Reed misheard that advice when his wife of many years died. He actually moved in . . . to her tomb.

Mary Reed died in March 1893. She was interred in the mausoleum of her still-living father in the Evergreens Cemetery in Brooklyn. Her husband, who was a retired businessman in his 60s, visited her every day, although not in the "I miss you in my life" kind of way . . . more so in the "What do you want to do today?" kind of way. His daily visits lasted from the creaky opening of the cemetery gates to the ominous finality of their shutting for the night.

Soon, Reed was forbidden by his father-in-law from hanging out in the tomb because it was, well, damned creepy. However, Mary's father died about a year and a half later, giving Reed the opportunity to move his wife's remains to a custom-made mausoleum elsewhere in the same cemetery, where he was free to again buck the "till death do us part" marriage vow.

Other than going home at night to sleep, and only then because cemetery rules forced him to, Reed lived in Mary's mausoleum. However, far from being too much of a ghoul, he turned the small stone enclosure into a nice little place to spend eternity. He decorated it with art and pictures, installed a stove for warmth, and moved in furniture. He and his deceased wife even shared a pet bird to help make their tomb a home, which eventually died but stuck around in taxidermied form, because, well, Jonathan kind of had a problem with letting go.

Reed would talk to Mary, eat his meals beside her, and it's even said that he had her casket custom made with a door so that he could see her when he wanted to. The first time you see your wife without makeup, it's a small surprise. The first time you see her without flesh, well, apparently love conquers that, too.

Some of his friends believed that he was under the delusion that Mary was still alive, although who knows? When you spend every day in a tomb stroking a stuffed parrot and playing peek-a-boo with a skull, your definition of life and death are probably a bit more complex than a mere binary perspective of OFF

and ON.

For more than a decade, Reed lived in his wife's mausoleum, hardly, if ever, missing a grave shift. As one would think, news of his eccentricity spread and he became somewhat of a sensation, with thousands of people visiting him at the tomb, where he rocked in his chair and jokingly flipping a thumb back at the old ball and chain.

Eventually, of course, it became a permanent arrangement, when Reed himself died in 1905. They found him unconscious on the floor of the tomb, and he was ruled dead sometime later and interred beside his wife, where to this day his story attracts visitors to their mausoleum.

In Reed's defense, the parklike Evergreens Cemetery (sometimes called Cemetery of the Evergreens) is a pleasant place to spend one's days. The cemetery, at 1629 Bushwick Avenue in Brooklyn, has accepted the dearly departed since 1849. It includes 225 acres of hills and trees and is the eternity of choice for more than 526,000 people.

There's plenty to see at Evergreens, in addition to nature and those who went against it. The cemetery claims the graves of such famous entertainers as Blind Tom Wiggins and Bill "Bojangles" Robinson, along with the world's first chess champion (who has a chessboard inscribed on his tombstone), and other notables. It also boasts connections to both the Revolutionary and Civil Wars, as well as being a hangout for science fiction author Isaac Asimov. The cemetery includes victims from both the Brooklyn Theatre Fire of 1876 and the General Slocum Tragedy of 1904, and a mass grave of unknown victims from the Triangle Shirtwaist Factory Fire of 1911 (see entries for all three in "Infamous Crimes, Killers, and Tragedies").

Still, Reed's tomb by itself is a good enough reason to visit. It is situated in the Whispering Grove section, which is in the southwest part of the cemetery to the left of the main entrance (downloadable maps with more than 30 locations of interest labeled are available on the cemetery website). The tomb is in a row of other mausoleums, all cut into a hill. Reed's Tomb is squarish, made of large blocks of stone, and is topped by a sphere. The front door has four small, wedge-shaped windows arranged in a circle and is protected by iron bars topped with maple leaves. Above the door it merely reads "Jonathan and Mary E. Reed."

Today, as it has been since Jonathan Reed's death, the door of the tomb is closed, and nobody will be there to greet you if you knock.

Staten Island Ruins
STATEN ISLAND

THE MIDDLE OF STATEN ISLAND is rotten with abandoned, decaying, and graffitied institutional complexes from the 19th and early 20th centuries. Most of them were constructed for medical purposes, and it's as if the facilities all caught the diseases of the patients that they housed, causing everyone to run screaming from the buildings, leaving them to the caprices of nature, time, squatters, and vandals.

The three main complexes thusly treated were the Farm Colony, Sea View Hospital, and the infamous Willowbrook State School. What remains of each are scattered throughout the 2,800 acres of the centrally located Staten Island parkland known as the Greenbelt. Often, it's hard to tell which building belongs to which facility, due to the degraded nature of the edifices and the surrounding forest. Also, the laziness of the researcher.

The Farm Colony was built in 1829 as a poorhouse, eventually becoming the New York City Farm Colony when Staten Island became a borough of New York City. The Farm Colony itself was basically a little city of its own, with facilities such as a hospital, an asylum, a school, and dormitories. In 1915 it merged with the recently built Sea View Hospital, which we'll get to in a second. Many thousands of people were housed at the colony for the duration of its existence, especially the elderly, but upon the establishment of the Social Security Agency, it became less needed and was closed in 1975. Its remnants are more or less located in the woods west of Brielle Avenue, behind the various sports fields currently lining the road.

Sea View Hospital was a compound of some dozen or so buildings originally built in 1913 as a tuberculosis center. It was designed to accommodate about 2,000 patients. Eventually, tuberculosis became less of a threat and the facility became more of a general one. As the hospital grew and changed, some of the buildings were abandoned and forgotten, although the complex still operates today in more modern facilities as the Sea View Hospital Rehabilitation Center and Home. The few ruins of its former self can be found on the east side of Brielle Avenue, some of which can be seen right from the road.

And then there's Willowbrook State School, the story of which is less one of entropy and more one of tragedy. This 375-acre complex was erected in the 1930s as a state-run institution for mentally handicapped children. However, World

War II intervened, and it was first used as an army hospital before eventually reverting back to its original purpose. So far, so decent.

However, in the 1960s it underwent a scandal, when it was discovered that healthy children were being infected with hepatitis so that doctors could study the effectiveness of potential treatments. On top of that, it was around this time that the facility started becoming overcrowded, with all the unpleasant ramifications of such a circumstance. In the 1970s, these unpleasant ramifications were documented by the local media, including a documentary in which a local TV reporter named Geraldo Rivera filmed Willowbrook's harrowing conditions of filth and neglect. Rivera then mounted its rubble to national fame, hosting television programs, cameo-ing in such shows as *Baywatch* and *Seinfeld,* and dramatically opening empty gangster vaults. Still, even with all the darkness that had come to light, it still took another decade for the school to finally and completely close.

Today most of Willowbrook's buildings have been renovated and annexed into the campus of the College of Staten Island (or CSI, as the campus's refurbished brick smokestack proudly proclaims) at 2800 Victory Boulevard. Only a few buildings still remain jumbled and weedy in the aforementioned Greenbelt.

Many of the ruins are relatively easy to access if you're okay with tramping through forests (and I say that with all cautionary caveats of danger and illegality). A quick spin through Google Earth will help you pinpoint most of them. I'm not sure how long the ruins will be able to hide in the Greenbelt, though. They've been steadily disappearing over the past decades, and one day they'll all be gone, demolished or revamped for safety or profit.

It'll be sad to see them go, just like it was sad to see them stay.

George Eastman Suicide Note
ROCHESTER

WE KNOW HIM AS THE MAN who put cameras into the hands of the masses. The Grim Reaper knows him as that impatient guy who cut in line. George Eastman was an inventor and the founder of the Eastman Kodak Company. He was also the author of the most compelling suicide note in the history of that literary genre.

Eastman was born on July 12, 1854, in Waterville, New York. His family then moved to Rochester, where he lived the rest of his life and where the Eastman Kodak Company is headquartered to this day. It was at the age of 24 that Eastman started experimenting with photography, during a time when that involved chemicals, plates, giant cameras, tripods, and portable dark rooms. He refined the cumbersome techniques, patented a device to produce large numbers of plates, and jumped into the camera business.

Eventually, he invented roll film, which changed everything, from making cameras truly portable and less expensive to paving the way for the birth of the movie industry. In fact, long before the digital revolution put cameras everywhere, cameras were everywhere . . . and that's pretty much thanks to Eastman. He wanted everybody to have a camera, wanted the devices to be as "convenient as the pencil." He even gave out free cameras to half a million 12-year-olds, to foster a camera culture. It was Eastman that launched the inexpensive Brownie camera in 1900, with the slogan "You push the button, we do the rest."

As to the other half of the company name, "Kodak" was just a simple trademark that Eastman invented, a word that would eventually overshadow his own name on the marquee.

Although he never found the time or will to marry, Eastman did finally slow down, and while he never fully left the company he founded, he dedicated himself to all the things that extremely rich people do—massive philanthropy and extravagant hobbies such as big game hunting.

Unfortunately, toward the end of his days, he developed a spinal condition that severely hobbled his lifestyle, and on March 14, 1932, at the age of 77, he shot himself in the chest with a Luger pistol.

And that's probably where the most interesting part of this interesting story is, at least to a guy writing a book about death-related sites and artifacts. Eastman left a handwritten suicide note, on a simple, yellow, lined piece of paper. Addressed "To my friends" and signed with his initials, his explanation for his self-demise was a mere six words long. It read, "My work is done. Why wait?" It's one of the few inarguable statements ever set to paper.

Eastman left marks all over Rochester, the surrounding area, and even the country. His Waterville birth home was moved to a museum in nearby Mumford, his mansion is now a museum operated by the University of Rochester and called the George Eastman House, his name adorns various institutions and localities, and he's had monuments and statues erected to him. His ashes are even interred in a memorial on the property of the company he founded, at 1669 Lake Avenue.

The memorial is publicly accessible in what's called Kodak Park, right on Lake Avenue itself. There, you'll find a brick and pink marble courtyard area anchored by a simple, low, film canister—shaped cylinder of the same pink marble and carved with a pair of human figures on opposite sides of the cylinder, a female form representing aspiration and a male representing science.

To find the cause of those ashes, all you have to do is visit the aforementioned George Eastman House, which is about 11 miles away, at 900 East Avenue. The 35,000-square-foot, century-old mansion features about 50 rooms on three floors, two stories of which are publically accessible. You enter the mansion from the back, where an art museum holds photography exhibits. However, once you're in

the mansion proper, it's mostly dedicated to the life and work of Eastman, with extravagantly decorated rooms filled with unique furniture and books and hunting trophies. And, of course, cameras.

The most interesting bit is in a small, blank room on the second floor that's part of a series of exhibits. In it, is a single, small glass case, within which is the sheet of paper upon which Eastman scrawled his final words to the world, after entertaining some friends and associates and then signing a codicil to his will naming the University of Rochester as his main beneficiary. Actually, the entire exhibit focuses on his death, with a piece of his coffin, that codicil to his will, his handwritten request to be cremated, his death certificate, dried roses from his coffin blanket, and a program from his funeral service, among other items. Pretty much everything except for the gun itself.

"My work is done. Why wait?" I don't whether it's the succinctness of the message or its humility in not trying to impart any wisdom gleaned from a life-time of success and experience, but the note is completely arresting. And that's whether you're merely reading the words in a book or seeing the simple yellow piece of paper firsthand.

And, of course, I took a picture of it.

Forest Lawn Cemetery
BUFFALO

F OR A CEMETERY TO COMPETE as a tourist attraction in a major city, it needs at least one of four elements: a long history, a beautiful natural environment, compelling works of funeral art, or graves of the famous dead. Forest Lawn Cemetery has all four and is, as a result, one of the more interesting places one can visit in the city of Buffalo, even if you don't find curated icky bits of the dead intrinsically fascinating.

Let's start with history. Forest Lawn was established in 1849 by a lawyer named Charles E. Clarke who was looking to capitalize on a booming Buffalo population that eventually had to fizzle somewhere. Now, more than 160 years later, the still-active Forest Lawn covers 269 acres and 152,000 remains.

However, Clarke didn't set out to just make mere rows of stones and bones. He, like so many cemetery creators before and after him, was inspired by Paris's famous Père Lachaise Cemetery, which was and remains as much a park and an exhibit space as a graveyard.

To that end, Clarke preserved and supported many of the natural features of the landscape, including shade trees and lakes, expansive hills, and a creek. Today, the property's 10,000-odd trees represent about 200 species.

Clarke added to this natural aesthetic with man-made ones, and it's a practice that the cemetery continues to this day. Scattered throughout the grounds are works of art that have nothing to do with marking the spot of the monied dead. For instance, the blazingly white, 16-foot-high abstract sculpture by John Field, of an angel plucking a limp form from the ground, dominates an otherwise empty hill that could just as easily have been filled with squat, square tombstones.

Elsewhere are more classic-style sculptures, such as the giant bust of Giuseppe Verdi, the 19th-century Italian opera composer who isn't buried in the cemetery, or the fountain statue called *The Three Graces*, in which three nude bronze women wash in the center of a lake.

But that doesn't mean that the funereal sculptures themselves don't beat out the art for art's sake. Take the Blue Sky Mausoleum, for instance. Designed by famed architect Frank Lloyd Wright, the mausoleum completely eschews the stacked dead approach and instead staggers its 24 white granite crypts in such a way that each one is open-faced to the sky. The effect is like a set of stairs from some Grecian monument. It descends a gentle hill from a set of benches and a pillar to the edge of a pond.

Greeting visitors and mourners just inside the cemetery's Delaware Avenue

gate is a large statue on an even larger pedestal of Chief Red Jacket, the famous Revolutionary War–era Native American orator, which marks the spot on this white man's holy ground where his remains have been interred.

However, the most fantastic grave on the premises can be found just past Chief Red Jacket's statue. The Blocher memorial was built in 1888 and is basically a gigantic, sealed, bell-shaped granite room. Floor-to-ceiling glass windows offer a view inside of four life-size marble Victorian figures. In the scene, parents John and Elizabeth Blocher stand over their dead son Nelson, while above an angel looks down on the scene, waiting for its tip, I suppose. Surrounding the memorial are benches where one can stew in jealously over the fact that we'll just end up sifted into an urn or planted under a simple square stone.

Of course, nature and art and history are all great . . . but they're still just school subjects. The coolest thing a cemetery can have is a dead celebrity. It has that in common with the best parties, I think.

And the famous who decay in Forest Lawn run the entire gamut of celebrity. There are the historical ones, such as President Millard Fillmore, who is buried with his family under a simple obelisk. There are the pop culture ones, including super freak aficionado Rick James. There are even obscure ones, such as Frederick A. Cook, the guy who may have faked the first trip to the North Pole, and Alfred P. Southwick, the dentist who invented the electric chair (see "Infamous Crimes, Killers, and Tragedies").

Forest Lawn Cemetery has two main gates, one at 1411 Delaware Avenue, where the office is located, and another more majestic one, with triumphal arch-type gates, at the intersection of West Delavan Avenue and Main Street. Either one takes you directly to dead people.

Utica State Asylum
UTICA

I WANTED TO INCLUDE every single one of New York's many abandoned asylums in this book. However, they all have the same basic story, one common to old asylums across much of the country. Erected sometime in the 1800s with grand intentions and wide definitions for the diagnosis of insanity, these massive and elegantly designed buildings started out with lurid-sounding names

that included such words as *insane* or *lunatic* and were then rechristened to something less grim, often including the phrase *state hospital*. Eventually, these institutions were closed due to being overcrowded and too large to fund, as well as their becoming more irrelevant as treatments evolved. Left with no purpose and no money for upkeep, the buildings decayed in abandonment over the decades while a struggle ensued between those who wanted them preserved as historical landmarks and others who wanted them developed by commercial entities into modern medical facilities or condos.

Such is the story with Binghamton State Hospital, Buffalo State Hospital, and Ovid's Willard State Hospital, for instance, all of which to one degree or another are still standing. I have featured several other asylums when I could find other angles on them, including Willowbrook State School, for the neglect and abuse scandal that occurred there (see "Infamous Crimes, Killers, and Tragedies"), and Rolling Hills Asylum, for its embrace of the paranormal (see "Classic Monsters").

And, as you can see from the title of this entry, Utica State Asylum also made the cut, for two reasons: its unique architecture and the infamous Utica Crib.

Opened in 1843 under the name New York State Lunatic Asylum, this institution was the state's first attempt at a mental home. Its story is pretty much exactly as laid out in the first paragraph about other asylums.

However, the construction of Utica State Hospital predated by about half a decade the influential Kirkbride Plan. This was an architectural philosophy, developed by psychiatrist Thomas Kirkbride, for constructing mental hospitals in such a way that the building itself contributed to the health of its patients. Basically, that meant plenty of windows for sunlight and fresh air, lots of outside space, and aesthetically pleasing architectural ornamentation.

As a result, unlike its peers, the Utica State Hospital isn't a sprawling Victorian-style building. Instead, it's an imposing Grecian edifice with thick, towering pillars and a blocklike shape. The dark gray stone makes the building seem almost tomblike, and its sheer size and structure tend toward the monumental. It's certainly a beautiful building (at least to someone not confined there, I guess), but it's also an intimidating one.

Meanwhile, the hospital became infamous not for its look, but because it was on the premises of the asylum that the Utica Crib was invented in the 1840s. This was a device for restraining patients. It consisted of a low, coffin-shaped structure surrounded on all sides by slatted walls like a crib. Unlike a crib, it also had a slatted roof that could be secured to keep patients from escaping. Basically, it was a horizontal cage. The hospital administrators realized that somewhere around 1887 and stopped using it.

The asylum itself shut down in 1978, but still looms unused and empty at 1213 Court Street. A nicely treed lawn leads up to it, stopping at a barbed wire–topped chain-link fence that bears signs that read, "No Trespassing: Violators Will Be Prosecuted" and "Danger, Hazardous Area: Keep Out." However, it's in a residential neighborhood and you can drive right up through the lawn to the fencing, which basically means you can stand right in the chilling shadow of the structure itself and think about how much dark gray pillars look like iron bars.

Other, newer buildings on the grounds are still in use for various purposes, but the main building of the former lunatic asylum that was Utica State Hospital just sits there, silent and impassive as the ivy slowly covers its flanks and the barbed wired gradually rusts.

Washington Square Park
MANHATTAN

IN MANY WAYS—metaphorically, symbolically, historically—we all walk on the backs of the dead. However, if you've ever been to Washington Square Park in Greenwich Village, you've done so literally. On the backs of 20,000 of them, in fact. Heck, you've probably eaten lunch, walked a dog, used the restroom, and played chess on them, as well.

Named for the same guy that 75 percent of the country is named for, Washington Square Park is a 185-year-old public park covering almost 10 acres of lower Manhattan. Before that, it was a marshy area that, like the rest of the central borough, was the territory of the Lenape tribe of Native Americans. Then the

Dutch grabbed it, eventually giving it to their African slaves (see the African Burial Ground entry, page 259). In 1797, it was bought by the city of New York to use as a graveyard for the poor, and, on occasion, as a grounds for execution.

After packing the sod with 20,000 of the city's indigent for about a quarter of a century, New York stopped using the area as a cemetery in 1825 . . . depending on how one defines *cemetery*, I guess, as the bodies remained below. As Manhattan grew and the living needed more space than the dead, the surface was ploughed into the park it is today, give or take a redesign or three. Apparently it's an easy magic trick, turning a cemetery into a park. A little sleight of hand, a few bulldozers pulled out of a hat, and suddenly what was once a place you whistled quickly past becomes prime real estate for throwing Frisbees and eating street vendor pretzels.

Today, the park is mostly cement, with regular patches of grass and trees. It has a large central fountain, various recreational game areas, a bust of the metallurgical innovator Alexander Lyman Holley, and a statue of Italian nationalist leader Giuseppe Garibaldi. It's most distinctive feature is the massive 77-foot-tall marble arch centered on the north side of the park, which stands like some giant tombstone for the park's soil layer of dead.

Actually and less aptly, the Washington Square Arch was erected in 1892 to replace a temporary wooden version built to celebrate the centennial of the inauguration of George Washington. It was designed by Stanford White and was based on the large Roman-style arches common in Europe that have blocky outer frames and rounded inner ones. On the north side of the arch, two statues of George Washington frame the entrance. Once upon a time, when Fifth Avenue continued through the park, cars drove right under it, and, assumedly, all over the aforementioned dead.

The park has a rich postcemetery history, from being the scene for political events and cultural movements, to a venue for musicians and performers, to filming locations for a range of movies. At some point in the late 1880s, Robert Louis Stevenson and Mark Twain hung out here together; and in 1989 it was used in *Ghostbusters 2* (see "Horror Movie Filming Locales") for a quick shot of a large pinkish ghost between the two pillars of the arch that, when I watch it, I like to pretend is the collective and pissed-off souls of all the Washington Square Park dead and forgotten. I go back and forth about which of those two anecdotes is my favorite.

The park, at the lower end of Fifth Avenue, is bordered by streets named after it (Washington Square North, South, East, and West). A good portion of the surrounding area is owned by New York University. In fact, just a block away is the façade of the house where Edgar Allan Poe once lived (see "Legends and Personalities of the Macabre") and which is now a part of NYU's Law School building.

As to its morbid past, every once in a while restoration work or new construction (including that of the Washington Square Arch itself) turns up a few skeletons, which are dutifully logged and studied by archaeologists and then properly reburied on the premises (the park is for the enjoyment of all, after all).

But despite having so many dead bodies feeding the few manicured spots of nature and its proximity to the residence of Poe, the only real ghastly myth about the park centers on a 110-foot-tall, 300-year-old English elm looming in the northwest corner. It's known that hangings occurred in the park, but no one is sure exactly where. However, the tree is still called the Hangman's Elm, probably due to a few large perpendicular branches that look as if they could hold the limp bodies of murderers and thieves.

Still, even if historians are unsure where exactly the bodies hung above you in Washington Square Park, they know for a fact that they're below you. Throw them a Frisbee or drop them a pretzel sometime.

Frank E. Campbell Funeral Chapel
MANHATTAN

How do you become one of the most famous funeral homes in the world? By catering to the bereaved of some of its most famous citizens, of course.

Founded in 1898 by its namesake, the Frank E. Campbell Burial and Cremation Company was instituted in Manhattan to fulfill a new funerary need. The story goes that in a time where funerals were often conducted in private homes, and in a city like Manhattan where most people lived in apartments, an accessible space was needed for mourners to go through the somber rituals that help get one past the death of one's loved ones and back to working on one's own.

Campbell apparently nailed that coffin, as the funeral home still operates to this day, albeit under corporate ownership, in its current spot at 1076 Madison Avenue. In fact, Campbell is credited with being at the fore of influencing American funeral customs in general.

And while molding funeral culture might earn you renown in mortuary circles, it's the chapel's clientele list that makes it known to the rest of us laymen who spend most of our life trying to not think about death. It turns out that setting up shop in Manhattan had even more business advantages than Campbell at first realized.

After all, the famous die, too.

The first forays of this gentle house of death into the world of celebrity funerals started with Rudolph Valentino back in 1926. The silent film actor was one of the first gigantic stars of movie culture, and his death at the early age of 31 from complications following emergency appendix surgery burned his name even more starkly into the celluloid strips of popular memory. As a result, a reported 100,000 fans attempted to see his body to either pay their respects or fulfill their fandom. It's even rumored that Campbell himself manipulated some of the crowd as a publicity stunt for the chapel.

As a result of being tasked with editing Valentino's end credits, Campbell had to learn how to provide shade to the limelighted bereaved. He accomplished it by maintaining high levels of secrecy and security, as well as the occasional use of decoy remains. His staff also had to learn crowd control for the occasions that the celebrities had public viewings. As the chapel's success in that area grew, it made it the go-to hotspot for high-profile cadavers. Its clientele list sounds like a red-carpet movie premiere or a history of culture, and includes such familiar letter strings as Irving Berlin, James Cagney, Joan Crawford, Judy Garland (who was basically laid in state, as some 20,000 mourners were allowed to view her glass-topped coffin), Jim Henson, the Notorious B.I.G., Jacqueline Kennedy Onassis, John Lennon, Ayn Rand, and many more.

In fact, before social media started RIP-ing people before they were dead, a great way to know someone famous had died was to see whether a huge crowd of media and fans was staking out the entrance to the funeral home.

The chapel has moved a few times since its original establishment more than a century ago. These days, it's in somber four-story building, especially low key compared to some of the other highly visible edifices on Madison Avenue. When I walked by, there were no policemen in front of the door, no mobs of fans held back by barricades, and no media attempting to shove recording devices through its doors. Just a simple, brown, corner building quietly hiding things we mortals find disturbing to think too much about.

Not wanting to party crash a public viewing, I tried to wrangle an official peek at the interior of the place, but that privacy the chapel prides itself on covers nosy book-writers gawkfesting in its inner sanctums. Of course, if you or a loved one dies and you have the money for what's been called the "Tiffany's of funeral homes," that's an instant VIP card, but if it's your funeral, you still won't get to see much.

Grant's Tomb
MANHATTAN

A LOT OF US ARE GOING TO END UP in a hole in the ground. None of us will end up in a hole in the ground as grand as that of Ulysses S. Grant, though.

Grant was, in no particular order, the 18th president of the United States and the Union general credited with winning the Civil War. Basically, he earned his

hole . . . although that's not going to stop me from using that phrase as my own epitaph.

Born in Ohio in 1822, he began his military career with his graduation from West Point, after which he fought in the Mexican War. He eventually left the military to try more civilianized pursuits, but found himself back in the army again when the Civil War broke out. On the battlefield, he quickly accrued a winning average to rival that of the best sports teams in history and rose to the rank of general, culminating with his acceptance of General Lee's surrender at Appomattox in 1865.

Thanks to his role in the Civil War, he became popular enough to win the presidency in both 1868 and 1872. However, his life wasn't all overachieving at the highest levels of American society. Along the way he found himself in quite a few holes besides the magnificent one he ended up in, including failed business ventures, political scandals, and bankruptcies.

After his final term as president, he took off for a two-year tour of the world, after which he settled in New York in 1881. Almost three years later, he was diagnosed with throat cancer and, in 1885, moved to a cottage on Mount McGregor in the Adirondack town of Wilton, near Saratoga Springs, in an effort to ease his health problems. They were eased. He died there about a month later, just days after finishing his memoirs, which were published by his friend Mark Twain. Today, the house is preserved as a state historic site.

The good thing about losing a hero is that we inevitably gain a monument. In Grant's case, that'd be his tomb. He was born in Ohio, lived large spans in Illinois and Missouri, spent time all over the country fulfilling military assignments, and certainly earned a place in DC, but it was New York that got his body. History does not record their gloating, but I have to assume that they did.

According to his wife, Julia, Grant was buried in New York because that was where she lived, because that's where she thought he wanted to be buried, and because New York assented to letting her be interred with him in whatever was constructed. So overall it was basically musical chairs. New York just happened to be where the music stopped for him.

Officially called the General Grant National Memorial, Grant's Tomb is touted as the largest mausoleum in the country. It was built in 1897 in the prime real estate of Riverside Park on the upper east side of Manhattan in an idyllic spot overlooking the Hudson River (see the following entry, for more about the area).

Designed by an architect named John Duncan, the sturdy granite and marble building looks as if it should be on the Mall in DC. The squat square base is topped by a circular turret surrounded by pillars and capped by a broad conical roof. The whole thing looks easily defensible for the military man buried within.

Riverside Drive splits around the tomb, and a tree-lined walkway takes you right up the stairs, through the double row of entry pillars, and inside. Admission is free, and the weekday morning that I visited I had the tomb to myself, not counting the single staff member and the two sets of august remains I was there to see. Inside, the space is vast and open and relatively plain, as far as these things go. Above is a dome, the windows of which are pretty much the only source of natural light for the dim interior. A handful of mosaics depicting Grant during some of his most historic moments are set high up in the walls, and the two back corners each open into small reliquaries that contain Civil War flags.

Upon entering, it's hard to notice any of that right away, though. As soon as you step inside, directly in front of you is a large hole that dominates the floor and is surrounded by a 3-foot-tall wall. About a story or so down into that hole are two red granite sarcophagi bearing Grant and his wife, who died in 1902, five years after her attending the dedication of the tomb.

Fortunately, like Grant's wife, you, too, can go down there and mingle. A set of stairs at the back of the tomb takes you right down to the bottom so that you can get within fingerprint distance of the sarcophagi, which sit side by side on a short dais.

In alcoves in the walls around the sarcophagi are five bronze busts of Grant's lieutenants, staring directly at the coffins like the sentinels of some Egyptian tomb. I'm not going to lie to you: that part felt creepy.

And that's about all there is to Grant's Tomb. Across the street is a matching stone pavilion that overlooks the Hudson and beneath which is a small visitor's center and gift shop. There, you can learn everything that the tomb (and I) have left out about the robust life of our country's 18th president whose body you just visited.

The historical. The macabre. Same stuff more often than not.

Grave of an Amiable Child
MANHATTAN

IN THE PREVIOUS ENTRY, I emphasized the idyllic, exclusive bit of Hudson River property in Riverside Park on the upper east side of Manhattan that was awarded to the remains of President Ulysses S. Grant and his wife. Turns out, it's actually a little less exclusive a graveyard than it would at first appear. Just a few yards from the massive Grant's Tomb is the humble 200-year-old grave of a four-year-old boy.

If it were anywhere else besides a major park in one of the largest cities on the planet, the solitary grave would probably be called a lonely one. Its marker is

about 4 feet tall and consists of a squat gray Barre granite base topped by a large funerary urn of the same material.

Around it is a black wrought-iron fence to protect the memorial from visitors. And around that is an identical fence to protect the visitors, themselves, from tumbling down the cliff just a few feet away to the Hudson Parkway below.

There's not too much of a story about this strangely placed grave—it's the fact of it that's intriguing—and most of the story is encapsulated in the brief epitaph:

Erected to the Memory
Of an Amiable Child
St. Claire Pollock
Died 15 July 1797
In the Fifth Year of His Age

The back of the monument adds to the pathos of a centuries-old child memorial with a quote from Job 14:1–2: "Man that is born of woman is of few days and full of trouble. He cometh like a flower and is cut down; he fleeth also as a shadow and continueth not."

A nearby placard from the Department of Parks and Recreation elaborates somewhat on the incongruent death marker. It postulates that little St. Claire died by falling down the nearby cliffs into the river, and that the grave was preserved in the sale of the property over the years at the original request of a George Pollock, who was either the father or the uncle of the boy. In a letter he wrote to the neighbor to whom he sold the property a couple of years after St. Claire's death, he asks that the "remains of a favorite child" at the edge of the property be kept "always enclosed and sacred."

Other ideas about the boy's death state that the place where it occurred had nothing to do with it, that whichever of the many causes that could kill a child back then happened to the boy, and the site of the grave was chosen merely because it was a nice spot for the start of a Pollock family cemetery.

Although the details of the boy's death are mysterious, nothing about the monument is, as it and the area around it are well documented with property records and pictures, plus the fact that the construction of Grant's Tomb in the 1890s brought more press to the spot.

The area has changed drastically over the years, and today the location of the boy's grave perhaps reflects somewhat the area's original rugged majesty. It has a great view of the Hudson River and the cover of the many shade trees that grow in the park. Specifically, you can find it behind Grant's Tomb, on the other side of Riverside Drive and up a bit from the visitor center for the presidential monument.

It's surprising that once this pleasant place came into the possession of the civic powers that be in 1860, they not only left it standing but even replaced the memorial a couple of times. In 1897, they crowned it with a new urn, and in 1967, they completely replaced the monument when the original became badly deteriorated by age and elements. Guess it's harder to pick on one decomposing boy than on a whole mass of decomposing people (see the Washington Square Park entry on page 245). The replacement is an exact replica in shape and size to the original, which the exception of the materials; the original was made of a sandstone base with a white marble urn.

The little saint was further paid remembrance by a stretch of road in his (misspelled) honor. He's the namesake of St. Clair Place, an area of 129th Street just a few blocks away.

Most parents try to secure a future for their child, and the Pollock family somehow did it in a way that you'd have to, I don't know, be the parents of the president of the country to otherwise achieve success.

Body of Mother Cabrini
Manhattan

IT TOOK A DEAD BODY to get me back into church. And I'm not talking about a funeral. I'm talking about the perennially displayed corpse of Mother Cabrini in Manhattan.

Saint Frances Xavier Cabrini was born Francesca Cabrini in 1850 in the city of Sant'Angelo Lodigiano, in northern Italy. She added "Xavier" to her name while a nun. The "saint" part came after her death. However, most people, then and now, just call her Mother Cabrini.

Mother Cabrini really wanted to marry Jesus. She was refused a couple of times due to her poor health, but eventually was able to take the vows in 1877. Her first major initiative as a nun was to become the superior of an orphanage, but that institute closed soon after.

Her next act was to lead a group of her sisters in Christ to found a missionary order called the Missionary Sisters of the Sacred Heart of Jesus. The named barely fit on the cover of their debut album.

She founded various institutions in Italy, but her long-term goal for the group's missionary work was China. However, in 1889, she was sent by Pope Leo

XIII himself to the United States, because it was a wretched hive of scum and villainy. Or because the young country's burgeoning Italian population needed some homeland-style ministering.

So that's how the Missionary Sisters of the Sacred Heart of Jesus found themselves in New York. And while New York remained a home base of sorts, Mother Cabrini traveled extensively across the country and the world throughout the duration of her ministry. She was a veritable Johnny Appleseed of humanitarian institutions, establishing some 67 of them across the country and world. They ranged from orphanages and nurseries to hospitals and schools, many of which are still around to this day.

A lot like Mother Cabrini herself.

I mean, sure, she died and was buried. However, for a saint, that's when life starts getting interesting. Her death occurred in Chicago in 1917 at the age of 67, and she was buried in West Park, New York. She was exhumed in 1933 and interred in the chapel of a high school named in her honor. A few Vatican-validated miracles later, Mother Cabrini officially earned her halo in 1946. In fact, because she became a U.S. citizen in 1909, she was the first American to be canonized by the Catholic Church.

As a result, her body became a relic. Two sets of relics, actually. At some point, her head and hands were sent back to her home country, and in 1957, the rest of her body was placed in a glass case in a purpose-built shrine dedicated to her on the grounds of the high school.

The shrine is situated at 701 Fort Washington Avenue, in the Washington Heights neighborhood of northern Manhattan. It's a pretty busy thoroughfare, and when I visited, it was a pretty busy shrine, with activity streaming through the warren of rooms and hallways within the building. However, the chapel itself was tranquil and empty.

Mother Cabrini's body is mostly bones at this point, but those are hidden beneath her black robes. A wax face and hands fill in for the parts sent to Rome. The glass coffin is ornate and set on a dais at the front of the chapel facing about 20 rows of pews. On the walls around her shrine are murals depicting key moments of her life.

The back of the chapel is dominated by a two-story, stained-glass window depicting the saint, below which is an exhibit, accessible through a pair of glass doors, of artifacts from her life, including clothes and photographs, her cane and eyeglasses, and other things worth stealing from her grave if she had one. There were also papal artifacts and an instrument of penance that Mother Cabrini used—a beltlike strip with half-inch tacks sticking through it, which apparently tenderized her enough for heaven.

Today there are institutions all across the country and world that bear her name, either as a direct result of her work or as a means of honoring her life. In fact, this shrine is one of at least three in the United States, the other two being in Chicago, where she died, and Denver, where she started a camp for orphaned girls.

One of my favorite things about Catholicism is its obsession with the dead, both the soul and the body. And when I need to sate my desire for the macabre, religion in general never fails me.

Grave of George Frederick Cooke
MANHATTAN

IT'S THE ONLY SURVIVING COLONIAL-ERA CHURCH in the entire city of New York, and it has the headless corpse of an actor buried in its backyard. God-damn right, it's haunted.

Saint Paul's Chapel was built in the mid-1760s, and was a place of worship for none other than George Washington, himself, back when New York City was the nation's capital.

Behind every great church is a graveyard, and behind this one is a small one, although many of its humble headstones date impressively back to the 18th century. The most notable monument, both in size and story, is a tall square pillar made of stone and topped by a flaming urn. It's located right in the center of the graveyard and marks the final resting place of the famous Shakespearean actor George Frederick Cooke.

Cooke was born in 1756 in England to an Irish father and a Scottish mother. He spent most of his acting career performing there, where he achieved great fame both for his onstage acting and his offstage acting out. Apparently, his love of the thespian was often usurped by his love of booze, which he would drink to the point of being undependable for performances. He would also disappear for long stretches of time and was known for spending his money as quickly as he earned it.

In 1810, he came to the United States to try on our stages for size. About two years later, after finding success here, he died in New York of a cause often attributed to cirrhosis. Because of that aforementioned lifestyle, he shuffled off this mortal coil with little to his famous name and was buried in the stranger's vault of Saint Paul's Chapel.

About a decade later, another famous British stage actor, Edmund Kean, who was a great admirer of Cooke, had his remains moved to the burial ground and erected the memorial about a decade later. Its inscription states: "Three kingdoms claim his birth / Both hemispheres pronounce his worth."

And while that was a nice thing to do on Kean's part, here's where Cooke's posthumous legend kicked in. During the exhumation, Kean was supposed to have taken with him as a relic a digit from the body—either a toe or a finger, no one's really sure. But what is certain was that they discovered that somebody else had already taken Cooke's skull.

The story goes that the skull fell into the possession of his treating physician, a Dr. John Francis, who kept it in his collection of anatomical curiosities. At one point, on a whim, he loaned it out to be the prop for Yorick's skull in the grave-digging scene of *Hamlet*. Other accounts say it has been used multiple times in that role throughout its existence.

The skull was then passed from physician to physician. Today, it resides in the archives of the medical college of Thomas Jefferson University in Philadelphia, except for one tooth that fell out and was gifted to 19th-century actor Edwin Booth, the older brother of the man who shot Abraham Lincoln. That bit of dentine ended up in the collection of the Player's Club of New York, which Booth founded and which still gathers in its 160-year-old mansion at 16 Gramercy Park.

The cemetery where the nonsouvenir parts of Cooke lie is surrounded by gates and only accessible when the church is open, which it is daily for a limited number of hours. However, if you arrive when the church is closed, you can still see the marker pretty easily through the iron gates.

Today, despite the intriguing post-death tale of Cooke and the 250 years of history in general, Saint Paul's is now better known for its connection to 9/11. The Episcopal church, at 209 Broadway, is just across the street from Ground Zero (see "Infamous Crimes, Killers, and Tragedies") and has become somewhat of its own memorial to the tragedy. It was used as a staging area for rescue attempts during the attacks and was actually closed to the public for two years after, for clean-up and repairs.

In 2001, the graveyard where Cooke's headless corpse is planted was strewn with burnt office and building paraphernalia from the collapse of the towers, although the building itself remained relatively unscathed. To walk into the church now is not to get a lesson in its 250-year-old history, but to see mementos from just 11 years ago that run along both sides of the walls and include everything from images to uniforms of rescuers to cots used during the aftermath, to pieces of that aforementioned debris.

As to any headless ghosts wandering around, there are tales, of course, but the sum total of them seems to be "the headless ghost of an actor wanders the grounds," which is so much less, well, dramatic, than the truth of the headless corpse and the acting career of its absent skull.

African Burial Ground
MANHATTAN

W E'VE ALL SEEN THE SAME TEASER used on a thousand detective and police procedural shows. A front loader does its dirt-lifting thing at the bustling construction site of an urban building project. Suddenly, somebody shouts, and the camera pans to a bunch of sweaty, burly men scratching their hard hats and staring at the ground, where a single skull stairs up at them with a "Hi, there!" look. One of them curses. Cut to the opening title sequence.

And that's just about the way it happened, minus the opening title sequence, during the 1991 construction of what is now known as the Ted Weiss Federal Building at 290 Broadway in lower Manhattan.

Except that the disturbed remains ended up being not that disturbing. It wasn't a missing person or a murder victim. Turns out, it was the first of more than 400 different sets of remains, officially making the location an archaeological dig instead of a crime scene.

It also stopped the grounds temporarily from becoming a building site. A different type of digging later, it was discovered that these remains were of African slaves. The area was a graveyard dating back to the 17th century, which had been lost to history due to the rapid and massive growth of the city.

Back then, New York went by its maiden name of New Amsterdam, and it

was a Dutch colony. Like the rest of the European settlers, the Dutch imported Africans to their new colonies as slaves. Slavery in New Amsterdam was a bit different than how we normally think of it. These slaves were allowed to own land, for instance. They also had some rights and protections within the society. They were almost more like medieval peasants. Except that, well, they were humans forced into the servitude of other humans.

Later, when Britain took over the area and rechristened it with a pithier name, life got worse for the Africans, and many joined in the Revolutionary War efforts of the colonials. Of course, that change also didn't help them out too much. Meet the new boss, same as the old boss.

Anyway, that part of the story, you know.

Back to the present day, once things got all historical, the General Services Administration, which was in charge of the building, revised the plans so as to include a visitor center inside the building, dedicated to the story of these forced African immigrants. In addition, in 2003, the administration erected outside the building a monument and spot for reinterment for the remains.

The bones were reburied in small, beautifully adorned boxes carved in Ghana and placed in vaults beneath seven human-size burial mounds. You can find the memorial and those mounds at the side of the federal building where Duane and Elk Streets intersect.

The dark granite memorial is difficult to describe in words. Let me show you. It's large, shaped almost like a mini-arena, round with no roof. You enter the round part through a spiral ramp that leads you, fittingly, below ground. Etched prominently into the walls are various spiritual symbols from Africa, Latin America, and the Caribbean. The middle of the arena is a flat, open space, and the floor is covered by a map of the world with the continent of Africa centrally placed.

Jutting off from the circle is a set of stairs that leads you up through a thin, 24-foot-high, triangular corridor called the Ancestral Chamber that deposits you back at ground level and directly across from the seven grass-covered humps of reburied remains.

Even though they reinterred those 400, there's still an estimated 200 remains somewhere on the grounds of the memorial that didn't need to be moved for the construction. And since the original burial ground was some six and a half acres in size and contained some 15,000 to 20,000 people, it probably means that most of the surrounding buildings on Foley Square are haunted.

Unearthing the remains of African slaves on U.S. soil was fortuitous. It gave New York a chance to celebrate and help preserve the culture of some of its most mistreated citizens, and reminded us all that no matter our skin color or other superficial differences, we're all the same inside. Bones.

Wilder Brain Collection
ITHACA

So I WAS LOOKING AT A ROW of human brains in jars when it hit me. The central mystery of life might be encapsulated in this single relationship of a living brain's examining a dead one. Somewhere therein is the answer to all of our fundamental moral, religious, and scientific questions. Something about . . .

Steve Martin! That's who starred in the 1983 comedy *The Man with Two Brains*. I've been trying to come up with that . . . all . . . day.

The eight brains that comprise the publically accessible part of the Wilder Brain Collection at Cornell University in Ithaca is, in my opinion, one of the more fascinating things you're going to find in this book. In fact, the collection has about three layers of immediate interest, but let's start with its history first.

The original collection was started in 1889 by Dr. Burt Green Wilder, a former Civil War surgeon who founded Cornell's anatomy department. The purpose of the collection was to see whether differences in character, intelligence, and race were correlated by physical differences in the brain. Basically, could you pick out a murderer from a scientist just by cracking a skull with a rock.

Wilder amassed hundreds of brains, some 600 according to most estimates, while simultaneously documenting whose

Used with Permission of the Wilder Brain Collection at Cornell University

brains they were. Eventually, the research floundered because, apparently, even the most important part of the human person couldn't tell us much about the human person, so the brains were eventually ignored.

By the late 1970s, the collection had languished to the point that most of the brains were desiccated and disintegrating. Seventy were salvaged. Eight, with death dates ranging from 1871 to 1944, were put on public exhibit in Cornell's Psychology Department, where they float in jars of solution to this day in a nice in-wall display. You can find that display in an otherwise bland, featureless hall on the second floor of the Uris Building at the corner of Tower Road and East Avenue (look for the giant, metal, naked statue of Herakles in front of the building . . . some brawn before your brains).

And that's where the second layer of interest comes in (the first, being, of course, publically accessible human brains in jars). More than mere faceless brains, seven out of eight of the floating gobs of tissue belonged to men and women who were distinguished, and often renowned, in their respective field. They include a political economist, a physiologist, a biology professor, a suffragist lecturer, an experimental psychologist, a pathologist, and Dr. Wilder, himself. Each one is labeled with a placard featuring photos and biographies that, I'm sure, are much more informative than the mere gravestone that each body got.

The eighth brain is where the third layer of interest comes in. At 3.9 pounds, it's believed to be one of the largest ever measured (second-largest, to most accounts). But that's not even the most interesting part of the story of this brain. You see, it's the brain of Edward H. Rulloff, a man also distinguished in his respective field: murder.

The brain, crimes, academic career, and restaurant of Edward H. Rulloff all deserved their own entry in this book, which can be found in "Infamous Crimes, Killers, and Tragedies." It's okay if you go right there and don't finish this entry.

All told, these eight brains that won't die are a fascinating exhibit, compellingly macabre in the best way that memento mori can be. Heck, I don't know any Latin, but I'm sure there are quite a few other words that could follow *memento* when it comes to his display. I mean, drop a few wrinkled hunks of tissue into clear jars and suddenly you're faced with some of the biggest questions one can ask about oneself. Is man no more than this, indeed.

Obscura Antiques and Oddities
MANHATTAN

EVAN MICHELSON AND MIKE ZOHN have almost double-handedly made commerce in dead, dark, and disgusting things fashionable.

Since the 1990s, the coproprietors of Obscura Antiques and Oddities have quietly sold fascinating and often morbid items out of a tiny shop at 280 East 10th Street, in the East Village of Manhattan: antique mortuary equipment, menacing medical devices, articulated animal skeletons, mummified and pickled body parts, taxidermy.

Then, after faithfully stocking their customers' cabinets of curiosities for two decades, the partners got a new glass-fronted shop, this one in the living rooms of cable viewers. In late 2010, the Discovery Channel premiered *Oddities*, a reality show that purports to show Obscura's daily business of selling such things as medical arsenic and Victorian hair art, as well as the type of people who buy them.

Were Michelson and Zohn actors, they'd have been cast against type. They're both in the early 40s. Michelson looks somewhat like a kindergarten teacher, with her dark-framed glasses and curly blond hair cut short. Zohn's tall, stocky, usually disheveled, and would probably fit a hard hat pretty well. But the two are way more interesting than first appearances. Or at least their taste in collectibles is.

I'd seen a few of the episodes of *Oddities*, so while in the East Village I dropped by the store, located not even half a block over from Tompkins Square Park. It was a Monday around lunchtime, and they were in the middle of shooting episodes for their third season.

Two men in headphones and laptops sat outside, the store being too small for them to do their job anywhere else. Inside, through the large glass window bearing the name of the shop, I could see Michelson talking to a customer while a third party menaced her with a video camera.

I talked briefly to one of the crew, who said they'd be breaking in a half hour or so. When I returned, the crewmen and cameras were temporarily gone, and the tiny store was packed with customers, meaning about seven people.

The store is pretty much as it comes off on the show. Immortalized animal remains and strange metal implements and old jars and bottles full of mysterious substances and less unidentifiable objects were stacked floor to ceiling on

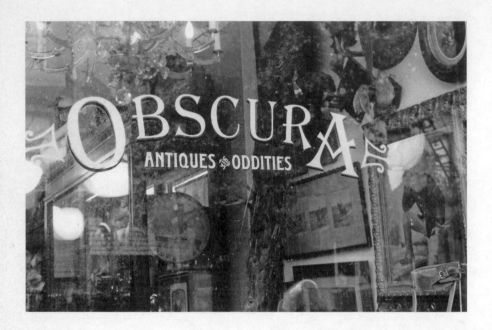

both sides of the shop, leaving little more than a hallway down the middle that ended at the checkout desk. Nothing appeared to be labeled or priced, which encourages discourse (and haggling) between customers and staff, furthering a store culture of people just hanging out and talking about weird stuff.

I got to talk briefly to Michelson and at some point Zohn came in bearing a taxidermied monkey of some sort. He was slightly out of breath, as if he'd had to chase it down. Because the two owners were busy with customers and shooting, I didn't stay too long. After I'd left, I quickly began to regret not having purchased something there.

As to the show itself, like all reality shows, it's a bit contrived. It tries too hard to tell a story around the "characters," focuses too much on the quirkiest customers, and sometimes forgets that the stars of the show are always the oddities. But, man, what cool oddities have been featured: shrunken heads, straight-jackets, mummy hands, electro-shock therapy chairs. Were it combined with PBS's *Antiques Roadshow,* the series might be more what I want throwing light on my face in my television room.

But people are apparently digging it as is. A couple of months after I visited, Michelson and Zohn began the process of moving to a bigger space a few blocks away from the original, at 207 Avenue A, the former location of a funeral home. Seems like the oddities business is a good one these days.

Girl in a Glass Coffin

OSWEGO

I HAVE THIS LOOSELY HELD IDEA that language constantly evolves because it's trying to find the perfect phrase. Once it does, I assume the language then dies, having fulfilled its purpose. *Girl in a glass coffin* isn't it for the English language, but it might be the closest we've gotten so far.

In turn-of-the-century Oswego, a pleasant town right on the shores of Lake Ontario, the phrase was more than just an evocative one.

In October 1899, the 11-year old daughter of one of the wealthiest families in the area died suddenly of appendicitis. Her name was Virginia Tonkin, and her parents placed her body in a hermetically sealed, glass-topped coffin. They held the viewing in the library of the house, and then afterward moved the fairy-tale coffin into her old bedroom, ostensibly until they could build a family mausoleum in a nearby cemetery.

However, as time went by, it became increasingly apparent, much to the morbid delight of both the newspapers and the town gossips, that the Tonkins weren't planning on interring Virginia anytime soon. The death of a child will excuse most types of behaviors, but there is a line. And I'm pretty sure it's drawn somewhere before months of nightly vigils over the decaying remains of the loved one.

Naturally, it became a tabloid story, and all kinds of untruths, half-truths, and truths were spread. After all, who can resist the tale of powerful millionaires powerless in the face of death and distraught to the point of bucking both propriety and innate human reactions of revulsion. I certainly can't, and, in fact, find it difficult to not invent ghastly practices just to make the story even more macabre. I mean, I can imagine the family using her casket as a dinner table, throwing tea parties for her with everybody in the house expected to attend, and introducing her to possible suitors. In reality, though, all the family ever admitting to was changing the flowers on her coffin and praying daily at Virginia's side.

Eventually, the authorities intervened, although for a while they weren't sure that they could as there were no actual laws on the books at that time for this particular situation. After putting up a fight, the Tonkins reluctantly complied and, about a year after her death, placed their daughter in the new family mausoleum.

Unfortunately, their newfound notoriety placed a further burden on the family. Not only had they lost one of their four children twice, once to death and once to a cemetery, but their youngest daughter, Rosamond, started receiving death threats from some anonymous deranged person who would send drawings of the daughter and the interior of the family house, as well as various scenarios describing her potential kidnapping.

The artist would demand ransoms to prevent such action, but would never instruct the family as to how to deliver the money. The mutilation and murder of a local child named Cora Sweet intensified the situation for the Tonkins, who then hired armed guards, tried to go into hiding at different times, and sheltered Rosamond in what basically amounted to a glass coffin.

Remarkably, this horrible situation actually went on for a few years, and, strangely enough, probably made a lot of people feel bad for intervening and forcing the Tonkins to stop treating their other daughter's corpse as a fetish.

The letters eventually ceased, and Rosamond grew up and married and was able to compartmentalize that relatively short section of her life over the long run. Nobody ever discovered the identity of the demented artist.

Today, the impressive Tonkin Mansion still stands at the northwest corner of West Seneca and West Fifth Streets in the Franklin historic district, although

it's a bit spookier these days. The enormous house is currently divided into apartments and is overgrown with creepers to the point that it looks like an ideal place for storing the cadavers of children. The mansion is officially known as the Perez House, after the builder of the place, but to those who like their history a bit more eerie, it's still called the Tonkin Mansion.

You can also pay your respects to Virginia herself. The Tonkin mausoleum is located at the back, more secluded area of the decent-size Riverside Cemetery, at 4024 County Route 57. The stand-alone mausoleum is made of heavy, gray stone with a green, bell-shaped roof. The surname of the family is proclaimed above the portal, and a lion's head beneath a palm frond decorates the metal door.

That door is more of an ornamental grate, though, so you can look through into the small area inside, and see the stone drawers, a couple of which have nameplates, including Virginia's. The small interior is lighted through a stained-glass window in the back that depicts a kneeling angel holding a scroll with the words, "For of Such is the Kingdom of Heaven." The window was damaged when we visited it, the glass broken in such a way that it completely decapitated the angel, making ironic the aforementioned caption.

The coda to this story is that we circled to the back of the square mausoleum, which was overgrown with grape vines and other plants, and saw a small, desiccated bat on the interior windowsill. It must have gotten trapped at some point between the stained glass (entering probably through the hole above the angel's neck stump) and the protective Plexiglas that had been placed on the outside of the window. There it died and was preserved, protected from the elements and all the death-feeders.

But *bat in a glass coffin* just doesn't have the same ring to it.

Haunted Barn Movie Museum

FIVE

Classic Monsters

*W*HETHER IT WAS 10,000 YEARS AGO around a fire at the mouth of a cave or yesterday on the $10 million set of a horror movie, every monster humankind has ever invented has given a face to death. And despite those faces baring rows of pointy teeth or slavering noxious liquids or bristling with hair or shimmering with scales, these tangible monsters make the vague, existentially terrifying, unknown reality of death more palatable . . . which says more than a library full of philosophical, religious, and medical texts about the horror of death.

But the creation of monsters isn't just an instinctive defense mechanism on our part. It's a coping one, as well. By taking the insubstantiality of death down a notch or two, by giving it physical form, by localizing it to a single or even multiple bodies we can better deal with it. Or at least pretend to.

Basically, humanity needs its monsters.

However, philosophical is the wrong tone to set with this section. I mean, this is the fun part. We're talking monsters, man. Popcorn-movie, campfire-tale, thriller-night, terrify-your-little-brother, Halloween-mask monsters. These guys make the party.

And within the pages of this particular party rave giants unearthed from the soil, demons capable of possessing entire houses, lake serpents that defy epochs, aliens that serve man, vampires from our childhood, ghosts and the people who talk to them, golems of literary fame, gargoyles who watch stoically over us, Sasquatches so fuzzy and so wuzzy you just want to give them a hug, mummies venerated in museums (attendant curses be damned), and a whole host of monsters of the more copyrighted sort from our films and books.

Now, while including a section on classic monsters makes sense in a book dedicated to death, the fact that creatures of this sort are imaginary seems to present a problem for a book also dedicated to the physical traces of its subjects.

But those physical traces are there, all over New York, and always human-created. Whether it's a statue of Bigfoot in a community park or an entire town that claims to be able to talk to ghosts, a werewolf-themed restaurant or an annual festival celebrating extraterrestrial visitors, these nonexistent monsters have left more of a mark on this state than have many historical personages who actually existed.

And all that said, I realize that some believe that a subset of the monsters herein discussed and tracked down are actually real, those being mostly the monsters that fall under the categories of ghost, cryptid, alien, and demon. And that's cool. All anybody needs to agree on for the purposes of this part of the book is that these monsters have stories. Truth and falsehood are refreshingly irrelevant here. Only the stories matter.

Before we jump into this, though, I'd just like to mention for my own obsessiveness of category that the two monsters that New York is probably the most known for, King Kong and the Headless Horseman of Sleepy Hollow, don't appear in this section. Not because there's nothing to see in the state related to them, but because I've covered them in other, more relevant parts of this grimpendium: King Kong popped up in "Horror Movie Filming Locales" and the Headless Horseman is in the Washington Irving entry of "Legends and Personalities of the Macabre."

So grab you silver bullets, your crucifixes, your EMF detectors, your tired, your poor, your torches, and your pitchforks, and let's go on a New York monster hunt. Last one to survive wins . . . temporarily.

Cardiff Giant
COOPERSTOWN

NORMALLY, THEOLOGICAL ARGUMENTS just end with, "I guess we'll find out after we die." However, in one particular case, it yielded a giant.

In October 1869, workers digging a well on a farm in the hamlet of Cardiff,

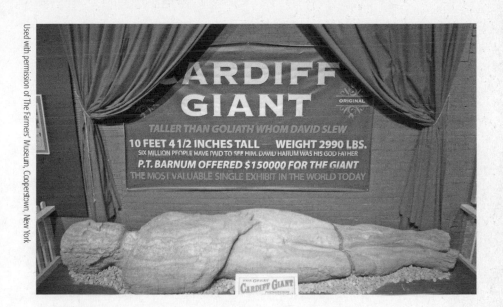

about 12 miles south of Syracuse, discovered what was thought by some to be an ancient, 10-foot-tall, petrified man.

Two months later, George Hull, the man who funded its creation and orchestrated its discovery admitted that it was a hoax. But a lot happened in those two months.

The idea came to Hull after an argument with a minister about the Old Testament assertion concerning the existence of giants in Bible times. To show that the gullibility of literal Biblical interpretation had real-world applications, Hull spent a year of his life and thousands of dollars on organizing the quarrying, sculpting, delivery, burial, and discovery of the statue of an oversize naked man.

The prostrate giant was a large block of gypsum stone cut in Iowa and carved by a cemetery sculptor named Edwin Burkhart in Chicago. It was then moved to New York by train, where it was planted, in more than one sense of the word, on the property of Hull's cousin, William Newell.

Whether the apparently ossified supercorpse fooled all of the people some of the time or some of the people all of the time is open for debate. As the story is usually told, no scientists bit at the bait, but Christians took the evidence as validation of every page of Scripture. Like everything, though, the truth is probably more complicated. After all, everybody says, "I knew it all along" in hindsight.

What is certain is that the Cardiff Giant proved wildly popular and netted Hull serious cash, both from the admission fee that he charged people to view it and then even more so when he sold his interest in the giant to a group of businessmen, who continued to exploit the statue as a biological wonder of the ancient world.

Meanwhile, P. T. Barnum, who hated any press not about himself, got into the act, first by trying to buy the giant, and then, when that didn't work, fashioning his own, which he then proclaimed as the true Cardiff Giant. "Your fake is a fake, sir." This is the situation that prompted the line, "There's a sucker born every minute," which was expressed by David Hannum, the leader of the syndicate that owned the original Cardiff Giant. Eventually the battle of the giants went to court, and amid all the sue-age, it was determined that everybody was being silly and they should just take their giants and go home.

In addition to inspiring eternally regurgitated and inaccurately attributed conventional wisdom about suckers, the Cardiff Giant also inspired such American literary giants as Mark Twain and L. Frank Baum, who both produced short humorous works about Hull's creation.

The absolute best thing about this hoax, though, is that even though it lasted a mere two months, now, almost a century and a half later, the Cardiff Giant is still on display in New York (and the P. T. Barnum knock-off, not to be outdone, is still on display as well, albeit in Michigan).

You can see the Cardiff Giant of legend, lore, and literature at the Farmer's Museum in Cooperstown, about 80 miles east of Cardiff. The multibuilding Farmer's Museum, at 5775 State Highway 80 (where a blue and yellow historic sign announces the location of the giant), is dedicated to 18th- and early 19th-century agricultural life. It features a working farmstead complete with livestock, a historic village re-creation, and various preserved buildings and artifacts.

When I visited, the giant was unashamedly exhibited a mere room deep into the main building where you pay admission. It reposed on a bed of pebbles on a small stage surrounded by a white picket fence. Multiple colorful and carnival-style banners with lots of exclamation points extolled its history, especially, I assume, for those who were just visiting to see a person in period costume milk a cow or shoe a horse.

In person, the colossus is certainly impressive, although it's difficult to form any objective conclusions about its fooling anyone at this stage. The sand-colored statue is large, with roughly sculptured features and details, and it lies on its back in a slightly twisted and purposefully unflattering position that a sculptor would never choose if he was going for a work of art instead of a prank. It also has exposed genitals large enough to make Madeline Kahn woof.

It's a strange commentary on us as a species that we hate lies yet love hoaxes. It's a little bit harder to understand why we draw the line—why when people such as George Hull and P. T. Barnum lie to us, we still revere them and their hoaxes 140 years later.

In other words, you can get us, but you can't get us.

Amityville Horror
AMITYVILLE

IN ATTEMPTING TO CATEGORIZE the story of the Amityville Horror for the purposes of this grimpendium, I had to ask myself, "What's more sensational, a mysterious familicide or a house possessed by demons?" And then I had to ask myself, "What kind of a world do I live in where I have to make that decision in the first place?"

A black one, man, a really black one.

Obviously, I made my decision about this infamous crime, killer, and tragedy that yielded a classic monster by going with the supernatural aspect. It's not that I wanted to treat lightly the shocking real-life 1974 murder of the Defeo family in their own home by one of their own, it's just that the subsequent claims of demon possession by later residents of the house is what really propelled the story into the pop-culture perpetuation that continues to this day.

Either way, the destination is still a large, three-story Dutch Colonial that has two stories, one involving mass murder and another involving paranormal terror.

Located near the southern coast of Long Island, Amityville should probably be known for quite a few things. After all, the place goes back almost 120 years as an official community; and the history of the region as a settlement, a couple hundred more. Still, in the Amityville version of the Marco Polo game, the response to "Amityville" is always "horror."

And that's because in the early hours of November 13, 1974, 23-year-old Ronald Defeo Jr., crept into the bedrooms of his family at their home on 112 Ocean Avenue and shot to death his mother, his father, and all four of his brothers and sisters, whose ages ranged from 9 to 18, while they slept. It only took about 15 minutes of his life to make the world a darker place.

The thing is, no motive has ever been found to explain the crime. Not even a demented one. Sure, Ronald Jr.—or Butch, as he was often called—had a history of drug use, criminal tendencies, and heated interactions with his father, but nothing that would draw a straight line . . . or even a crooked one . . . to killing everybody in his family.

But that just means he was broke in the brainpan, right? Insanity is by its definition inexplicable. Well, his defense tried that tactic, but the jury decided he was competent enough to be found guilty of six counts of second-degree manslaughter.

Butch's efforts after the crime seem to support his mental coherence. He methodically changed from his bloody clothes, hid all evidence, including the murder weapon, far away from the scene, and then went through a public charade the next day as part of an alibi process that ended in his rushing to his favorite bar to report the death of his family. He had even premeditated somebody to blame, a local mobster.

Fortunately for justice, he was a bad liar, and inconsistencies in his story quickly became apparent. He was sentenced almost exactly a year after his hor-

rendous crime and is incarcerated at the Green Haven Correctional Facility in Stormville, New York, to this day. There, he really should have moldered into obscurity, except for maybe the random news retrospective.

However, just before Christmas 1975, about a month after Butch Defeo's sentencing, a family by the name of Lutz—George, his wife, Kathy, and three children— purchased and moved into the property. Less than a month later, they ran screaming from it . . . straight to the press.

The ghost story they told was far from *A Christmas Carol,* though. According to the Lutzes, the house was full of evil—everything from demons to disembodied voices, apparitions to animated objects, physical attacks, blood and slime oozing from the walls, swarms of flies, and various disturbing incidents that seemed to connect the phenomena to the mass murder that had occurred in the very rooms that they had moved into. It was an American nightmare.

Of course, that nightmare turned into the American dream. In 1977, a book based on their "true life" experiences became a hit and spawned the 1979 horror movie classic *The Amityville Horror* starring Josh Brolin, Margot Kidder, and Rod Steiger. That movie, in turn, spawned some seven sequels and counting, a remake in 2005, and multiple documentaries on the story. Paranormal investigators swarmed on the house like the aforementioned flies, and George Lutz, who died in 2006, even trademarked the phrase *The Amityville Horror.*

All that's the fun part of the story, of course. The disclaimer is that critics easily point out more inconsistencies in the Lutz story than in Butch Defeo's original, but that hasn't stopped the popularity of the story. Just ask the people who live in the Amityville Horror house today, who claim that the only phenomenon they have to put up with are the tourists ("Hi, guys").

To dissuade some of that attention, the original address of the house has been changed from 112 to 108 Ocean Avenue. In addition, they've even gone so far as to alter the distinctive eye-shaped windows on the side of the house that have become the symbol for the whole affair.

The light-colored, five-bedroom Dutch colonial is located right on the water in a large, upscale neighborhood. At one point in the past few years, it was put on the market for a sum of $1.5 million. Strangely, the house is set perpendicular to the water, so that its front and back face the sides of the neighboring houses, only a few dozen feet away. This arrangement also has the effect of having the infamous (and altered) "eye" windows facing the street.

Incidentally, the house used in the filming of the original 1979 movie receives a similar level of unwanted attention, to the point that its owners have changed its façade as well, but that's a New Jersey story, not a New York one.

Just down the road about a third of a mile from the house is the bar where Defeo frantically started his alibi. At the time of the murder it was called Henry's, but these days it's a restaurant called the B&B Fish & Clam. Located at 180 Merrick Road, it is part of a small strip mall.

The Defeo family is buried in Saint Charles Cemetery at 2015 Wellwood Avenue, in nearby Farmingdale. Besides their death year, they also share a single gravestone cozily embraced by an adjacent bush. Because it's a Catholic cemetery, the shape, size, and style of all the tombstones are similar, so the Defeo marker can be difficult to find without knowing approximately where it is . . . which is Section 13, Range O.

In the end, if there ever is one, it's a mass murder, a haunting, a hoax, a book, a movie series, a phenomenon. It's all the Amityville Horror.

Peace Fountain
MANHATTAN

WHAT IMAGE DOES the word *peace* conjure for you? A dove? Lions lying down with lambs? A handshake between powerful politicos? A calm sea? Weapons beaten into ploughshares? Damned dirty hippies? How about the severed head of Satan dangling off a crab shell?

If you said *yes* to that last one, then you must be New York sculptor Greg Wyatt. I know this because I've seen with my own soul windows the macabre lunacy of your exquisite Peace Fountain.

Right beside the Cathedral of Saint John the Divine at 1047 Amsterdam Avenue, on the Upper West Side of Manhattan, is a bronze fountain erected in 1985. It doesn't always shoot water, but it's always eye-magnetic.

If the gate is open, you can walk right up to the statue, although you can also see it pretty well from the sidewalk on Amsterdam Avenue. According to a plaque at its base, it depicts the forces of Good kicking the smoldering ass of Evil. That part is understandably depicted as the triumphant Archangel Michael standing above the body of a defeated Satan. So far, so conventional.

However, it's the rest of the statue that makes you wonder how many of the prophecies of the Bible you slept through in church.

Michael is its predominant feature. He's muscled; armed with a long, downward-pointed sword; and his backs sprouts large, detailed wings that stretch to the apex of the sculpture. Mike celebrates his victory by cuddling a giraffe, while in line in a diminishing spiral, eight more giraffes await their turns for some festive intimacy. Below the angel lean the uneasily smiling disks of both a sun and a moon, each one obviously wondering what the heck they are doing in this piece.

All of these elements stand upon the spiky body of a large flat crab, its claws and segmented legs dangling down to the twisted base. Most strangely, upon its back is also the decapitated body of Satan—the reason this statue finds itself in this section of the book—lying prostrate in defeat. His upside-down, horned head trails below the crab, the innards of his neck gripped in one of its large claws. His visage bears the startled expression of somebody who, well, just had his head cut off after thinking he could take on God in the cosmic ring.

Basically, there's a graphic weirdness all about the piece, even when it includes more traditional imagery, such as the lion and lamb at the rear of the statue. Mercifully, the afore-referenced plaque does give some semblance of explanation. The crab represents the origin of life in the sea; the twisted pedestal is supposed to invoke a DNA strand; the giraffes represent more peaceful animals from the completely not-peaceful domain of nature; the sun and moon are the classic opposing forces that "God reconciles in his peace"; and the severed demon head is, well . . . sometimes a severed demon head is just a severed demon head.

I know just below nothing about art, so I'll refrain from judgments on its merits as such. I will say, though, that, thankfully, even though the piece is strange, at least it's rendered in a detail, texture, and arrangement that demonstrate definite talent and forethought. From the feathers on Michael's wings to the arm tendons on the corpse of Satan, the sculpture is well realized and encourages prolonged inspection.

All around the plaza are small plaques on stands dedicated to both religious and secular saints. One features Gandhi. Another, for John Lennon (see "Infamous Crimes, Killers, and Tragedies"), is inscribed with lyrics from his song "Imagine." These are examples of how everybody else likes to depict peace, of course. And there are a million more obvious ways to do that. Wyatt just happened to choose giraffe-archangel affection and a severed demon head for his Peace Fountain. I'm not saying he's wrong. Peace is crazy. That's probably why we're so bad at it.

New York Lake Monsters
PORT HENRY, PERRY

PEOPLE INVARIABLY ASK the wrong question when it comes to centuries-old giant reptile lake monsters. It's always, "Do they exist?" when the appropriate question should be, "Can we theme a party around them?"

The good people of Port Henry are among the few who've gotten it right.

Every year, on the first Saturday in August, that small village and its surrounding towns near the southern tip of Lake Champlain celebrate Champ Day, to honor the famous local lake monster that has been decent enough to not act like a lake monster throughout the 140-year existence of the town.

I mean, it might seem strange to celebrate a creature that could probably average two Port Henry families per meal, but in real life, all Champ does is pose for a few blurry pictures, practice avoiding sonar, and generally just do a good impression of an imaginary creature.

The history of this plesiosaur-like reptile with its serpentine neck, humpy back, and flippered feet goes back as far as we can stretch it, to the original Native Americans; continues through the 1600s to Samuel de Champlain, the explorer who gave his name to Lake Champlain and inadvertently to its resident dinosaur; and continues to the present day when everybody has cameras and video equipment complete with HD, auto-focus, and built-in lake monster blind spots.

Lake Champlain, where the monster hangs his cross-stitched HOME, SWEET HOME sign, is a massive body of north–south aligned freshwater that's the Pluto of the nearby Great Lakes. It's not really a Great Lake, but some people like to think it is. Still, this "just a lake" is about 500 square miles in size and large enough to extend into the territories of New York, Vermont, and Quebec. Plus, none of the Great Lakes have monsters as famous as Champ . . .

although I'm sure they have lake monsters. They are lakes, after all.

Champ's biggest PR move, the one that rocketed him to the top of the Forbes List of U.S. Lake Monsters, actually happened across the border in Vermont. In 1977, a woman named Sandra Mansi snapped a photo of what she and others claim to be Champ. It's blurry, has no scale, and could be 18 other things before it could be a lake monster, but it was enough validation to at least get Champ officially into the upper ranks of cryptitude.

Back to Champ Day, my travels found me in Port Henry, which is right on the Bulwagga Bay area of Lake Champlain, a few months too early to join in on those festivities, unfortunately. Nevertheless, signs that this town had a pet leviathan were pretty evident. I saw a Champ-shaped parade float moored in the front lawn of a house; a rough, green-painted, plywood replica of the beast on the side of the road; and, in the midst of all those telltale signs, an actual telltale sign.

On the southern end of the village, on the side of South Main Street near where it intersects Whitney Street, is a large, three-paneled Champ sightings board.

The maroon sign stands right beside a matching WELCOME TO MORIAH sign (the village of Port Henry is part of the town of Moriah), seems to be nicely cared for, and lists about 130 sightings, including the date of the sighting and the name of the person who saw him.

It starts in 1609 with Samuel de Champlain, takes a big jump to September 1972 with Alice Pratt (there are actually a lot of Pratts on this board), and then ends in August 1989 with a Shirley Marinello. Of course, that tells me not that there haven't been sightings of this immortal aquatic reptile for the past 20 years, but that either signs are expensive to update or whoever's project this was lost an election, moved away, or got generally disillusioned with his or her interest in Champ when it wouldn't show up for its festival appearances.

In my previous book, *The New England Grimpendium,* I classified Champ as a New Englander. After all, the town of Burlington, Vermont, on the eastern shore of Lake Champlain and about 40 miles north of Port Henry, has a small monument to it and named their Minor League baseball team after it. Now that I've been on the other side of the lake, I'm not so sure. There's probably enough of the behemoth to go around, though.

Interestingly, the Champ sightings board isn't the only lake monster sign I saw in my travels across New York. About 300 miles away from Port Henry and just south of Rochester, the entrance sign to the village of Perry proudly proclaims under the image of a green serpentine reptile, "Home of the Silver Lake Sea Serpent."

Granted, it's a bit of a contradiction in terms to have a sea serpent in a lake. Nevertheless, on a summer night in 1855, a group of fisherman witnessed a massive green reptile cavorting out in the middle of the local Silver Lake.

Once word got around, tourists and monster hunters flocked to the area, spending their time and cash trying to find it. Meanwhile, rumors of missing livestock starting circulating. To this day no one is sure what it was that was splashing in the lake and eating cows. Just kidding. Unlike the tale of Champ, the story of the Silver Lake Sea Serpent actually has an ending.

Two years after the sighting, a local hotel, the Walker House, caught on fire. In the course of saving it, a large pile of green fabric and coiled wire was discovered in the attic. When confronted with this evidence, the owner of the hotel, A. B. Walker, admitted that it was used to create a lake monster to boost the tourist trade for the benefit of his establishment. Lake monsters as marketing stunts. There's a long tradition.

Over the past five decades or so, the people of Perry have tried to kindle interest in their local hoax, but it hasn't seemed to really catch on yet, at least not like in the Lake Champlain area. The fact that the Perry monster was an actual wet blanket probably hurts their cause a bit. Still, if you look around the town, you can see the beast here and there, continuing its terrifying role as a marketing campaign.

So if you ever find yourself anywhere near one of New York's many lakes, keep an eye out for lake monsters. You couldn't miss them if you saw them, but you could apparently mistake them if you didn't.

Whitehall Bigfoot
WHITEHALL

THE WEST COAST, especially the Pacific Northwest region, pretty much owns U.S. Bigfoot mythology. Of course, the East Coast doesn't want to feel left out of any conversation, so we end up with a place like Whitehall, a small town just east of the Adirondack Mountains, which shoots its collective hand into the air like an overeager child to tell us its Bigfoot story.

Well, actually, it's probably not the town. It's too busy touting its place in U.S. history as the birthplace of the U.S. Navy. It's one of, like, six or seven towns in the northeast that does so, although, impressively, it is the only one without an ocean coast.

The people that really push the Adirondack-area Bigfoots are, naturally, East Coast Bigfoot enthusiasts who can't easily commute to the Bigfoot mecca of the Pacific Northwest and need some toys in their own backyard to play with.

Like everything, the Whitehall Bigfoot is traced back to Native Americans, who somehow ended up being some kind of monster legitimacy card for all sorts of legends and myths throughout the country. Then, once a monster claim is officially made, it self-perpetuates, so there will always be a recent sighting by some random guy.

However, the pivot point for the Whitehall Bigfoot seemed to come in 1976, when a series of sightings was reported of a large, bipedal, hairy creature that screamed like a young girl at the Nickelodeon Teen Choice Awards and walked like a gorilla with scoliosis. The first sighting was recounted by a group of teenagers who spied a brute featuring the classic Bigfoot description in the relative wilderness area of Abair Road, a 1-mile stretch of pavement connecting County Routes 10 and 11.

Later, more witnesses reported seeing the hairy beast or catching his glowing red eyes in the beams of their flashlight or coming across his tracks in the ground. Newspapers articles were run, books were written, and a few expeditions were organized, but, as these stories always seem to end, nothing really came of it. These days, the Bigfoot fervor of the area has died down somewhat, except when somebody needs content for their paranormal show or, uh, book and goes digging stuff up.

Still, the remnants of the Bigfoot craze are there, even if the Bigfoots aren't.

Abair Road is still the type of place where a strange animal sighting couldn't be immediately dismissed. It has a few houses, but it's mostly old farms and pastureland interspersed with tracts of forest.

The guaranteed Bigfoot sightings now happen downtown.

A couple of local businesses have incorporated the giant into their marketing identity, including the Skene Valley Country Club, a public golf course at 129 County Route 9A, which features a Bigfoot in its logo; and Bigfoot Wine and Liquor at 132 Broadway Street, which has gone even

further and installed at the side of its building a 6-foot-tall, welded-metal Bigfoot with a wide, friendly face that seems more come-and-drink-with-me than rip-you-apart-in-a-dark-forest.

Finally, another Bigfoot sculpture, this time of wood and not connected to any particular place of business, can be found in Canal Harbor Park, a strip of land that parallels the Champlain Canal on one side and Skenesborough Drive on the other. There, you'll find a 9-foot-tall carving of a rather slim Bigfoot that looks like a sloth with the face of Jesus. The statue seems pretty portable, but when I saw it, it was standing in front of one of the buildings in the complex, just south of the rotting remains of the USS *Ticonderoga*, a historic schooner built in 1814 that is now just a glorified woodpile in a giant chicken-wire cage.

I know this entry sounds skeptical to the point of being an unenjoyable read, but you can blame a mouse for that. In May 2011, basically just weeks before I wrote this entry, researchers in the wilds of Colombia discovered a single red-crested tree rat, a species thought to be extinct for over 100 years. This rodent is about 18 inches long. And they found it. In a South American forest. And they took indisputably clear pictures of it. Nobody's ever yet netted even in a single frame of film of an 8-foot-tall Sasquatch that screams at the top of its massive lungs and whose eyes glow in the dark, and which apparently has a U.S. distribution of both coasts and many large areas in between.

I mean, I like *Harry and the Hendersons* as much as anybody, but that just shows Bigfoot makes a better story than a reality. However, he's also pretty cool as a statue, too.

Mars 2112
MANHATTAN

I RECKON THAT WITH ALL the flashing lights, marketing stunts, strange characters, and general chaos of Times Square, were an extraterrestrial spaceship to land in its vicinity, nobody would notice. And if those same aliens opened up a restaurant at their landing site, people would notice, just as far as its being a new place to grab dinner and drinks. And then those extraterrestrials would wire home that humans were a pretty cool lot.

I knew that the address to the science fiction–themed eatery Mars 2112 is 1633 Broadway at 51st Street, and when we were about a block away I could see the tall metal shaft that was its sign blazing its vertically arranged name in red. But I couldn't see the restaurant, which was strange because themed restaurants usually go overboard to extend their theme their façade to grab people's attention, especially in a crowded marketplace like New York City. So where was it?

Finally, as we got within punching-in-frustration distance of the sign, we saw the restaurant. It really was at 1633 Broadway. Well, under 1633 Broadway, anyway.

Below us was a large, square courtyard sunk about a story or so into the ground. It was too regular for it to be the crater that the Martians had created on landing, but would have made for a great underground base. Yup, while we shake the perimeter fences of Nevada's Area 51 and scour the White Mountains of New Hampshire, the aliens were calmly serving us burgers in mid-town Manhattan.

The only object in the bare subterranean courtyard was a spaceship. Only is a bad modifier there. The identified flying saucer was about the size of a small car and set on a 7-foot-tall column. The entrance to the restaurant itself was across from it in a side wall of the submerged courtyard.

We walked in and were greeted by a less than enthusiastic man in sci-fi duds and a Doc Brown wig. He asked us whether we wanted to go straight to the restaurant or hit the simulator first, which, he was carefully to explain, wasn't a simulator anymore but just a movie.

Operating under the general assumption I have in life that a broken simulator is better than no simulator, we opted for it and were ushered into a small theater designed to look like the interior of a spaceship. We chose a couple of the two dozen or so seats that faced the screen, and, a few minutes of CGI-animated journey through space later, we "landed" on Mars and were ushered into the restaurant.

Or, more accurately, we were ushered into a rocky tunnel that wound past an arcade room, a bar room, and a few fake space hatches. Eventually, this tunnel opened out onto the main hall of the restaurant, which the website describes as "a 35,000-square-foot, bi-level, multi-dimensional, immersive environment."

I'm going to agree with that description while adding that it was, well, extremely red. The entire interior was decorated to look like a large underground Martian cave, lit or painted red, maybe both, and the glowing red atmosphere made me feel as if I was suddenly seeing in a different spectrum of light. The

ceiling had a fake skylight, showing a night sky, and was covered with helium balloons that children had let go in the course of their Martian spelunking.

One rocky wall was taken up by a giant screen where some kind of alien newscaster talked about the news on Mars for the day. Meanwhile, three costumed actors wandered the area, posing for pictures, handing out balloons, and generally just trying to act alien. One wore a short, three-eyed, mascot-type costume; another, a skin-tight leotard with a reptilian mask; and the third, an extravagant Martian queen dress with fiber optic highlights and a pointed forehead. Mars 2112 is an Equal Opportunity Employer.

Like most themed restaurants (see the entry on the Jekyll and Hyde restaurants on page 301), the food was unmemorable . . . because it wasn't the point. We ordered fish and ribs from whatever is the local fauna of Mars and got an expensive tab in return, especially because we ordered a few of their space-themed cocktails. It cost NASA $280 million to get a small robot rover onto the planet, so having to import whatever liqueur tastes like butterscotch probably affects the pricing.

Other than that, there wasn't a whole lot of interactivity to the theme of the restaurant. You're in a big red cave trying not to make eye contact with a three-eyed mascot and checking your bank balance on your smartphone, wondering whether you can afford another cordial because the only thing that whets alcoholism more than being in a surreal environment is being in a familiar one.

And if you have one too many of those, it's no problem. All the exit signs are clearly labeled "Earth."

Cup and Saucer Diner
Pine Bush

I F EXTRATERRESTRIALS INSIST on buzzing your town over and over again, you might as well capitalize on the new demographic and try to sell them some grub. I assume that's the motivation behind the alien-themed Cup and Saucer Restaurant in Pine Bush, anyway. To feed its aliens. Or the people that feed on alien mythology, I guess.

Pine Bush is what is known in the nomenclature as a UFO hot spot. It's supposed to be an area of historically congested UFO sightings or, at the very least, an area of historically congested crowds of people seeing UFOs. Basically, that means lots of tales about nightly visits by strangely shaped crafts with weird light patterns that yield a few articles in newspapers and become the subject of books, which then causes enough national popularity for a time that the FBI moves the town into the "keep an eye on" column for a few years before eventually releasing their records on the topic with heavy black lines through all the fun stuff.

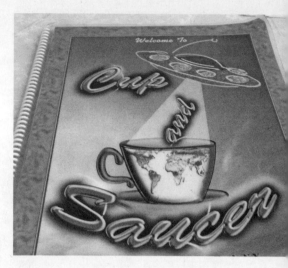

At least, that's how I think it went for Pine Bush, a small hamlet just west of Poughkeepsie and about 80 miles north of New York City. It's kind of hard to do research on UFO sightings, though. There's some weird stuff to have to sift through.

Reports for Pine Bush sightings seem to extend as far back as the golden age of science fiction, with some continuing to present day. There's always somebody who just can't let an era die gracefully. However, the UFO fervor seems to have hit a peak sometime in the 1980s, with a little 1990s bleed-over. This aspect of the Pine Bush sightings is a check in the "believable" column for me. If there was ever a time when we needed interference from advanced, extrasolar intelligences, it would be the 1980s: "Stop doing everything you're doing in this decade. You're embarrassing the universe."

Usually, I'm in the "small towns get bored" camp of explaining this kind of phenomena. Actually, I still am, but as with everything except my feelings toward anything the Keebler elves make, I have conflicting beliefs.

I mean, sure, superficially, it seems weird that advanced alien intelligences would choose to blink lights over random small towns. That's because we assume a lot about how advanced alien intelligences would act. In our fiction, aliens are exactly like us other than having bugged eyes or four arms or tooling around in antique police call boxes. When they invade, they're after the same resources we find important: our real estate or our natural resources or our bodies or our technology or our major sports stars. Things we value and would fight back over.

Chances are, though, that alien intelligences are so far different from us, that they're going to do weird things. Like beyond *Coneheads* weird things. Like steal all of our peanut-butter jar lids or try to communicate with humpback whales or make random lights in the sky.

Then again, it could be that these small-town UFO hot spots are often near air force bases, which need both the ground and air real estate to do things that urban areas would get ticked off about. In this case, Pine Bush is about 15 miles from Stewart Air National Guard Base, just outside of Newburgh.

Regardless of the truth behind the alien sightings in Pine Bush, the consequences are real: a footnote in the town's Wikipedia entry and an alien-themed diner at 82 Boniface Drive.

At least, I thought those were the only remnants of the town's UFO legacy. However, as we drove through the downtown area on the way to the restaurant, we started having our own alien sightings.

In just about every window in the retail district was painted an alien—the classic kind, bright green and thin with large, slanted black eyes set in an over-size bald cranium. Each alien was themed according to the nature of the business of the windows it adorned. The barbershop had a barbershop quartet's worth of aliens, all sporting thick black moustaches. The Mexican restaurant featured an alien in a sombrero, eating a taco. The beauty salon had an Edward Scissorhands alien. And the town hall was labeled "UFO Headquarters." We even saw a diorama in the front lawn of one business that included a short, green alien in a black cape standing beside a saucer-shaped UFO made out of an old satellite dish, the large, old-fashioned kind, back before the devices natural-selected to the size of household pets.

The place seemed to have more aliens per square foot than does the rest of our entire galaxy.

We were puzzled, but we were also hungry, and continued on to the restaurant. There we discovered it was one of those 1950s-style silver trailer diners that you see in every town, except this one had a sign with an alien saucer beaming something into a hot cup and saucer, in case you didn't get the pun just by the name itself.

Despite what the sign and name promised, inside, it was just barely extraterrestrially themed. The covers of the menu (giant spiral-bound tomes filled with everything from classic cocktails to omelets to steaks), the T-shirts that the waitresses wore (and which you could buy yourself at the counter), and a few plush aliens were as far as the theme went, and these had to battle with tropical-themed stickers in the windows.

On the way to the counter to pay for our meal, we let it drop that I was a travel writer (which we usually do around the time that the check arrives). At that point, the manager, who had been standing nearby, lit up and began regaling us with tales of the town's UFO past and how both the town and the restaurant had been featured in a bunch of publications that weren't at all being tongue in cheek in their coverage. I didn't catch everything he said (I was furiously attempting to calculate the tip), but I remember hearing "Roswell of the East" a lot.

Most notably, though, he mentioned that the next day was the town's first ever UFO festival, with a parade, costumes, lectures, and various other other-world-themed entertainment going on throughout the day. That was the reason for all the decorations downtown. I had missed a really good book entry by a mere 12 hours, it seemed.

Anyway, everybody with a sky has claimed a UFO sighting, but few towns have turned such events into a restaurant and an annual festival. When they do, I could care less whether the alien sightings were real, hoax, mass hysteria, or air force exercises. I think it says cool things about our species that we turn anything into a chance to party.

House of Frankenstein
LAKE GEORGE

IT WAS A NICE, WARM AFTERNOON IN JUNE, the sun was shining, a pleasant wind blew from the lake, and the town I found myself in was thick with people in sunglasses and shorts . . . so naturally I hid in terror from all that summer, inside the safety of a house of monsters.

The Adirondack town of Lake George and the 32-mile-long lake for which it is named has a history that goes back to its Native American populace, extends past its European discovery by Samuel de Champlain in 1609 and then the blood-shed of the War of 1812, and continues through to its prominence as a vacation destination from the late 1800s until the second you picked up or downloaded this book. Today, its main drag features all the usual vacation town amusements, arcades, restaurants, shops, attractions. However, right in the middle of all that

lakeshore leisure is the House of Franken-stein Wax Museum, where it has loomed for the past 40 years.

The place doesn't look too spooky from the outside, although it looks bigger than I was expecting. Its wide two stories are topped by a steeple of sorts, and a pair of white pillars almost as tall as the building flank the entrance. The upper story features a large picture window where the Phantom of the Opera smashes the keys of his pipe organ to the strains of what I assume to be "Louie, Louie."

Inside the foyer of the building, which is decorated to look like a stone castle, a Universal Studios–style Frankenstein's monster is secured to a metal contraption, while the doctor himself sits nearby in a protective cage. A display case full of movie monster statues and action figures stands in the corner.

But that's all you get for free. Before I paid the $9-plus-tax entry fee (prorated to $8 and $4.50 for students and children), the till girl pointed to a sign above her head. It explained that the attraction was scary and you can't get your money back for being a wuss. I pushed through the 10-year-olds in front of me, bravely gave her my money, and then slowly walked through a doorway into the dark unknown.

I was expecting a few rooms with badly put together monsters in awkward poses. What I discovered was an ascending series of black hallways lined with windows like some kind of old loony bin. Behind each of the windows was a dimly lit, room-size diorama featuring waxwork figures in scenes that ranged from monster attacks to gory torture sessions to elegant Victorian horrors to strange deaths by misadventure. A few of the scenes featured licensed characters, such as Freddy Krueger or the Predator, but most were just riffs on the classics, mon-sters, ghosts, zombies, murderers, vampires, mummies, and tons and tons of victims. Some were out of the history books, such as grave robbers Burke and

Hare, the Spanish Inquisition, and the Salem Witch Trials. Others were more literary. For example, Edgar Allan Poe made an appearance. Many were fantastical. All were monstrous.

As I walked through the darkness, eagerly shoving my face against each window as if the answer to life had been promised to me behind one of them, I could hear pneumatic hisses and taped screams and feel reverberations from future dioramas as other visitors accessed them. At one point in the blackness, the floor turned spongy beneath my feet and I was surrounded by a jungle scene. The Creature from the Black Lagoon poked his head out of the swamp.

Some of the windows had large buttons that, when pressed, spotlighted part of the exhibit, or set in motion some of the characters, or let one unwittingly play executioner. Eventually, I reached a spinning tunnel bridge, which deposited me back out into the foyer. I reluctantly walked back into June, wishing it was October.

The place isn't as shiny as a high-end Halloween haunted house, with its live actors and secret passages and gory set dressing, but that's not a bad thing. The House of Frankenstein is a unique experience—classic, bloody, atmospheric—with plenty to look at if you squint through the darkness. All told, I estimate there were a couple hundred characters in about 50 different scenes.

The wax museum, at 213 Canada Street, is open from mid-April to Halloween. If it doesn't completely scratch your dark spot, you can also head a few buildings down to its sister attraction at #115, which is Dr. Morbid's Haunted House, a conventional haunted attraction where people in costumes jump out at you. You don't get to push buttons to execute people there, though.

Castle of Count von Count
MANHATTAN

WITHOUT A DOUBT, the most famous vampire in the world is Count Dracula. He's just the apex of that widow's peak, no contest. However, the number two most famous vampire might take some debate. If you would be so kind as to permit me to start that discussion, I think, very possibly, that the second-most-popular vampire in all mediums would be a purple piece of felt in a cape and monocle.

Count von Count, *Sesame's Street*'s resident arithmomaniac, is one of the most famous characters of that famous public television program.

And while it might seem strange that an educational program for preschool children would include a traditionally evil monster as one of its characters from early on in its 40-years-and-counting career, the truth is, *Sesame Street* has always been overrun with furry, toothy, horned, heavy-browed things that they've always called, well, monsters. From Grover, Oscar the Grouch, Telly, Cookie Monster, Herry, and the Two-Headed Monster to even the modern-day darling that is Elmo, the creators of *Sesame Street* have apparently always believed that the education of our young should be a bit monstrous.

Sesame Street was created in 1969 by Joan Ganz Cooney and Lloyd Morrisett, a television producer and psychologist, respectively, with an enormous amount of help from Jim Henson of Muppets fame. You know what it's about: teaching children, ostensibly inner-city children, about counting and spelling and manners.

Three years later, in its fourth season, it debuted the Count, a relatively sinister-looking, angular purple puppet with black hair, wearing a cape and sporting a monocle over his left eye. Everything about the Count is pointy—

his nose, ears, eyebrows, tongue, beard, and collar all the way to the pair of white felt fangs jutting from his wide mouth. The Count lives in a spooky gothic castle in a perpetual lightning storm (despite the sunny days of Sesame Street that keep the clouds away) surrounded by cobwebs and bats shaking on sticks. Voiced by Jerry Nelson, the Count, like any respectable vampire, has an Eastern European accent.

The Count's purpose on the show was to teach the basics of counting, as well as to extol its joys. And nobody has ever counted with as much relish, no census taker, no sports statistician, no biodiversity specialist. The Count would count his bats, his spiders, lightning strikes, himself . . . and, when they eventually let him out of the castle, everything he could stick a fuzzy purple finger at.

For the first quarter century of its run, *Sesame Street* was filmed in a Manhattan film studio, before moving to Queens, where it is produced to this day. However, that's not why its resident vampire is included in this book, with its obviously loose use of the term *grim.* No, this has to do with Count von Count's home sweet home, where he wandered (and sang) beneath its cobwebbed chandeliers, played his pipe organ, and counted sheep in his canopy bed. When the exterior of the Count's castle was shown, especially in the older days of *Sesame Street* when they were less shy of letting the Count spook out, the shot was of an actual 150-year-old castle, a castle located to this day right in the middle of Central Park.

Belvedere Castle is situated just south of the Great Lawn, near the Delacorte Theater and right off the 79th Street Transverse. With its stone turrets and balconies, the castle was built to be a mere attraction, a nice place to look at while in Central Park, and a nice place to look at Central Park from. Eventually, the National Weather Service started using it as a weather station for recording wind speeds and rainfall, and then it was further multipurposed to house the Henry Luce Nature Observatory, with its many nature programs and exhibits. At Halloween, it is naturally turned into a haunted castle.

But *Sesame Street* had already done that years before by ostensibly basing its only living dead character among the Belvedere's stone corridors and stairways, where he entertained his multiple countesses, as well as, on one particular rainy night, Susan Sarandon.

Back to my original point of the Count as the silver-medal winner to Dracula's gold, *Sesame Street* has been influencing generations of impressionable children for almost half a century. It's fair to surmise that many kids watched this gateway vampire and were subconsciously primed to enjoy vampire stories, as well as horror stories in general, when they grew up. How many vampire movies, books, and television trends germinated in a dusty castle echoing with the staccato laughter of a counting fiend? Only the Count could count.

I remember my first vampire. Tell me the Count doesn't deserve a spot in this section of the book.

Haunted Barn Movie Museum
MONROE

THE GUY'S NAME WAS JOEY VENTO, and he told me over Facebook that I should visit his Haunted Barn Movie Museum. His avatar was a man in a gorilla suit. I decided to go. It's hard to say no to a gorilla suit avatar.

Sometime later, I was pulling into his front yard. Literally. He had a driveway, but that was reserved for said museum. Cars were demoted to the pasture. A small, stone house dating to the 1920s sat on a piece of land that bordered close to neighbors on one side but then expanded into a sizeable, lightly wooded property on the other. In front of the house was a restored 1800s-era black funeral cart, around which flat stones were planted on end like small tombstones (I would discover later that one of them actually was a tombstone). Every tree on the property had something quirky or strange nailed to it.

It was immediately apparent that the people who lived here were of their own sort.

Vento turned out to be a short man of about 50 with curly salt-and-pepper hair, a beard, and a diamond stud in his right ear. He was from Brooklyn, but had been living in the Hudson Valley town of Monroe for about a decade and a half or so.

He welcomed me warmly into his home, where I met his wife Diane and teenage daughter Jessica. After conversing with them for a while over tea and cookies, during which time I learned about Orange County's unique history for producing mastodon fossils, we walked outside into the freezing January afternoon for the main course: The Haunted Barn Movie Museum.

The museum was housed in a wooden outbuilding, smaller than the barn in its name but larger than residential sheds. The exterior was covered in those

ceramic faces you can buy at garden supply stores and all around its base were Halloween tombstones. Various other random ornaments hung from its flanks. The wooden sign above its purple door read THE HAUNTED BARN MUSEUM, with the word *movie* omitted for reasons of either length or accident or evolution, I don't know. Regardless, the exterior of the barn revealed no real clue as to the treasures inside.

Vento opened the door, and my first impression was that he had beheaded every movie monster from the 1940s to the 1970s and set the grisly mementos on his shelves. It was glorious.

Halloween skeletons and giant tarantulas and strings of purple lights hung from the ceiling, but other than that and a few other atmospheric flourishes, most every object crammed into the barn had its provenance from cinema or television.

I personally have a thing for monster movie props, and I was terrified I would miss seeing something that I would learn later was there, so I examined every label while he told me stories about how he had gotten this piece or the filming story behind this other piece. There were masks, costumes, concept models, prototypes, and promo items from, despite my original impression, just about every decade in film history, from bits as old as decaying foam rubber from the stop-motion brontosaurus in the original *King Kong* to a full-size vampire corpse from the 2007 version of *I Am Legend*.

Some of the finds in there included a concept head for the first act of Stanley Kubrick's 1968 *2001: A Space Odyssey* that was never used. A can of Soylent Green that Charlton Heston posed with in a promo ad for the 1973 movie of the same name. A Selenite mask from the 1964 adaptation of H. G. Wells's *First Men on the Moon*. The insectoid mask from the 1989 alien abduction flick *Communion*. A stunt helmet for Dracula's armor from the prologue to Francis Ford Coppola's 1992 version of *Dracula*. A silver child-size spacesuit from the 1960s *Lost in Space* television show. "Dead Nate's" zombie corpse head from the "Father's Day" segment of the 1982 anthology movie *Creepshow*.

Honestly, this article should really just be a catalog of everything he had in there. Much better than my narrative.

But there was one definite motif running through all the articulated dinosaur models and life masks, autographs, and pictures. Apes. Damned dirty apes.

Vento had amassed enough masks, facial appliances, props, costumes, and salvaged bits of set dressing from the original Planet of the Apes movies to start his own ape revolt. In addition, he had various generic gorilla costumes, as well as props and models from the different *King Kong* incarnations. He himself had been present in New York City as a kid for the filming of the 1976 version and had piece of Kong's hide in the barn as a memento. His first ever piece of primate, one that he'd had from childhood and the one he'd grab if there was a fire, was a gorilla background mask from the 1970 *Planet of the Apes* sequel, *Beneath the Planet of the Apes*. Suddenly I got his Facebook avatar.

But the museum wasn't just an exhibit. It had a practical purpose, as well. The Haunted Barn Movie Museum is a movie venue during warmer seasons. Desks and chairs are arranged at the back, and a 6 by 6-foot collapsible widescreen is placed up front. Vento often runs shows there, especially for kids, who are enthralled by his collection and often send him their own crayon drawings for it. He keeps those examples of refrigerator art alongside the work of such magicians as Marcel Delgado and Ray Harryhausen and Rick Baker.

Later he toured me around the rest of his property. To the side of the house was an outdoor theater setup. From there, the remnants of a haunted walk from the previous Halloween led to a large, cement-floored gazebo where sat a black-robed mannequin with the face of Jeff Bridges from the 1984 *Starman*.

Now, you'd think with such a collection as Vento's, he would never leave his barn. However, he continues its spirit with the family business. He, along with his wife and daughter, run Movies to Go, an entertainment company that shows films for both private and public events in both indoor and outdoor venues.

Vento's interests stem from the influence of his father, Sonny, who jump-started Vento's passion for movies, monsters, and collecting at various times during his childhood. According to Vento, his father was a Brooklyn long-shoreman and, as a result, would often land incidental background roles. In fact, he's been in the frames of such ticks of film history as Alfred Hitchcock's *The Wrong Man, On the Waterfront,* and *The Beast from 20,000 Fathoms* (see "Horror Movie Filming Locales"), for which he was paid in Scotch.

I never got to visit the Ackermansion. I've never been invited down into Bob Burns's basement. I haven't even taken the public tour of Universal Studios Hollywood Archives and Collections Department. I have to imagine that the Haunted Barn Movie Museum gives one a strong glimmer of that same feeling of awe that those famous collections inspire at the work of the special-effects masters of cinema. Keep collecting, Joey.

Haunted Dark Rides
Sylvan Beach, Brooklyn, Rye

STRICTLY DEFINED, a dark ride is any track-based amusement park or fair ride located in an enclosed space. Often, these rides are scenic, with various three-dimensional dioramas from history, folklore, or fancy, depending on the theme of the ride. However, there is a subgenre of dark ride that is much darker. Because you know what goes great in the dark? Monsters.

Somewhat like riding a coal car through a Halloween haunted house, haunted dark rides feature dimly lit, kinetic ghouls and ghastlies for scaring you, eerie noises and music for unnerving you, and pitch blackness and sharp turns for discombobulating you. However, unlike their seasonal cousins, haunted dark rides are open almost year-round and are rarely staffed by human spooks, instead using mechanical monsters and effects.

Even more differentiating, dark rides don't let you take the horror at your own comfortable pace. You can't pause to gather your courage or run screaming in the other direction. You're stuck in a small car heading in a predetermined

The Flying Witch

direction toward various unknown scares at the speed the controller deems best for heightening the thrill. Think the chocolate river tunnel scene in the movie *Willy Wonka and the Chocolate Factory.*

The most famous haunted dark ride of this type in the country, and probably the world, is Disney's Haunted Mansion. From there, the quality of most dark rides drops precipitously. However, as with horror movies, being B grade is sometimes a more desirable trait.

Of course, haunted dark rides are an entertainment form from another era, so there aren't too many left and the ones that survive can be pretty dated. I was able to track down five in New York, and rode through the darkness of all but one that was shut down the day I was there.

Laffland

SYLVAN BEACH AMUSEMENT PARK in Central New York is a small, humble park, and its haunted dark ride, called Laffland, is a microcosm of that. However, what the park and ride lack in spectacle, they make up for in history. The amusement park is right on Oneida Lake, and has been there in some form since the late 1800s. Laffland itself was erected in 1954, and it looks as if it hasn't changed much since that time.

At Sylvan Beach, you pay per ride, as opposed to paying for entrance into the entire park. When you enter that strip of park, you'll be able to pick out Laffland right away due to the two large clown cutouts on the roof. Below them are images of a skeleton, a devil and a flapping colony of bats, pretty much the only outside features that let you know that the interior is a spook show. Also prominently featured are the phrases "World's Craziest Ride" and "You'll Laugh, You'll Scream, You'll Holler, You'll Howl."

The ride is about two minutes of curving tracks running through about 20 cheap but vintage monster displays (often called stunts), all of which seemed more dimly lighted than they should be, but also which don't seem as toned down spook-wise as the undersell of the façade seems to indicate. While it's not the most compelling of rides, it is quite the time machine.

Ghost Hole and Spook-A-Rama

NEXT IS THE FAMOUS CONEY ISLAND, the more-than-100-year-old collection of amusement parks at the southern tip of Brooklyn. Here, haunted dark rides have come and go, most recently Dante's Inferno in the now-defunct Astroland, which was closed, except for its signature rollercoaster (see *The Beast from 20,000 Fathoms* in "Horror Movie Filming Locales") sometime around 2008.

Two haunted dark rides still squat ominously amid all the cheery food vendors and brightly colored coaster tracks: Ghost Hole and Spook-A-Rama.

Unfortunately, Ghost Hole was closed the day I visited, and if the ride is anything like its façade, that's a real miss for me. Decorated like an old stone castle with various creatures painted across it, the building's crowning feature is a large, three-dimensional McFarlane-esque demon centered right in the middle of the overhang like some kind of morbid hood ornament. This modular dark ride has been set up at Coney Island since the late 1990s and was at a park in Maryland before then.

Spook-A-Rama, on the other hand, was open for its ghastly business, as it has been since 1955. Back then, it was a much more ambitious ride when it was billed as "The World's Largest Spook Ride." These days, it has been scaled down from its original quarter-mile track. Its façade has also been scaled down, with its most notable feature today being a three-dimensional skeletal demon on its roof.

Inside, the track runs throughout an open space and is less claustrophobic than Sylvan Beach's tunnel-like ride. The track seemed to take random turns not possible in such a space, which was possibly due to the fact that the ride uses high-backed parallel couches as opposed to linear roller-coaster-type cars. The stunts were also more lurid than at Sylvan Beach.

Both haunted dark rides are easy to find. The amusement park area of Coney Island has shrunk over the years, and even though there are technically multiple amusement parks, they are all small and connected, meaning you can meander through them all without noticing the divisions. As at Sylvan Beach, you only pay per ride

Zombie Castle and Flying Witch

FINALLY AND ULTIMATELY are the pair of haunted dark rides at Playland in Rye, just above New York City. Playland has been around since 1928 and is the only amusement park in the country operated by its state government, although that's only as of the writing of this entry, as plans are in place for redevelopment of the money-hemorrhaging park.

Playland is probably most famous for being featured in the 1988 Tom Hanks comedy *Big*. When I visited, a Pepsi machine stood in the location of the Zoltar fortunetelling machine from the movie. The only wishes it grants are for bottles of soda.

At this park, you pay an entrance fee, so it can be a more expensive experience. Fortunately, the two haunted dark rides featured here are the best of this particular bunch.

Zombie Castle is housed in a tidy-looking castle with various demons and vultures and, naturally, zombies adorning the façade. Built in 1934, about six years after the park opened, this dark ride is nestled beneath the giant green dragon tunnel of the Dragon Coaster. Inside, you'll find variations on the theme of the living dead—zombies, corpses, skeletons—all in such situations as graveyards and torture chambers. They scream and shake at you, and it all adds up to an almost ideal haunted dark ride experience. The only major flaw is that Zombie Castle is overshadowed by its sister ride, the Flying Witch, right across the concourse.

The Flying Witch beats all the dark rides in this entry, both in appearance and ride quality. It was installed in 1971 and features an enormous exterior wildly painted with every monster that has ever sprung from the collective human nightmare, all painted in a style of art heretofore only found on vans from the 1970s and '80s.

Zombie Castle

There's a windmill at the corner of the building, the rotating blades of which are covered in demons. Three-dimensional characters line the ride overhang, including Dracula, Freddy Krueger, the Grim Reaper, a dragon, and, of course, a flying witch on a broom. Most prominently, the giant livid red face of a demon emerges three-dimensionally from the wall.

Inside, the quality of the stunts was high, with a pleasing (and terrifying) variety of kinetic monsters that include the dying, the dead, and the deadly assaulting you from all sides and above. The ride also utilized its darkness well, and multicolored lights gave the ride an eerie atmosphere. Meanwhile, an unrelenting soundtrack thick with the tumultuous noise of the damned make pointless the act of covering your eyes in terror.

Although the Flying Witch is my favorite, all the rides listed herein maintain the same basic appeal. Excellently macabre façades, the clacking tracks and vibrating cars, the patches of complete blackness that make you wonder what's ahead, the loss of control, the pneumatic hisses and statical groans, the Halloween feel in the middle of summer, and the nostalgia of the bygone. The light at the ends of these tunnels is always disappointing, because it means the ride is over.

Unfortunately, these rides are always in danger of being over permanently. Entertainment has become increasingly more complex and sophisticated, and papier-mâché demon heads, cardboard zombies, and mannequins in rubber chains and masks just don't do it for enough people. So ride these highways to hell while you can, before their elaborate haunted houses are dismantled; their zombies, stomped back into their graves, their witches, yanked from the sky; their demons, exorcised into oblivion; their maniacs, jailed in padded rooms forever. Before the dark rides themselves go dark.

The Jekyll and Hyde Club
MANHATTAN

I CAN DO THIS INVESTOR PITCH in four words and an initial: "Chuck E. Cheese with monsters." And I can predict the response in one: "Brilliant." The Jekyll and Hyde Club is part restaurant and part horror-themed, live-action, and animatronic entertainment venue, although, like its namesake Robert Louis Stevenson split personality, it's the eatery's monster side that dominates.

There are actually two of these themed establishments in Manhattan, the original and smaller location in lower Manhattan, often referred to as the Jekyll and Hyde Pub, and the four-story, much more over-the-top version in midtown that goes by the slightly broader moniker of a "club."

Disclaimer: Much of the experiences chronicled in this entry were influenced by many overpriced gin and tonics.

I visited the latter Jekyll and Hyde first, at 1409 Avenue of the Americas, just a block or so south of Central Park. However, its four-story façade makes it seem more like a Times Square venue, with its faux-crumbling exterior covered with Egyptian iconography and skeletons.

At street level, a couple of posed skeletons and an 8-foot-tall Hyde character props stand as either bouncers or photo ops, and a caped staff member cajoles passersby into becoming patrons.

Upon hearing our own intent to enter, the doorman had us wait while he went inside. Shortly after that, another costumed character, this one spouting a barely intelligible Cockney accent and walking with a hunch, ushered us in. We walked down a short, dim hallway to an inner door that he pretended not to be able to open. The lights went out, he started making strange noises, and suddenly a screen lit up and we were addressed by an animated skeleton, who mostly cracked jokes and bantered with our host (or vice versa, I guess). Finally, after the ceiling started shaking and dropping down on us, our host opened the door into the restaurant proper.

From here, we were in control of our own destiny and, after we gave our name to the hostess, we were startled by a fake head popping up from its secret location in the hostess podium. From that point on, the restaurant was less haunt and more just monster mash.

We went up one level to the library, where we waited for our table, had a couple of drinks, listened to the animatronic Edgar Allan Poe and Jules Verne busts behind the bar tell each other jokes, and surveyed the restaurant.

The walls of the second floor were lined with books. The shelves were also adorned with portraits with their eyes knocked out and interspersed with glowing-skull sconces. At our end of the floor, a crocodile head with lighted eyes was mounted to the wall; and at the far end, a similarly mounted shark head

would sometimes open its jaws to reveal a scuba diver's head inside, which then addressed diners and staff members alike with jokes about his lot in life.

Bolstered by those aforementioned gin and tonics and the general carousing atmosphere around us, I would later make my way to the upper floors. Although unused and empty at the time of our visit, each one had its own theme, laboratory and attic, with more seating and various arcade games. A final set of stairs was blocked by a sign that declared that level "The Tower" and warned of torture and experimentation of the type to drive men insane, and that nobody was allowed past that point. I was to learn later that it was control center for all the restaurant's special effects.

All of the floors were also balconies, as each overlooked a central chimney lined with animatronic effects and the stage below on the ground floor. Special effects included a giant Sphinx face, a zombie band, a jungle explorer trapped in a cannibal pot, a towering black statue of Zeus with lighted red eyes, and a mad scientist in a control booth of sorts. Throughout our meal, these characters variously came to life. A few times an elevator lowered topped by a talking gargoyle. Inside it, Jekyll would theatrically transmogrify into Hyde while the zombie band played David Bowie's "Changes."

Meanwhile, live actors would interact with the animatronics and the diners. Throughout the course of our meal, five or six different characters dropped by on our table multiple times, from a gypsy that stole our silverware to a giant monster who had to be led around by another character lest he upset tables with his massive costume or topple to the pit below.

If that all seems like too overwhelming an experience for you, the Jekyll and Hyde Pub, at 71 Seventh Avenue South in Greenwich Village, is more low-key, with more of a pub/restaurant setting. This Jekyll and Hyde is just around the corner from the Slaughtered Lamb Pub (see page 307), which is owned by the same proprietor as the Jekyll and Hyde restaurants.

I visited the downtown Jekyll and Hyde early in the afternoon. Only a couple of tables were filled, and I was able to strike up a conversation with the manager, who took the opportunity of the lull in patrons to show me around the place.

The pub has only two floors, and the upper floor is more of a function room area. It also holds a closet-size control booth, complete with microphones and video cameras and all kinds of switches for reanimating the various monsters that decorate the walls and ceiling of the pub downstairs, which the manager was kind enough to do for me.

These animatronics included a few that were at the club version of the establishment, another mad scientist, the ch-ch-changing Jekyll and Hyde, and
another talking gargoyle, but also featured a few unique ones, as well, such as a
mounted werewolf head and a matching mummy one, a skeleton organist, and a
Frankenstein monster on a slab that lowered from the ceiling.

After a certain hour, the manager told me, this Jekyll and Hyde also employs
live actors, but I must say I enjoyed the experience of not having to banter with
them. Instead, I could just soak up the monstrous ambiance and watch mechanical monsters do their thing here and there. I'm rarely a fan of theatrics but am
completely a fan of special effects.

Fair warning, the entire club experience was fairly expensive (I didn't eat at
the pub), but you're in Manhattan and you're probably prepared for that in general. At the club, four drinks, a burger, and a quesadilla ended up being a $90
expenditure that your purchase of this book went only a tiny fraction of the way
toward allaying.

Of course, you're paying for far more than just a burger. You're paying for a
good fright night out on the town.

H. Leivick's Golem

QUEENS

NOT COUNTING ISRAEL ITSELF, the New York City metro area has the largest
Jewish population in the world, so it makes sense that we include one of that
ancient culture's monsters in this section. And the most famous of them, with the
exception of Satan himself, has to be the golem. And H. Leivick was a Yiddish
playwright who helped popularize the monster in contemporary times.

A golem is a humanoid creature made out of mud and animated by magic.
It's super strong, is created to protect Jewish communities, and acts under the
control of the rabbi who imbues it with life, although the drama in golem stories
is often drawn from the inability of the rabbi to do so completely. The only way
to stop the golem is to reverse the magic spell that energized it. For some perspective, Frankenstein is often considered a modern golem story. In real life, so
was André the Giant.

The idea of the golem is traced back to the Bible itself and the animation of

Adam, who is made from the "dust of the ground" and quickened with the "breath of life," although the first use of the word *golem* seems to be in Psalms 139:16 and has nothing to do with a juggernaut dirt creature smashing the heads of anti-Semites. Certainly, it can be argued that the Bible needs some of that, though.

The creature does pop up regularly in Jewish texts and folklore, and its most famous legend coalesced sometime in the 1800s. Taking place in 16th-century Prague, Judah Loew ben Bezalel, the chief rabbi of the city and an actual historical figure also known as the Maharal (a play on words designating him as an influential teacher), raised a golem to defend the Jewish community there from persecution.

Many writers have taken that particular version and run with it, the most famous in mainstream culture being the classic 1915 German silent film, *Der Golem*, which was written and directed by Paul Wegener and Henrik Galeen, the latter of whom also wrote the script for the 1922 F. W. Murnau film *Nosferatu*.

On the literary side, one of the most famous incarnations of the dirt monster of Prague is the 1921 dramatic poem *The Golem* by H. Leivick.

Leivick, whose real name was Leivick Halpern, was born in 1888 in Belarus to a large traditional Jewish family. He grew up during the turbulent Russian Revolution, in which he took an active part. In fact, he was arrested by the powers that beat and sentenced to four years of imprisonment followed by exile to the still-dreaded Siberia. It was during his imprisonment that he wrote his first dramatic poem, "The Chains of Messiah." He was eventually smuggled to the United States in 1913.

From there, he garnered literary fame for his Yiddish poems and plays, with his most famous being his long-form poem about the golem.

Originally written in Yiddish and often staged as a play in various languages, Leivick's *The Golem* departs from the traditional use of the golem in many ways. It's still raised by the Maharal, in this case to fight against the blood libel, in which Jewish people were accused of killing gentile children to use their blood in sacred rituals. However, instead of being an ass-kicking automaton, the golem in Leivick's story is extremely humanlike, tormented by warring desires, confused by its place in the world, buffeted by feelings that span the entire spectrum of emotion. Of course, he can still smash gentiles with whatever the Yiddish equivalent of élan is. And he's able to turn invisible at times.

The Golem is a thickly symbolical play, and the entire thing reads like one long bad omen. Also, even though the narrative has phantoms and spirits,

corpses rising from the grave, violence and more violence, and the golem crea-ture itself, the tone of the poem is almost more meditative than monstrous. But it is monstrous.

Leivick spent most of his American life in New York, although he lived in cities as diverse as Philadelphia and Denver. Like the golem itself, Leivick even-tually reverted back to the clay from which he came, in 1962.

He's buried in Queens in Mount Carmel Cemetery, on the border of Brooklyn and Queens that, like so many of its fellow Jewish graveyards in the area, is stuffed to the gates with tombstones so that there's hardly enough ground between them to make a midget golem. Mount Carmel is also the final resting place of convicted child killer/martyr Leo Frank (see "Infamous Crimes, Killers, and Tragedies").

The website for Mount Carmel (mountcarmelcemetery.com) has an excel-lent search feature, as well as maps of the five different sections of the cemetery. The main gates of the cemetery are at 83-45 Cypress Hills Street in Glendale, although Leivick's section can also be accessed at 66-02 Cooper Avenue. He is buried in Section 3, Block B.

His tombstone is on the outer rim of a teardrop-shaped cul-de-sac, right on the edge of the road beside a thin concrete path labeled "6." That's important information because finding his exact stone isn't as easy as looking for his name.

His stone is entirely in Yiddish. According to Jewish scholar David Roskies in his book *The Jewish Search for a Usable Past*, the epitaph translates as:

> *I lie covered over and hear my own star*
> *Conveying my name to the Lord of the Stars.*

I'm told that the left side of the dual stone shows Leivick's wife's name and her birth and death dates, and that the right side shows Leivick's. The first character on the top line (Yiddish, like Hebrew, is written right to left) is a single initial, ה, so that's him. The only thing that I personally can confirm that is written on the stone is "endowed care."

Anyway, while the golem hasn't had any real phases of popularity like vampires and zombies and other monsters, it has simmered for centuries without disappearing . . . and there's always a pile of dirt handy.

The Slaughtered Lamb Pub
MANHATTAN

STOP ME IF YOU'VE HEARD THIS ONE. Two American backpackers walk into a pub in northern England, get scared away by the locals, and are then mauled by a werewolf.

If you haven't heard that one, it's pretty much incumbent upon you to watch John Landis's 1981 horror comedy, *An American Werewolf in London*. This book is a success if just one more person is introduced to that classic. Also, "mauled by a werewolf" is a great punch line.

In the first scene of the movie, the two young men stumble across a pub called the Slaughtered Lamb after a cold day of roaming the moors and hitching rides on sheep wagons. The sign for the establishment is illustrated with what looks like the severed head of a wolf on a pike.

"What kind of ad is that for a pub?" one of the travelers asks. I know he meant it rhetorically, but the answer is, "Good enough of one for real life, if the Slaughtered Lamb Pub in Manhattan is any indication."

Owned by the same people as the Jekyll and Hyde restaurants (see page 301), the Slaughtered Lamb, at 182 West Fourth Street in Greenwich Village, is a slightly themed werewolf pub ostensibly inspired by the pub from the Landis movie.

Outside, the pub bears a sign with a wolf's head, albeit a less gory one than that of its namesake pub. However, the establishment makes up for it by adorning its exterior with three or four full-size skeletons scattered across its blue awning.

In the movie, the pub was a warm oasis full of men in wool caps and tweed jackets throwing darts, telling jokes, and just generally being the quintessential English pub.

Inside the Manhattan version, it had all the requisites for a cozy pub . . . just missing the people, tweed-clad or not. The only other person I saw was the bartender. That's my fault, though, as I stumbled in during the early afternoon from my day of riding sheep wagons. My drinking clock runs a little fast, I guess.

Unfortunately, from the small bar area, you'd never know there was a were-wolf themed. My disappointment only went as far as my first gin and tonic, though. That's usually the way it goes. Also, because as my eyes adjusted to the dim interior, I saw in the corner a barred door through which could be seen a staircase leading down into what a bloody sign, in the shape of a guillotine, labeled "the Dungeon." The staircase was decorated with what I assume to be a Health Department—approved skeletal corpse hanging from the wall.

Unfortunately, after conversing with the bartender, I learned it was the game room, which would be open later in the evening, and that little of the monstrous was down there. I asked her whether there was anything to validate the name of the pub, and she told me, "Not so much," but vaguely gestured to the dining area, which was in an adjoining room behind the bar.

In that back room, I started to see a bit of theming: a portrait of a werewolf in dapper clothes above a mantelpiece, restrooms adorned with his and her decapitated heads, an ad for Full Moon Ale that implored drinkers to "Wolf it down!," and a pair of clothed skeletons sitting in a booth under a Plexiglas-covered metal cage.

Like I said, slightly themed, and the only testament to the actual *An American Werewolf in London*, besides the name of the establishment, was a framed movie poster.

But then I saw it. If this were a romance story, it'd be the person I fall in love with. Or, if a horror story, the monster I flee from. Turns out, it's the monster I fall in love with. In another display case, this one without the bars and set on a rotating pedestal, was a full-size werewolf, sinking its teeth into the neck of a buxom female victim.

The werewolf was gray, of the humanoid sort, and not based at all on *American Werewolf*'s quadruped lycanthrope. The victim had long, blond hair and a lacy, sheer dress. A thin line of blood dribbled from the werewolf's maw down her neck and chest. Disturbing and sexy.

Actually, the pose of the two was much more of a vampire one, but people have to eat bangers and mash and shepherd's pie around it, so they couldn't really depict a full-out bestial feast-orgy. Health Department, again.

"Not so much," indeed. For some reason, the bartender completely under-sold the fact that they have a large werewolf that is eating a woman on the premises. I probably should have tried to get her to unlock the basement for me. "Nothing much" probably meant Uzi-wielding Nazi mutants.

But that single display was glorious enough, and that plus my two gin and tonics meant the visit was a worthwhile one.

Now, as I mentioned, I wasn't there during the restaurant's peak time, so for all I know, when the place is more packed in the evening it earns its theme. Maybe there are wolf howls over the stereo system or fresh pentangles on the wall drawn in tomato paste. Maybe visitors are implored to wear puffy red jackets at the time. I at least hope the pub plays "Blue Moon."

And even if they don't, they still have a large werewolf eating a woman to season your dining experience.

Gargoyles and Grotesques
MANHATTAN

WHEN YOU LIVE OR WORK in a city full of skyscrapers, you get used to the feeling that somebody is looking down on you. However, it's not always just the unfocused and disinterested glances of office workers and penthouse dwellers behind the tempered plate glass of high-rise windows. To walk the sidewalks of New York City is to be subject to the stony stares of a thousand monsters perched on the ledges and wedged in the crevices of the building-scape that Manhattanites call sky.

Gargoyles and grotesques have a long history of adorning buildings, especially churches, where they had multiple uses. Practically, gargoyles were water spouts, channeling corrosive rain water away from the erosion-susceptible brickwork. But they were also ornamental, and in the case of churches, didactic, symbolizing, like *kill* stickers on a fighter plane, the evil that the church was there to keep at bay.

Grotesques, on the other hand, while having both of the latter purposes, lack that hollow feeling inside that would make them gutters. They're basically stone sculptures stuck to buildings, but both gargoyles and grotesques are a way to make your building stand out when you're in a city crowded with the giant boxes.

Because both gargoyles and grotesques (from here on just referred to as gargoyles to give my *G* key a rest) were used as symbols of evil, we often think of them in their more monstrous forms. Heck, the classic gargoyle is a horned demon with bat wings. In actuality, many aren't even sort of monstrous. They range from the comical to the dramatic, from animals and people to more abstract forms, and Manhattan showcases the gamut, including monsters. However, you might need a zoom lens or masonry crampons for some of them.

Obviously, it's impossible for me to list all the best gargoyles in New York City in this entry because, well, I don't know them all. But here are some great ones that I did find. For a better sense of all the city's high-up horrors, the Internet, as always, is the place to go. Entire websites are dedicated to the topic, and a quick search on any photo sharing website will produce some great finds.

For instance, take the 23-story Farmer's Loan and Trust building at 475 Fifth Avenue, just across the street from the main branch of the New York Public Library. Its roof is lined with both demons and dragons, the latter of which jut out the side of the building just below the roof. It looks like a medieval battle scene

atop some besieged castle, with the demons as the soldiers and the dragons as the cannons. I guess that's what the war in heaven was like back in the day. These gargoyles, like so many, are pretty much at the height that only other passing demons and dragons could see them in any real detail unaided.

At a different extreme, and even farther up New York City's vertical skyline, the eagle-shaped gargoyles on the Chrysler Building at 405 Lexington Avenue are famous both for being made out of stainless steel and for being inspired by the hood ornaments of that company's classic automobiles.

If you want to see some gargoyles close up, the Britannia building at 527 West 110th Street is a good place. Usually, anyway. Even though this 100-year-old edifice is nine stories tall, its series of limestone gargoyles are placed only a few feet above the heads of passersby. Depicted is a series of four squat human figures that, even though they're meant to be portrayed as engaged in basic activities— eating, cooking, writing—seem somewhat sinister due to the angular planes of their faces and their deeply lidded eyes.

Unfortunately, when I visited, the building was under construction and the middle two were either removed or were covered up in the canopy. Still, two were visible.

If you just want to see a general selection of these monsters of masonry, walking some of the city's most famous streets will certainly help you meet that questionable goal. I mean, Broadway, Wall Street, and Fifth Avenue are all places you're going to end up at some point anyway, so you might as well look up every once in a while (and then duck when you see the hideous countenances looming above you). Of course, it goes without saying that the city's old churches are great places to find these brick beasties in the wild.

For instance, the distinctive 120-year-old, six-story building at 716 Broadway (where it intersects with Washington Place) is lined near the top of its red façade with gilded demon faces and features two more beasties at the corners of its roof. Nearby, about half a block down Broadway where it intersects with East 4th Street, is a building with a first story decorated by owl sculptures.

Personally, I'm a fan of the classics, and in this case that means the afore-mentioned demons with bat wings. A good example of this species of gargoyle can be found on the Berkshire Bank at 4 East 39th Street. Its horns, wings, and slightly simian face (pictured) protruding from the building are pretty much the image that our collective unconscious associates with gargoyles and grotesques.

There's a reason why urbanites don't look around when they walk the streets of New York City. It's not because they're jaded by the thousands of wonders constantly surrounding them. It's not because they're rude or calloused by the masses of people they rub shoulders with every day.

It's the monsters above them.

Rolling Hills Asylum
EAST BETHANY

I T WAS A COLD, gray January afternoon. Snow was coming down in what can only be described as a spiteful fashion. A wild wind was blowing through the holes of the 185-year-old abandoned asylum, giving every single ghost inside its decrepit walls a voice. Fortunately, I was not alone inside. I was with the current owner, Sharon Coyle.

Rolling Hills Asylum is located on the edge of East Bethany, between Buffalo and Rochester. It was built in the early 19th century as a poorhouse called the Genesee County Poor Farm. Here the county would shelter the impoverished and the sick, the criminal and the mentally off—basically, whoever couldn't take care of themselves or were dangerous to others. The residents or inmates who were able to would work the surrounding farm, raising crops and animals.

Eventually, as the needs of the county changed, the building became a nursing home. Then in 1972, it followed the plot of most asylums from the period and was completely shut down. However, instead of "rotting to this day," in the early 1990s it was turned into a little museum called Carriage Village, which was then turned into a quaint mall of specialty shops. After about a decade or so as a retail establishment, that black mark against its spooky cred quaintly went the way of the poorhouse and nursing home before it.

Today, the 53,000-square-foot, Y-shaped building at 11001 Bethany Center Road sits on 11 acres and is backed by the Genesee County Park and Forest.

In the late 2000s, it was bought by private owners and turned into a "paranormal research center" with a trademarked name and everything. That basically means that the owners create some income off it by letting ghost hunters run through it with night-vision camcorders. These spook chasers include those with their own television shows, as well as those who just want to kill a Saturday night—professionals and amateurs, the two groups would be classified in any other field.

And that's what Rolling Hills Asylum has become better known for these days, instead of its history. Its haunted status is attributed to the usual reason: the many lives and deaths of the unfortunates who called Rolling Hills home. According to Coyle, at least 1,700 people died on the premises, many of whom were buried in unmarked graves in the potter's field at the rear of the property.

Outside, the red brick building spreads its front two wings in some kind of dark welcome, the interior rot clearly evident. Inside, the warren of hallways and rooms and underground tunnels is a confusing place, perfect for running around in with a flashlight and a camera, reveling in both the boredom and the thrills that come from participating in the controlled illusion of urban exploration.

Of course, that's not what I was doing. I was being led through the building by the person who is currently the most intimate with it, who knows its passageways and ghosts better than anybody does.

Coyle loves her asylum. It's massive, difficult and expensive to upkeep, and can easily turn into a life's work for her, if it hasn't already. I can barely stand having a small lawn to mow at my own house, so I suggested half-jokingly that she get rid of the place. She just looked at me as if I'd asked her to eat her pet dogs.

As we walked through dank, dark halls leprous with peeling paint and water stains, she would greet ghosts by name to let them know that I was cool and that we were just here to look around. It took us about an hour and a half to get through the whole place, Coyle's pointing out to me the various uses of the rooms, kitchen, morgue, chapel, and sickroom, some of which she had re-created with antique-store finds.

From certain vantage points, you could see down the lengths of entire wings, an arrangement that I hate almost to the point of arson. My imagination always conjures the simple image of a barely glimpsed human form walking briskly across the hall between rooms. Also, multiple times I heard definite noises that I doubt could be attributed to the wind, but which I did anyway. I don't at all believe in ghosts, but being secluded in an echoing, decaying, two-century-old building is a great time to throw that back in my face.

Although it was the first time I'd ever stepped hesitant foot inside Rolling Hills, that cold, creepy day was actually the second time I'd seen the place from the outside. A few months previous, I had driven by on the way to some other oddity for this book. It was a summer morning, sunny, dewy, and I got out of my car and stood at the Jordan-esque crossroads right in front of the building. On two sides of me, green corn stretched to the hills beyond. A third side showed an empty field. And on the fourth, the one I wouldn't turn my back to, was the 185-year-old abandoned asylum. At the time, I couldn't figure out whether the scene was idyllic or spooky. Now that I've walked its diseased intestinal tract, it can only be the latter for me.

Lily Dale Assembly
POMFRET

As near as I can figure it, there are four types of people who visit Lily Dale Assembly, the 130-year-old spiritualist community on the western edge of New York. There are the sincere, who are looking to communicate with the dead. The curious, who are looking for any experience out of the ordinary. The adamant, who are looking for a fight. And the apprehensive, who are looking to write a book. I can personally attest that one of these four types of people can have both a really awkward and a really good time.

Lily Dale is a hamlet located in the town of Pomfret, about 60 miles southwest of Buffalo and about 15 miles from Lake Erie. To get there from where I live, I had to drive the entire six-hour length of New York, the whole time dreading the one thing I had to do in Lily Dale . . . get a one-on-one reading from a medium.

Because that's the entire point of the place. After all, in this town where every other resident is a medium, some 25,000 visitors a year arrive looking to hire an envoy to the other side, in addition to attending spiritualist seminars and connecting with like-minded folk, both living and dead.

In the mid-1800s, spiritualism—that hazy belief the central tenet of which is that the dead don't die, they just get more talkative—was in its heyday in New York. Such sites as the Georgetown Spirit House (see page 326) and the popularity of the Rochester-area Fox sisters (see "Legends and Personalities of the Macabre") reveal that, at that time in New York, the dead were much more interesting people to talk to than the living.

The area that is now Lily Dale started out as an informal camp for people of the "free-thinking" persuasion, as they sometimes styled themselves, to meet. In 1879, the land was purchased for the official establishment of a spiritualist community and eventually named Lily Dale Assembly.

Every year, this 130-year-old community of some 250 spiritualists hosts conferences, services, and personal and public readings, usually during the summertime. In fact, so many people visit during that season that the residents charge an entry fee then, just to get into the town.

I personally tried to set up an advance appointment with a medium for a weekend in August and went through more than a dozen with zero space on their calendar. The town has about 40 registered mediums, meaning they've been vetted and found genuine by the governing body. It wasn't until I moved my trip to the off-season in September that I was able to secure a half-hour of a medium's time.

Driving past the open gate where we'd have paid ten bucks per person just a few weeks before, it was immediately apparent that Lily Dale was almost supernaturally quaint, as if all the state's grandmothers got together and started their own enclave. Victorian houses, many of which bore small neat shingles stating which medium was in residence there, were set close together on a handful of parallel streets. You could run around the whole residential area in seconds without spraining a lung.

We parked in the small, empty dirt lot reserved for visitor parking. Few visitors walked the streets, and the place seemed like a different kind of ghost town than it was vaunted to be. We timed it so that we

could get our readings, one for myself and then a separate subsequent one for my wife, out of the way first, but in the interests of narrative, I'll save that experience for last.

There's actually quite a bit to explore in the tiny hamlet. Lily Dale is cradled between the idyllic three-bead necklace that is Lake Cassadaga and the old-growth Leolyn Forest, which is full of trees hundreds of years in age.

Maps of the town are easy to get online, but unnecessary due to its size and the fact that there are small signs pointing out the main attractions. We headed down one of the forest walking trails, which meandered past a pet cemetery and on to the Forest Temple, a simple clearing filled with rows of benches facing the fabled Inspiration Stump. For the past century, mediums and other speakers have led services and conferences from the pulpit of this dead tree. Today, the stump has been buttressed with cement and is protected by a low iron fence. It's become more of a symbol than a soapbox. On its cement slab top were placed pictures, jewelry, and other mementos of the dead.

Next, we visited the former spot of the original home of the Fox sisters. In 1916, the cottage where the sisters first claimed to be communicating with the dead was transplanted from Hydesville (modern-day Newark), just outside of Rochester, to Lily Dale. This acquisition raised the profile of the town as a spiritualist mecca considerably. Unfortunately, the cottage itself was razed by a mysterious fire in 1955. These days, a plaque and a small garden area commemorate the foundation-print of the cottage.

Finally, we visited the Lily Dale Museum, which is basically the town attic. The pink and gray building itself was once a one-room schoolhouse that dates back to 1890. Although it is normally only open in the busy season, the curator, Ron Nagy, was kind enough to meet us and show us around. The small building is packed with pictures and artifacts and records going back beyond the town's formation 130 years ago. Examples from every type of spirit communication were there, including spirit painting, slate writing, and ear trumpets, as well as more conventionally historical objects.

Also included were artifacts from famous mediums, including the Campbell brothers, the Davenport Brothers, and the Bang sisters (bring a medium was apparently a family business back then). The central exhibit is probably the case of artifacts salvaged from the Fox cottage fire, including the infamous trunk where the supposed remains of the supposed murdered salesman were supposedly found. In fact, a large model of the cottage dominated the central table of the museum.

As I mentioned, we saw all this historical oddity in the context of having just had our first personal experience with spirit-channeling, so we found it especially fascinating . . . and especially dubitable.

The medium with whom I made the appointment was an older woman, as are many of the mediums in town. I sat in her front room, tidily kept in floral and lacy patterns. She inserted a blank CD into a machine so that I could have a record of the session—all part of the $60 service (long-distance rates over the Great Divide can be pretty hefty). She sat down across from me, prayed . . . and then the dead came.

I was first visited by a preacher, whom I couldn't place, and then a grandmother, whom I also couldn't place even though I had a 50-50 shot. She (or the dead people behind the curtain) missed horribly on my occupation, missed some pretty major events in my life from the past year, and made a few solid but unsubstantiated bets (that I would have another child, that I would do well at my job, etc.).

At some point I actually began rooting for her to get something correct or conjure some relevant information in my life (a feeling I could easily see being transmogrified into a readiness and a need to believe for those under the duress of extreme grief over lost loved ones). For instance, she'd sometimes give image impressions, including a random caterpillar image in one instance and nuts connected to my deceased grandmother in another, and I would strain to make a connection.

As is often the case with such vague suggestions, I was eventually able to make the inevitable tenuous connections thanks to feedback from family members (my mother-in-law had recently bought some caterpillar-themed decorations for any possible future grandchild, one of my grandmothers lived on Walnut Avenue, etc.). If that is evidence of the afterlife, then so be it.

I was uncomfortable enough about it all that I couldn't help but turn some of my paid time with her into an interview about life after death. I learned that, according to this particular medium, death is a process of letting go of earthly things so that the soul can go on and do other things more soul-worthy and probably incomprehensible to material minds. I also learned that the same goes for serial killers and genocidal dictators, who end up at a slightly less pleasant but still vague place where they're stuck until they can come to terms with their crimes. It all sounded inoffensive enough to be completely made up.

The one thing that I was pretty positive of was that the woman was sincere. That she believed that the random sensory impressions and brain flashes that, honestly, we all get, were actual communications from an invisible realm. The best ruses are the sincere ones.

All in all, the half hour was packed with vague information and obvious guesswork. My wife had a similar experience to mine, except that the medium was even further off in her observations, despite having the head start of conversing with me beforehand. Incidentally, I transcribed the aforementioned session recording, and it can be found on my website, OddThingsIveSeen.com ("Medium . . . Well, Parts 1 and 2").

Obviously, I can't say I went into it all with an open mind. I find it difficult to talk to live people across town over cell phones, and I just can't believe that people can talk to the dead wherever they are. However, the fact that we have to endure our loved ones dying sucks, so screw it. If you've lost someone dear to you, do whatever you can to feel better, even if that means hanging out in the cozy illusion that you can still communicate with the person.

And none of it changes the fact that Lily Dale is a pretty nice place, if you can stomach the ghosts.

"Ghostbusters Ruling" House
NYACK

THERE ARE ABOUT 120,000 WORDS in this grimpendium. You can skip all of them without any detriment to your life (and possibly even with improvement to it) except for the following nine: "As a matter of law, the house is haunted."

Those are words straight out of a decision by the New York Supreme Court.

The house at topic is a 4,680-square-foot, 120-year-old Victorian on the banks of the Hudson River in Nyack, within view of the Tappan Zee Bridge. In the late 1960s, Helen Ackley, her husband, George, and their four children bought the house, which had been vacant for seven years previously, and moved into it. They found the place to be, well, pleasantly haunted.

We know this because of a May 1977 *Reader's Digest* article that Helen wrote, explaining how they would hear footsteps, feel beds shaking, and even see multiple full-bodied specters in the house, usually in colonial period garb.

Apparently, the whole experience was more amity than Amityville Horror for them, as the ghosts left small gifts of gold rings and silver tongs and favorably weighed in on the Ackleys' choices of décor. In fact, the tone of the article exhibits the type of fondness reserved for recently deceased household pets or long-gone Christmas memories. She even ended it with wistful regret at the prospect of ever leaving her ghostly housemates.

But she eventually did. In the late 1980s, after two decades with their friendly phantasms, the Ackleys put it on the market. A man from New York City named Jeffrey Stambovsky liked what he saw and put down a deposit of $30,000 on the large house.

However, before signing all the paperwork, he learned about the house's public past as a place of poltergeists . . . and wanted out of the deal forthwith. "Man, you didn't tell me there were ghosts," is how I imagine that conversation went. I'm also imagining him as Owen Wilson, for some reason.

That's the story, anyway. It seems to me it could easily have been a matter of

cold feet as opposed to chilled spine. After all, he had basically just committed to a $650,000 purchase and found a possible way to get out of it. But who knows, maybe it was the ghosts.

We do know that Stambovsky took the Ackleys right to court over the matter of the surreal estate, and promptly lost. He appealed, so in the middle of deciding the bounds of human rights and the future fates of accused men, the Appellate Division of the New York Supreme Court had to figure out whether having Beetle-juice in the attic was something home sellers had to disclose prior to a sale.

The decision is a blast to read, and is famous for referencing (it's extremely tempting to use the term *citing* here) the movie *Ghostbusters* and its theme song—which is how the house got its name—and making a haunted house's worth of ghost references and puns. Judges are smart, and they can see a once-in-a-life-time opportunity when it comes.

Incidentally, the context of the phrase "As a matter of law, the house is haunted" in the decision is basically that the reputation of the house as haunted had to be accepted based on Helen's public declaration of it in *Reader's Digest*, as well as a few local publications, so the justices could get on to the actual crux of deciding whether it was relevant to caveat emptor laws.

Perhaps surprisingly, Stambovsky won one for the afterlife and was able to get his money back. However, he probably should have gone through with the sale because by this time the house was getting tons of press, and the Ackleys had no problem selling it afterward.

Today, the house at 1 Laveta Place is still a private residence, and is assessed at a value of some 2.5 million. Laveta Place is basically a giant hill that dead ends at the river, and the haunted house can be found at the very bottom on the right as you descend. It has been repainted away from the pinkish-red that it was at the time of all the litigation to a cooler blue and is well maintained. A large tree in the front yard does a good job of shielding the house from the cameras of tourists with questionable itineraries . . . unless you go in the winter. Still, the asymmetrical shape with its prominent cupola is perfect for a haunted house.

Incidentally, the house is right across the river from Sleepy Hollow, where residents relish their local haunts (see the Washington Irving entry in "Legends and Personalities of the Macabre").

Castle of the Lady in White
ROCHESTER

IN "HORROR MOVIE FILMING LOCALES" is an entry with a similar title to this one. That entry was about the Rochester-area filming locations for a movie based on a legend native to those parts. This entry is about the site of the legend itself.

There are about as many variations on the Lady in White legend as there are times it's told, yet averaged out, the story seems to go something like this: Once upon a time, in the days before substantiating evidence, a girl disappeared. Her mother, accompanied by her two large dogs, looked for her for days, only to eventually find her violated and murdered. Despondent, the mother threw herself into the cold waters of Lake Ontario. However, death was not the panacea she was hoping for, and she wanders the grounds of what is now Durand-Eastman Park with her two ghost dogs, eternally looking for (or mourning) her lost daughter.

And, apparently, she's also doomed to a monochromatic fashion palette.

I'm guessing there are a lot of places around the world with some kind of lady in white ghost folklore. Certainly, I've found myths of female ghosts in a crayon box worth of colors just in the few places on the map that I can stick a "visited" pin into. However, the reason I've included this story in this volume, over the hundreds of New York ghost stories I've come across, is that anytime people tell the story of the Lady in White, they always point to the remnants of her castle in Durand-Eastman Park.

Durand-Eastman Park is located on the border of Rochester and Irondequoit. It began as a donation in the early 1900s of some 500 acres by a surgeon named Henry Durand and the founder of Kodak Eastman, George Eastman (see "Notable Graves, Cemeteries, and Other Memento Mori"). Since that time, it has doubled in size to almost 1,000 acres of land, including about 5,000 feet of Lake Ontario beach.

I wanted to see the remnants of the Lady in White's castle, but I figured such a mysterious chunk of abandoned building must be hidden somewhere almost unattainable by the lazy likes of me. Turns out, it's right on the main road. Lake Shore Boulevard skirts the northern end of the park right on the edge of Lake Ontario, where everybody parks for the beach. There, right between the small Durand and Eastman Lakes and just a few dozen yards from a parking lot across the boulevard, was the well-preserved stone structure of local lore.

It was a single wall, about a dozen feet tall, and made of natural stone cemented together. It stretched less than 100 feet and featured cylindrical bulges on either end, as well as a third one directly in the middle.

A set of stone stairs curves up to and just behind it. I took them, and ended up on the top of a wooded hill with a great view of the Great Lake. Most of the wall was built into the hill, but several feet of it protruded higher. The few feet of its interior and the top of the wall, the parts that couldn't be seen from the road, were covered in graffiti. All of it white paint, naturally. Among the usual curse words and racial epithets and drug references and Nazi swastikas was the phrase "Castle of the White Man" or something along those lines anyway.

Unfortunately, I didn't visit the castle of the Lady in White at night, when she (and apparently kids with thematically colored spray paint cans) is wont to wander. Certainly, at the very least, the rampart has no purpose currently and must have been left over from some previous structure the origins of which, if not the home of the tragic story of a mother and her daughter, must be at least equally mysterious.

Well, not really.

The wall is actually a lookout point left over from an eating pavilion that had been there sometime in the early 1900s. The funny thing is, I'm not being a curmudgeon by pointing this out. Most people's accounts end the same way, and the site itself, right at the base of the hill in front of the wall, even bears a sign with the name "3 Lakes Pavilion," called such because of its placement right in the middle of Lake Ontario, Durand Lake, and Eastman Lake.

Nevertheless the Lady in White story persists in captivating generations of western New Yorkers because, well, it's way more interesting a tale than "once upon a time [moves flashlight closer to chin] people used to picnic right on this spot."

Cave of Evil Spirits
LEWISTON

NOT TO PROMOTE STEREOTYPES, but caves are spooky. Just are. And when the cave is found beside the remnants of a stream called Bloody Run in a ravine named Devil's Hole, Cave of Evil Spirits is almost a redundant name for it.

Devil's Hole State Park is a 42-acre strip of land on the banks of the Niagara River in northwestern New York. The park straddles the city of Niagara Falls and the village of Lewiston. It gets its name from the ravine on the Lewiston side of the premises that cuts down to the Niagara River Gorge, where the river relaxes a bit from its famous fall a few miles previously.

The ravine was formed by a river tributary that was awarded the name Bloody Run due to a battle/massacre (depending on which side you were on) that took place there. So, as my third grade teacher used to open class every day, "Let's start with the bloodshed, shall we?"

In September 1763, during a time of territorial squabble between the British, French, and the indigenous tribes that were in French employ, a wagon convoy of British soldiers was ambushed above Devil's Hole Ravine by a few hundred members of the Seneca tribe. The story goes that more than 80 British soldiers were killed, the entire wagon train was pushed into the ravine, and not a single Native American lost his life.

Eighty dead soldiers is a lot of ghosts to have wandering around, so it makes sense that they holed up all these limbo years inside, well, a hole. And that hole is the Cave of Evil Spirits, located on the side of the ravine named after a different hole than the cave, apparently.

The infamy of the cave is supposed to predate the slaughter, although the only story I've been able to dig up on it was that in 1679, French explorer Robert de LaSalle went inside the cave after being warned of its evil spiritedness by his Seneca guide. Bad luck was supposed to follow whoever entered. LaSalle did so, and then had a bunch of bad stuff happen to him over the course of the next two years, culminating in his murder by his own exploring party.

As of the writing of this sentence, it's been a little over six months since I myself entered the cave, and the only misfortunes I can claim in that time are a flat tire, a rescheduled Halloween due to an unseasonably early snowstorm, and having to sit through the movie *Basket Case* to be able to write about it in an earlier section of this book.

Today, Bloody Run is all but dry, with only a bare trickle down the steep slope of the ravine on my visit. Its steep descent down the ravine is eased by a series of hundreds of stone steps leading down to a path that parallels the Niagara River. It is just off those steps that you can find the Cave of Evil Spirits . . . if you dare. Or just want to.

It's extremely easy to get to, as long as you don't make the same mistake I did and take the aforementioned set of steps all the way to the bottom, hike too far along the trail, and then double back and ascend the steps, sweaty, breathing heavy, and suddenly not caring if you find it or if you have to kick it out of a book about spooky stuff. Here are the directions, so that doesn't happen to you.

Devil's Hole Park can be accessed via Robert Moses Parkway, and there's no fee to visit. Just a few steps from the parking long is a low wall, over which you can see an amazing view from about a height of 300 feet of the river, the gorge cliffs, and the nearby fortress-like power plant. A trail wends along the wall and right to the aforementioned set of stairs. About a third of the way down these stairs, a vague dirt path forks off and up to the right. That'll take you to the cave. No other path forks off the stairs, vague or otherwise.

As I mentioned, the remainder of the descending steps past the cave path can be laborious, especially because you have to make the return ascent, but it takes you right down to the river's edge and the hiking trail. It's cool, but it's no haunted cave.

The limestone cave was supposed to be a lot bigger in the past, but today it's about 4 to 6 feet or so high, and about 30 feet deep, so you'll always see the entrance even if you go all the way to the back wall. A large rock sits at the entrance, which itself is framed in colorful graffiti and Che Guevara stencils, so if you're there, your interests coincide with those of uninspired teens (I've long come to terms with that myself).

The foot-high remains of what looks to be a man-made wall of undetermined past use stretch across the back of the cave a few feet beyond which the cave ends. Once you're inside the Cave of the Evil Spirits, unless you brought a can of spray paint, there's nothing to do but turn around and exit . . . and then decide whether to continue down the steps or head back up for the view and picnic tables.

Devil's Hole sounds like something your Sunday School teacher would warn you about, but it's a beautiful place despite its name, violent history, and the fact that it has a cave full of bad mojo. When in the Niagara Falls area, go see it . . . after you witness tons of water famously falling over a cliff, of course.

Georgetown Spirit House
GEORGETOWN

IN THE SMALL, CENTRAL NEW YORK TOWN of Georgetown is a quaint white house with green shutters and a green door, the kind your grandmother might live in . . . and she just might be, assuming that she's dead.

Besides quaint, the house is also curious. The box-shaped frame is covered in divotlike notches that give the exterior a strange texture, and its roof is lined by three tiers of lacelike trim that make it look as if the house is covered with overlapping doilies. However, the most curious part about this house is the plain brown historic marker in front of it that states simply, "Spirit House."

Those two words are the only immediate indication that this house was once a grand hub of spiritualism—the belief that people could chat with the souls of the dead—during the heyday of that movement in the latter half of the 19th century.

The house was personally built by a man named Timothy Brown, who was born in Vermont in 1815 and moved to Georgetown in 1855. He wanted a place that could be a spiritualist temple of sorts and even went so far as to claim that he was actively guided by spirits in its construction. According to the story, Brown had no skills in this area himself.

After 10 years of work under his ghostly foremen, the house was completed in 1868. Other than the strange façade, there weren't really any aspects that proclaimed it as a house for the dead. Interestingly, Brown designated the closets of the house as ghost green rooms of sorts for them to hang out in, before the mediums and other séance participants called them onstage.

I always assume that every number I see anywhere is exaggerated, but according to many accounts, thousands of people made the trek to this spirit box to communicate with the dead. Enough, in fact, that Brown had to expand the house by buying an empty church and adding it on, as well as purchasing about a dozen more acres of property.

The prominence of the Spirit House in the busy New York spiritualism scene lasted about a decade. Its fall is often attributed to a waning of interest in the movement, although the movement stayed popular in general for a few more decades and is still practiced today (see the Lily Dale entry, page 315). It's also attributed to the story that a notebook was found on the premises bearing information from one of the local graveyards. A medium's cheat sheet.

Brown himself eventually switched sides in 1885, converting from spiritualist to spirit, and ownership of the house trickled down through family members and others. Over the years, it underwent a churchectomy, reverting back to its original box shape and the property was paired down to about three and a half acres. The house itself stands at 2,640 square feet. Nobody has lived there since 1989, although some spirits might have deaded there since then.

The house is at 916 Route 26 South, right on the street and just below the intersection of Routes 26 and 80 that marks the center of Georgetown. The property is nicely treed and sits beside a Baptist church and graveyard. A white picket fence lines only the front border of the property, on which is a brief informational sheet installed by the Georgetown Historical Society that explains why a house would have a historical marker proclaiming it as a spirit house.

A peek inside revealed that the Spirit House was completely gutted, and a sign in the front yard announced that it was for sale. The asking price at the time was $88,000. I assume they throw in any lingering ghosts for free.

Since my visit and despite a fund-raising attempt by a local spiritualist group, the property was apparently purchased by a private interest. As of this writing, the reports don't seem to indicate who it was or for what purposes the buyer would want a gutted ghost house out in the middle of nowhere.

But I do know one thing. If this was a ghost story, that's what would be called an "inciting incident."

Tahawus Ghost Town
Newcomb

JUST IN THE COURSE OF WRITING THIS BOOK, I've visited dozens of cemeteries, city blocks worth of historic buildings and landmarks, and scores of sites connected with violent death and/or intense evil. I've seen disembodied brains, empty skulls, and mummified cadavers with my own moist eye jellies. But I never once saw a ghost. I did, however, see a ghost town.

In my experience, ghost towns in the northeast area of the country contain little more than vague cellar holes and generally must be hiked to for even that meager reward. However, there's one ghost town in the Adirondack region of New York that not only has actual buildings, but can be driven to directly on nicely laid asphalt. Heck, it even has a historic connection to a past president of our country.

Tahawus, also known as Adirondac or Adirondak (which won't make sense in the audio version of this book), was a small community established in 1827 in the northern part of the town of Newcomb, near the headwaters of the Hudson River. It sprang up to support a mining and iron smelting operation run by the Adirondack Iron Works. Three decades later, in 1857, a combination of factors that included ore impurities, local flooding, and financial pressures caused the people of Tahawus to say, "Screw it, you can have your stupid town back," leaving the dozen or so structures to the whims of the wild.

In 1943, some of the town was reclaimed from the ghosts of the Adirondacks to support further mining operations necessary for the efforts of the Second

World War. Some of the still extant buildings from the earlier settlement were used. However, in 1989, the mine and the town again fell into disuse.

Meanwhile, throughout the late 1800s and the course of the 1900s, local hunting and fishing clubs started leasing the area, and it became a popular hiking destination with the creation of the gigantic, 6-million-acre preserve known as Adirondack Park being officially put on the books in the 1890s.

In fact, then vice president Theodore Roosevelt was availing himself of the area in 1901 when he learned that President William McKinley was about to die from an assassin's bullet in Buffalo (see William McKinley Assassination Site and Gun entry in "Infamous Crimes, Killers, and Tragedies").

The buildings of Tahawus continued to decay, as they had since 1857 despite their random use, until the early 2000s, when a well-funded preservation group called the Open Space Institute (OSI) dropped $8.5 million to purchase the town and a surrounding 10,000 acres. It has since started conservation efforts in the region.

Today, you can drive right up to this ghost town, the buildings of which range in condition from virtually intact to rotting piles of lumber, on a freshly laid asphalt road, waving politely to all the sweaty and burdened hikers as you pass them. Most of Tahawus's half-dozen or so remaining buildings line the road; a few are located farther back in the forest.

To get to the ghost town, take County Route 25 north toward Henderson Lake. It will dead end at a trailhead parking lot, but Tahawus will be visible just before the dead end, the decimated front porches of the buildings mere inches from the road. Here are some GPS coordinates that might help you out: 44.089146, −74.056386. Double-check them first, though. I might've confused them with my save point of the nearest McDonald's to my house.

The first structure you'll come across is the 150-year-old blast furnace that towers about 60 feet tall over the road on one side and the stream on its far side that is ever on its way to becoming the Hudson River. The rectangular furnace could belong in some distant Amazonian jungle, with its giant chunks of dark, rough-hewn rock and plants growing through its crevices. When I visited, it was artfully adorned with DANGER signs.

The rest of the buildings of Tahawus are more residential and look as if they've all seen the wrong end of a meteor shower. The roofs are caved in where they're not missing, there are holes in the floor, frameworks are exposed, rusty protrusions run a two-for-one special on impalement and tetanus, and when

the wind is just right, you can catch the delicate fragrance of asbestos, mold, and animal droppings. One building looked as if it had been chopped in half by the hand of a god who had been practicing his karate moves.

There were no furniture or household artifacts that I could see amid all the building rubble, and the only recognizable structures in the interior were the doors and fireplaces, askew and hanging from brittle hinges in the former case and decades to centuries cold in the latter.

The one exception to all that eerie damage was a pale yellow house with carefully boarded-up windows. Called MacNaughton Cottage, it was here that Vice President Roosevelt had his home base when he heard about his impending promotion. The building stands in such good condition as a result of being stabilized by the OSI.

Tahawus, as it stands/decays now, anyway, gives the impression that you should earn entry into its squalid, spooky environs by hiking miles over mountains and across rivers with nothing but a faded map, a compass that always stick to the southwest, and a rumor of glory directing your quest. Instead, you can (carefully) explore the houses and area with your car from a heartening 10 feet away, while the strains of "Men Without Hats" waft comfortingly from the radio. It's a great way to experience the world sometimes.

New York Mummies
MANHATTAN, BROOKLYN, BUFFALO

THERE ARE SO MANY EGYPTIAN MUMMIES scattered across the United States, it's as if somebody grabbed Cairo and shook it upside down above us. Heck, the ACLU should start defending them as an underrepresented minority. In New York, the best place to see theses desiccated corpses in their unnatural habitat is at either the Metropolitan Museum of Art or the Brooklyn Museum.

The Met is, of course, one of the most famous art museums in the world. It's been around since 1870 and at its awe-inspiring current location in Manhattan since 1880. Its massive stone façade at 1000 Fifth Avenue, on the east edge of Central Park, dares passersby to enter and be overwhelmed by an amazing quantity and quality of artifacts from all the foundational cultures of this planet: earthy African art, eloquent Greek statues, ornate Asian sculptures. Of course, I'm the type that'll breeze through artifacts from all the foundational cultures of this planet just to see millennia-old linen-wrapped corpses.

The Egyptian collection at the Met is supposed to be the largest outside of Cairo itself, with some 26,000 pieces, most of which are on display and arranged throughout a staggering 39 rooms. You will get lost. You will be surrounded by images and artifacts that spark latent images of Christopher Lee shuffling after his victims. You will have an amazing experience that would only be topped if they handed out complimentary pith helmets at the entrance to the wing.

I honestly don't remember there being so many rooms, not that I was counting, but certainly, there are hallways and galleries full of Egyptalia, statues, jewelry, pottery, carvings, and all the funerary artifacts that gave ancient Egyptians the immortality they always sought.

Heck, while I always assume every piece of Egypt I see was looted from a tomb, the Met has enough artifacts to decorate about ten thousand Egyptian living rooms.

Most noticeably, they've rebuilt a tomb that you can walk through to see the carvings on the wall, as well as reassembled an entire temple, the Roman-period Temple of Dendur, in the Sackler Wing, which was one of the places that Harry met Sally.

And the mummies are everywhere, mostly in those colorful sarcophagi covered in markings that make me wish they offered hieroglyphics as a second language, instead of Spanish, in high school. There were also specimens from the Roman period, of the sort where the Egyptian morticians placed a two-dimensional painted portrait of the embalmed on top of his or her face.

Unfortunately, you'll find no grisliness at the Met. No half-opened mummies, no gaping rag-festooned skulls, no impossibly shriveled bodies. I have to admit, I look for that in an Egyptian museum, even if we do have medical scanning technologies and better formed ethical systems to prevent it. Still, I have to take away a star for that.

But as much as the Met is an elegant experience far above my commentary, so is the Brooklyn Museum in its own way. But here's my commentary.

Just a borough away, in Brooklyn, is the much less overwhelming Brooklyn Museum, at 200 Eastern Parkway. This massive 115-year-old, statue-bedecked and pillared edifice is no less impressive, but inside, its five floors don't boast the diversity or sheer amount of artifacts as the Met (even if that means that the Brooklyn Museum only has about 1.5 million pieces in its collection). As a result, I felt less guilty breezing past mind-staggering works of antiquity to hit up the Egyptian dead on the third floor.

The best part of the Brooklyn Museum's Egyptian galleries is how they are arranged. Various rooms filled with artifacts lead in a generally linear direction

Metropolitan Museum of Art

Brooklyn Museum

to dead end at a single, tall doorway. Up to that point most of the rooms are painted a plain light beige to better accentuate the artifacts, but through that doorway the walls are black. Above that portal is the simple but dramatic name "The Mummy Chamber." Style points.

Inside is a small but well-arranged and diversified collection that includes a handful of human mummies, along with animal mummies such as a cat, a small alligator, and an ibis. There are canopic jars, framed strips of mummy linen inked with spells to help the dead, and another spell, this time on parchment, which stretched the width of the chamber under a glass counter. A short clip from the 1933 Universal Studios *Mummy* plays in a loop on a monitor affixed to one of the black walls. More style points.

Again, nothing grisly, but a placard on the wall explains why they don't unwrap mummies anymore (for the understandable but still disappointing reasons I already included earlier in this entry). There was also an explanation of their code of conduct for legally acquiring Egyptian artifacts, as apparently the trade in such is dominated by artifacts that have been looted, stolen, and sold on a black market that I can't seem to find myself.

Both museums are worth seeing, spending an entire day at, and buying a small condo next to.

Incidentally, if you are the interminable length of the state away from New York City, you can get your mummy fix at the Buffalo Science Museum. I wasn't able to visit this exhibit (if only one could embalm deadlines), but apparently it has one entitled, "Whem Ankh: The Cycle of Life in Ancient Egypt," which features a couple of hundred artifacts and a pair of mummified priests, who, if you catch them in their more unguarded moments, can be heard whispering dustily to each other, "Did you ever think we'd end up in Buffalo?"

ACKNOWLEDGMENTS

I'M NOT SURE WHETHER EVERYBODY to whom I owe a debt for the completion of this macabre little book wants his or her name anywhere near it, but here goes. My apologies first, then my thanks.

And that thanks goes to Lloyd Kaufmann and Michael Herz, of Troma Studios, as well as staff members Chelsea and Mike, for taking the time to meet with me and leading me through the entrails of their HQ; Joe Coleman and his wife, Whitney Ward, for giving me one of my favorite memories of this book adventure; Joey, Diane, and Jessica Vento of the Haunted Barn Movie Museum for giving me another; Joanna Ebenstein of the Morbid Anatomy Library for the great space and the great conversation; Richard Nagy for opening the Lily Dale Museum out of ghost season for me; Jana Eisenberg of the Buffalo and Erie County Historical Society for sacrificing a part of her holiday weekend to satiate my morbid curiosity; Jim Logan at Sleepy Hollow Cemetery for being the best source of information about the area; Anne-Marie Johansson of the Ashokan Dreams B&B for the in-depth telephone tour of West Shokan; Sharon Coyle of Rolling Hills Asylum for introducing me to her ghosts; and anybody that sent me suggestions for potential New York sites.

On a personal note, I would like to thank Shawn Keefe and his amazing talent for cemetery navigation for helping me with one of my New York City trips and then (despite his experience) joining me again for a Long Island jaunt; Mike Colombo for braving sexagenarians in rainbow clown wigs with me during a two-day Finger Lakes trip; Brian Weaver for legitimizing another *Grimpendium* with his excellent cover art; Kermit Hummel and the staff at Countryman Press for wanting to do another book; and everybody who bought the last *Grimpendium* or supported my OTIS website through the years, without whom this book wouldn't have been made.

I'd like to thank my family, of course, for all the usual sappy reasons and especially my wife, Lindsey, for too many things to write down, but in this particular case for all the trips, all the camera work, all the support, and above all, keeping me sane on a schedule packed to the point of preposterousness.

I'd also like to thank Google Maps and whoever invented consumer-level GPS, without both of which I would never cross my property line.

Finally, my appreciation goes out to anyone in the Empire State who has ever dedicated any part of their life to death, including those who've honored a memory in a tangible way that enabled others to partake of it by merely showing up, those who have dedicated their efforts to continuing and maintaining somebody else's legacy, no matter how macabre (almost used the word *immortalized,* an enormous faux pas in a book about death), and those who have found unabashed fascination in the monstrous or were inspired enough by the words *The End* to create or preserve something worth visiting.

INDEX